# THE GOOD ENOUGH CATHOLIC

## Also by Paul Wilkes

# THE

# GOOD

# ENOUGH

# CATHOLIC

## A Guide for the Perplexed

# PAUL WILKES

BALLANTINE BOOKS

NEW YORK

Grateful acknowledgment is made to the following for permission
to reprint previously published material:

*America* Magazine: excerpts from: "Divorce, Remarriage and Reception of the
Sacraments" by John S. Grabowski, October 8, 1994; "Sex and the Single Catholic:
The Decline of an Ethic" by Andrew M. Greeley, November 7, 1992; "Perspectives"
by Catherine Walsh, February 11, 1995. Reprinted by permission of
Rev. George W. Hunt, S.J., President and Editor-in-Chief, *America* Magazine.

*Church* Magazine: excerpts from: "The Practice of Priesthood: Working Through
Today's Tensions" by Rev. James J. Bacik, *Church* Magazine, Fall 1993, p. 12;
"Sexual Activity Among Teenagers" by Gerald D. Coleman, *Church* Magazine,
Summer 1991, p. 41. Published by the National Pastoral Life Center,
18 Bleecker Street, NY, NY 10012. Used by permission.

*The Tablet*: excerpts from: "Joy of Our Desiring" by Basil Hume, April 29, 1994;
"Asking Too Much" by Clifford Longley, January 6, 1996. Reprinted by
permission of *The Tablet*, the international Catholic weekly.

*Theological Studies, Inc.*: excerpt from "Development in Moral Doctrine" by John T.
Noonan, December 1993. Reprinted by permission of Theological Studies, Inc.

*U.S. Catholic*: excerpts from "Religious Symbols Belong in Your Home" by
Patrice J. Tuohy, April 1993; "Small Faith Groups Help the Good News Hit Home,"
interview with Father Arthur Baranowski, January 1992. Reprinted by
permission of *U.S. Catholic*, published by the Claretians.

http://www.randomhouse.com

Library of Congress Cataloging-in-Publication Data
Wilkes, Paul, 1938–
The good enough Catholic : a guide for the perplexed / Paul Wilkes.—1st ed.
p.     cm.
Includes bibliographical references and index.
ISBN 0-345-39543-3
1. Catholics—United States—Religion. 2. Catholics—United States—
Social life and customs. 3. Catholic Church—Doctrines.
I. Title.                                                      96-38528
BX1406.2.W55   1996
248.4'82—dc20

Manufactured in the United States of America
First Edition: November 1996
10 9 8 7 6 5 4 3 2 1

*For my Tracy, Noah, and Daniel—*
*Good Enough Catholics All*

If a collision occurs, it is not enough to say that you followed the rule, for the rule requires that you take whatever action necessary to avoid a collision. This means that if the give-way vessel fails to act appropriately, the stand-on vessel may actually be required to violate the rules, if that is what it takes to avoid a collision.

—U.S. COAST GUARD AUXILIARY
*Boating Skills and Seamanship* (10th ed.)

And as he sat at table in the house, behold, many tax collectors and sinners came and sat down with Jesus and his disciples. And when the Pharisees saw this, they said to his disciples, "Why does your teacher eat with tax collectors and sinners?" But when he heard it, he said, "Those who are well have no need of a physician, but those who are sick. Go and learn what this means, 'I desire mercy, and not sacrifice.' For I came not to call the righteous, but sinners."

—MATTHEW 9:10–13

# ❧ CONTENTS ❧

# INTRODUCTION

With a good measure of hope and even more humility, I want to propose a new approach to living the life of a Catholic today—The Good Enough Catholic.

I say "new," and yet what is ever really new in Catholicism? I say "good enough," yet might that not be construed as a lukewarm response to such a magnificent and mighty faith?

If I might explain both of these half-truths.

In a period spanning little more than a generation, we Catholics have been witnesses to perhaps the most sweeping revolution in church history. Once we were required to follow strict laws obediently, and to parrot precise answers to a series of catechism questions in defense of the "one, true church." Suddenly, we were given license to employ our intellects and consciences in reaching decisions about our lives, our beliefs, our approach to God.

The event that caused this upheaval on what had been a tranquil and seemingly fixed Catholic landscape was, of course, the Second Vatican Council, held from 1962 to 1965. With some distance from Vatican II, it is apparent that the conclave was hardly an anomaly, and certainly not a blip on history's screen.

It is not that Vatican II was the first—or will be the last—of the signal events that occur unpredictably and fitfully to shape religious life. Catholic history hardly began with Vatican II. The church has witnessed a long, sometimes glorious, sometimes inglorious history, filled with saints and sinners, wise and hollow judgments, oppression and transcendence.

In essence, the conclave was a response to almost unbearable tensions within Catholic doctrine, outlook, and practice that had built up and needed to be released. Surely, the scriptural metaphor of old wineskins and new wine has application here.

We can now see (as those involved in the council could hardly have comprehended) that Vatican II was a stunningly forward-looking effort, a moment of seismic upheaval in the bedrock of the institutional church that both reflected and foretold changes in the secular world. An old order was dying in the postwar world; a new order was being born. A church that had demanded rote uniformity in worship and creed, that had effectively walled off itself and its people from the supposedly corrupting forces of the surrounding culture, saw that it, too, needed to change. It, too, needed to atone for sins of commission and omission.

Remarkably, the church—virtually overnight, in terms of its long history—opened itself to diverse approaches to God, announcing that the world was no longer to be piously shunned. Instead, the world outside the church would also be looked upon as God's domain—and, regarded in this way, should be transformed by a Catholic presence that included not just the hierarchy and clergy, but lay people as well.

A call for a new Catholicism had been sounded.

With such a recent and fundamental reorientation in a church that had seemed impervious to change—as well as the backlash it produced—it is hardly surprising that so many Catholics today find themselves conflicted on how, and whether, to live as a Catholic. Such rapid shifts, however needed or overdue, extract their own cost.

To both the promised enfranchisement of Vatican II and the traditionalist reaction that followed in its wake, the response of Catholics ranged from the easily predictable to the absolutely unthinkable. Some turned away—not only from Catholicism, but from all religious observance. For these, the world appeared no longer to have need of, or use for, institutional belief. Others sampled from the rich offerings of other faith traditions—from ancient Buddhism and Islam—to New Age methods and "human potential" movements. In the American mind, therapy seemed to replace religion as the path to inner fulfillment. Still others recoiled and tried to rebuild the mighty fortress, opting for a fundamentalism stripped bare of doubt or questioning.

But by far the vast majority of Catholics—despite their wide variance in observance and in their acceptance of church doctrine and teachings—still cling to Catholicism. Within this majority are people who attend mass regularly, participate in parish life, educate their children in Catholic schools—and those who do none of these things. Regardless of their individual approach, each, if asked, would proclaim themselves Catholic. We have, in essence, a "real" Church and a shadow Church—both, in remarkable ways, Catholic at their core.

Some would maintain that such widespread disaffection and varieties of religious experience are evidence of a church profoundly out of touch with its people. Equally, others would counter, we the people are a hopelessly relativistic lot, with ego gratification, rather than God's will, as our goal. We are out of step with a church that has kept truth alive, through Dark Ages and Enlightenment, for 2,000 years.

## THE NEED REMAINS

My own feeling is that we just haven't yet figured out how to be Catholics at this transitional time in history.

Admittedly, this is not an easy task. Catholics are understandably unwilling to abandon the individuality they have struggled painfully to discover, only to return to a cookie-cutter approach to religious belief. Yet, on the other hand—as many a seeker has found—when that unique *me* is the centerpiece of worship, and the mystery of God has been shoved off to the side, a hollowness results.

This period we are in, I sense, marks a certain kind of Catholic spiritual adolescence—one beyond the time of complete parental constraint that marked the pre–Vatican II church, yet one terribly unsure of what is to be done with newfound freedoms. Whatever stage we may be experiencing, and however we may be able to articulate the current faith dilemma, the old and basic need for a divine presence in our lives has not gone away.

What we seek is a belief at once transcendently compelling and eminently practical—a true, reliable, and lasting light to illuminate our lives; a spiritual force to infuse our beings and inform our judgments; a compass by which to set our course. We want something to help us live life and confront death, a way to shape our morality, a set of principles we can take into the bedroom as well as the boardroom—a faith that can weather our various trials, moods, and seasons. We yearn for a life rooted in, but not stunted by, religious tradition; a value structure that can wisely assay the worth and role of secular culture, yet preserve us from being enslaved by it.

In the midst of the social and religious turmoil that surrounds us, many Catholics simply walked away in frustration or marginalized themselves from their faith; indeed, an entire generation of Catholic-born children have been raised with little knowledge or understanding of the religious beliefs that shaped their parents and the American Catholic ethos. We are now witnessing the rise of the best secularly educated group of cradle Catholics ever born—and, religiously, the least literate. Their parents had a rich Catholic culture and faith as their foundation and guide—something to live by, return to, or continually rebel against. Their children, while calling themselves Catholic, have no such baseline. As Stephen Carter has argued in *The Culture of Disbelief*, religion, once central to an individual's core identity and outlook, has been trivialized to the status of a hobby. God has become optional. Yet many Catholics today, sensing an emptiness in their lives, are reconsidering their attempt to opt for life without God. What once seemed like greater freedom now seems only deeper darkness.

# A NEW CATHOLICISM

It is the premise of this book, and the conviction of its writer, that there is a Catholicism—a new kind of Catholicism—that is exactly right for this spiritually hungry, morally unsure, and self-reflective time. I think Catholicism, properly understood, offers a unique, total, satisfying, diverse approach to living, one far too valuable and tested to shun because of disagreements with certain of its teachings, or remembrance of pain inflicted. Father James J. Bacik, a Toledo priest, has summed it up well:

> Our culture needs precisely what the Catholic heritage has to offer. Our tradition of community and our parish structure are vital antidotes to rampant individualism. Our insistence on discipline and simplicity of life counters the materialism and hedonism which threaten the cultures. Our understanding of sainthood is helpful in a society whose heroes are less than exemplary. The Catholic imagination has an appreciation of the mystery dimension of life, which challenges the one-dimensional outlook of our secular world. Our insistence that moral values are best grounded in religious convictions provides a useful antidote to the moral relativism which weakens society. We bring to a world grown pessimistic about solving great problems an abiding hope that history will reach its goal and that God will ultimately reconcile the human family.[1]

While agreeing with this appraisal, some might contend that fundamental change must come to the church before it can be their home. Yes, change may come to Catholicism—from birth control to divorce to married clergy—but, meanwhile, our lives must go on. To wait for a perfect church (or *our* idea of a perfect church) is to wait in vain. Many are adrift in heavy seas—and this bark of Catholicism, though fragile and sometimes uncomfortable, is at hand.

I believe that there are ways to live out a Catholicism today that is at once faithful and thoughtful, a Catholicism offering the freedom both to participate in its life and to disagree genuinely with some of its ways. It is a Catholicism that can enrich a person's life and help that person transform family, community, and world. It is a Catholicism rooted in the life and inspiration of Jesus Christ, a Catholicism that can spring up in the good soil of this world, at this time in our lives.

I am a member of that vast majority of Catholics I spoke of earlier— those who find themselves at odds with certain teachings and practices of the church, but are unable to stay away from what has been the single most formative influence in our lives. As I am presuming to say something about how and why to live a specifically Catholic expression of Christianity, a few words may be in order about myself and how this book came about.

I was raised in St. Benedict's, a Slovak Catholic parish in Cleveland, Ohio. Both Catholic and ethnic identity were strong in those days; not only did we not know Protestants or Jews, we didn't even know Catholics of other ethnic backgrounds. I eventually went to a Catholic high school, Cathedral Latin, and a Catholic college, Marquette University.

With seventeen years of Catholic education behind me, I surprised even myself when I married—for, it would turn out, the first time—outside the Church. I did not attend Catholic churches for many years. I eventually divorced. In the course of a life rooted in the pre–Vatican II church, and lived in a vastly different church, I embodied what was good in Catholicism, founding and working in a homeless shelter. I was also a rather multifaceted sinner, succeeding in breaking virtually all the rules I had learned to regard as sacred. Mine has hardly been a seamless Catholic life.

Many times I have found myself at odds with Catholic doctrine— appalled by the inadequacies of the clergy, hurt by the insensitivity of hierarchy, and disillusioned by the hypocrisy of lay people. But I have never found a more sensible and holy way of living a life. When I was younger, I thought Catholicism was *the* way. I have found, instead, that it is *a* way. But it certainly has proved to be *my* way. The Catholic faith of my childhood faith has grown, just as my body has matured. Each has weathered storms. Each, though dramatically and irrevocably changed, is still with me.

So, here I am—Catholic, father, husband, journalist, pilgrim on the face of the earth, but neither a theologian nor a Catholic apologist—seeking both answers to life's questions and examples on which to pattern my life.

# VOICES

This book about Catholicism came to be, first, through a visit to a twentieth-century bookstore—and then by way of journeys into the mind of a modern-day child psychologist, and a twelfth-century philosopher. Both of my educators are, oddly enough, Jews.

I don't know whether my struggle to be a decent parent or a decent Catholic in today's world was more on my mind when I wandered into a bookstore in Worcester, Massachusetts. As a new and somewhat unsure parent, I was scanning the "child rearing" section when my eyes settled on the spine of a book. Amidst the hyperbole and catchy covers, this one title appealed to me with its modest claim. The book was *The Good Enough Parent* by Bruno Bettelheim. I flipped back the cover and read the flap copy.

"Child rearing is a complicated undertaking, different for every parent, demanding in different ways from one day to the next, impossible to define with hard-and-fast rules, baffling, instinctual, as daunting a task as it is rewarding." I could feel a tingle of recognition ripple along the nerve endings at the back of my neck. *This man knew my heart!*

When I reread the flap copy later, I realized I had unconsciously inserted the words "Catholicism" and "person" into the respective places of "child rearing" and "parent." Thus began the reading of a book that proved to be a good primer for this inexperienced parent—and an even more useful approach for understanding and living out Catholicism today.

Bettelheim, an eminent child psychologist, had expanded on the concept of the "good enough mother" of D. W. Winnicott, another wise observer of parents and children. Key to the "good enough" concept was the idea that, while the caretaker-parent need not be perfect, there needed to be a sufficiently healthy and nurturing ("good enough") relationship—so that the child, with a certain sense of security, could eventually develop a wholesome sense of self. This bond needed to be strong, reassuring, and in certain ways ever-present; but eventually the child would have to grow, leave the protected environment of the home, and face a world that would not hold his or her best interests as primary. The child would grow into an adult confronted by the necessity of making decisions unprotected by familial love. The child would no longer have the parent's reassuring presence *in person*, but would carry it internally, psychically. The basic relatedness was always there.

Bettelheim's book was certainly not meant to be a new catechism for modern-day Catholics. But as I thought further about his approach, I realized that it contained many nuggets of wisdom easily applicable to a Catholic's religious pursuit and spiritual life. For, only when we can receive reinforcement for our best efforts—only when we feel loved and accepted by God—will we have the courage to go on to develop a good and moral life. By contrast, if we are continually told that we are inadequate, bad, and unworthy—in short, not good enough—our spiritual selves will be stunted, and we will simply give up trying.

The anxiety produced by constant feelings of inadequacy or guilt was ultimately counterproductive, Bettelheim argued, and corrosive to human growth. Yes, guidelines needed to be drawn and reinforced; total permissiveness was an insidious form of neglect. But mistakes made would be more than compensated by the many good and right things the "good enough" parent would do. For within one's self was a reservoir of instinctual behavior that could be relied upon. Common sense, and our basic good instincts, were more often than not a very accurate guide. There was not one correct way to act, making all other ways incorrect, invalid, and potentially damaging.

What was most amazing to me was the notion that being "good enough" was actually being *quite good*, and hardly a small achievement in itself. It did not mean there were no rules or boundaries, nor any need for self-examination. Being "good enough" represented a thoughtful, heart-ful response to the myriad issues with which life confronts us.

The person who is at once relaxed and alert, at turns compassionate and unbending—depending on the situation—will end up being an exemplary parent and person, producing equally thoughtful, balanced children. Bettelheim, in essence, was calling for excellence, but not demanding perfection—and all the while validating the role of inner experience.

Soon after discovering this "good enough" concept, I came upon another man who also had clearly understood the complexity of twentieth-century Catholic belief. Moses Maimonides (d. 1204), one of the greatest medieval philosophers, was essentially a religious and philosophical rationalist. He was roundly attacked, and his books were banned and burned—all because he was impious enough to assert that it was within human capacity to discern the reasons for God's laws. To the Jewish religious leaders of his day, this was heresy of the worst sort. Maimonides fought bitterly against those who merely proclaimed laws and cared little about their underlying rationale, their difficulty, or their consequences. His ringing praise for the majesty of God and God's laws, and his stinging criticism of the hidebound rabbinic interpretations of those laws, was set forth in a volume gamely titled *Guide for the Perplexed*.

Faith and intellect were partners in the makeup of Maimonides' ideal believer, producing a person who could live a life close to God while withstanding the storms of the individual mind as well as the shifting tides of public sentiment.

You could find God *while* being perplexed, and *in being* perplexed, Maimonides maintained.

"Good Enough." "Perplexed." They added up—for me—to a way to be formed, and to live, as a Catholic.

# ACCEPTANCE AND DEMAND

For I sensed that if Catholicism, lived out in this day by us ordinary people, was to be the universal, open, embracing religion that the word "catholic" implies—if a church founded upon the life story of a man who preached and practiced love and acceptance was to fulfill his mandate—then the pathways to union with God, though strewn with roadblocks and crises, must be paved with compassion, forgiveness, and hope as well. Religion, after all, is not an absolute science; it is an art and a continuing discovery.

As I set out to gather the stories and information that would eventually make up this book, I quickly saw that it is only our own myopic vision (and often a good dose of lingering Catholic guilt) that keeps Catholicism one of the most misunderstood treasures, and least tapped resources, of our lives.

I found that Catholicism is being lived out in America in a variety of wonderful and enriching ways, each true to a vision at once authentic to that person and still well beneath the wide and sweeping tent pitched for this community of believers. Indeed, there is more room in Catholicism than a person might imagine. From Bible-quoting fundamentalist Catholics to Catholics who have found a spirituality rooted in Buddhist meditation, from Catholics who celebrate the mass in an uproarious charismatic celebration to those who prefer the quiet dignity of a Tridentine Mass, the church is broad enough for all. I found masses begun with the gentle tinkle of a bell, or a blast through a conch shell. The range is almost embarrassingly inclusive. Catholicism's faithful need not believe themselves to be part of an "either/or" religion, but rather one that espouses a "both/and" approach. There is unity, to be sure, but not uniformity.

Most would not claim my term as their own—and in fact may feel they are nowhere near "good enough"—but I found that Good Enough Catholics already abound; they have naturally evolved. They are fueled and inspired by Catholic teaching, sacraments, and community. They are also frustrated at times—both with the responsibilities of being a moral, religious person in a seemingly amoral, secular world, and with an institution that seems painfully slow to change and downright heartless at times. Yet they go on, even as authoritative voices within the church proclaim that unless you believe *this* and reject *that,* you cannot consider yourself a Catholic. Those voices will continue to be heard. But a more powerful voice is that of Christ, whose message was far less dogmatic and certainly more enigmatic. There is a dialectic—seemingly a contradiction—present in the life and teachings of Christ, a tension that puzzles, prods, and undergirds Catholics. Christ reached out his arms and said that God loved all people, no matter how far they sought to run away; the worst sinners were welcomed. Yet, almost in the same breath, he pointed a finger and said we can never do enough. There is room enough within Catholicism for us to rest secure in Christ's love, and to be challenged constantly.

# THE APPROACH

This book is focused on three purposes.

First, we all need to know the tradition in which we are rooted. For Catholics, this means trying to understand how human history and church history have transpired to influence church teaching and, through it, the lives of ordinary Catholics. A group of them—us—are alive today; and like Catholics throughout our rich history, we, in our own set of unique circumstances, seek a way to battle our inner demons and doubt, honor our God, and find happiness and fulfillment on this earth.

We do not need to reinvent the Catholic Church in our day; we need to reinterpret it. Our rich history stands behind us, not only sanctioning our pursuit, but urging us on.

For classical Catholic tradition holds that not only must *ecclesia docens*—church teaching—be used to guide the right conduct of the faithful, but so must the *sensus fidelium*—the response of the faithful—be considered. Both are crucial elements for the formation of a truly Catholic view of ourselves and the world. Neither is supreme; taken together, they represent a partnership we need to understand better, a partnership that has been, sadly, forgotten.

It is my hope that, through its short summary of various aspects of Catholic tradition, *The Good Enough Catholic* will offer some degree of education (as I was educated in researching it)—a refresher course for the initiated, new and crucial information for the many un-churched young Catholics, and a helpful guide for people with no faith background looking to the church as the place where they might find their spiritual home.

Second, as it moves from part to part, chapter to chapter, *The Good Enough Catholic* provides a way of addressing the most elemental and crucial parts of our lives, and help in answering the often vexing questions that any moral person faces. It needs to be said that this is not a book of sure answers. It is not a "how to" book. The intention is more to engender an *attitude*, a way that will provide readers the tools with which to fashion their own, individual lives—or, to put it another way, the moral building blocks of life. Institutional, spiritual, and human dimensions will be taken into account, for, while we all are part of Catholicism, each Catholic's experience is unique. We live in a variety of contexts—family, neighborhood, work, country, church—and each needs to be considered.

In essence, *The Good Enough Catholic* seeks to lay a firm foundation upon which to build a life, a new kind of Catholic life. The experiences of the people within this book are testimony that Catholicism can be lived in creative fidelity to both the church and to one's conscience—with elements of faith, of intellect, of experience.

Third, *The Good Enough Catholic* presents a challenge, a call to begin a transformation. At the end of each chapter, a number of suggestions are offered for putting theory into practice—gently, quietly, not perfectly. But Good Enough.

Please do not consider this a workbook. These are not chores to perform, or forced exercises. They are suggested as a natural progression for those who want to experience in practice what they can see makes sense in theory.

We live in an era of enormous freedom, freedom that carries with it equally enormous responsibility. Sometimes the freedom is dizzying and disorienting, and the responsibility seems overwhelming and daunting. And yet we want our lives to stand for something; we want challenges, not placebos. Catholicism can provide the guidelines, the encouragement, the sustenance, and the support system.

There is power in commitment. There is power, largely untapped, in the Catholic Church and in Catholic belief. And there is power within you beyond anything you have yet imagined.

One final note by way of introduction. In the course of doing the research for this book, it was my privilege to meet with scores of Good Enough Catholics all across the nation, to hear the stories of how they have lived out this faith we share, and to learn from them the ways in which they have struggled (often more successfully than I have) with the issues I wanted to address in this book. It soon became apparent to me that what I wanted to say would be greatly amplified by what they had to say to me. As a result, you will find throughout the chapters that follow the voices of a number of Good Enough Catholics. They are real people, living real lives, and working out a real faith—within the Catholic tradition we share. They did not always agree with me, or indeed with each other; but that is the whole point of the genuine quest that stands at the center of being a Good Enough Catholic. They were a source of tremendous inspiration to me, and I am deeply grateful to each of them. Occasionally, because of the circumstances of someone's life or the things they wanted to say, it seemed appropriate and right to protect their identity through the use of a pseudonym. When I have done so, an asterisk (*) follows the name I have given to that person.

# THE GOOD ENOUGH CATHOLIC

# ❦ PART I ❧

# THE INNER LIFE

*Without an inner life, we are wayfarers in the blackness of night without a light to guide us, lonesome travelers on life's road.*

*For the Good Enough Catholic, that inner life begins in the mystery of God and the reality of the man, Jesus Christ (chapter 1). We seek God, but God is unseen. Jesus Christ, who walked this earth, was a visible expression of God, a sign of God's hope for the human race.*

*The mass, and its central focus on the Eucharist (chapter 2), provides our primary sensory and spiritual encounter with God and Jesus Christ. The sacraments (chapter 3) are signs of the continuing presence of God in the world, offering sustenance and inspiration for our journey.*

*In prayer and the nurturing of a spiritual life (chapter 4), we reach out to God and, in turn, he touches us. Strengthened, we go forth into the world to live a moral life (chapter 5).*

# CHAPTER ONE

# JESUS CHRIST
## Wistfulness, Wishful Thinking, and Reality

Jesus Christ, the central figure of history, is the link between the historic covenant made by God with the wandering people of Israel, and another covenant, made by a God who chose to be physically present on earth in order to proclaim a message of timeless reconciliation between humankind and its loving creator. While certainly distinct, both covenants had the same object: to show God's nature to his people, and to reveal a plan for people to live in relationship with him and in harmony with their neighbors. God chose to be known in, and through, these covenants.

In essence, both covenants were unique points of contact between God and the beings he had made, beings whose very nature summoned them to transcend their earthly limitations and seek the divine.

To introduce a divine presence and make known a divine plan was a major order at both of these moments in history, 4,000 and 2,000 years ago. When God vowed to be the God of Israel and the Jews agreed in turn to be his people, the world was largely a chaotic, pagan place. Human sacrifice was widely practiced; the strong ruled, while the vast majority of humanity lived in constant fear and wretched poverty. There was no concept of the dignity and destiny of each person. In this setting, a tiny tribe of Israelites sought an alternative, vowing to live by a code of laws that sanctified daily actions and regarded all people as equal before their creator.

In what Catholics call the Old Testament, God spoke directly to and through the prophets, forming the people of Israel with both laws and direct intercession. The Jewish people were at times rescued and sustained, at other times punished and admonished, as they observed or ignored the way he had ordained for them.

With the birth of Jesus Christ, God stepped beyond using intermediaries to bring his message, and, Christians believe, came to earth to live as a human being. Jesus' message was clear and revolutionary to a world that, while certainly more advanced than the world of the early Hebrews, still had little regard for the worth of every individual. The message was this: No longer was the tribe or nation into which you were born a measure of your humanity. Whether you were highborn or low, man or woman, Greek or Jew, slave or free, made no difference. All people were children of God, loved equally by a creator in heaven. The social, economic, ethnic, sexual, and religious distinctions so tenaciously held and harshly imposed could no longer be used to elevate the few and denigrate the masses. Compassion and justice were the hallmarks of God's nature.

Throughout his life, by his example and by his words—both in the allegorical stories of the parables and by his direct exhortations—Jesus taught a moral code, a way of life ordained by God. In the words of St. Cyprian, "The commands of the gospel are nothing else than God's lessons, the foundations on which to build up hope, the supports for strengthening faith, the food that nourishes the heart. They are the rudder for keeping us on the right course. . . ."[1]

As we begin to consider what it is to be a Good Enough Catholic, we need first to understand, as best we can, who it is that founded our faith. Who are we following? What kind of man was Jesus Christ in his lifetime—and what kind of presence can he be in *our* lifetime?

# SHROUDED AND REVEALED

The person of Jesus Christ is enormously complex, at once vividly and poetically detailed in Holy Scripture, shrouded in history, and wrapped—often smothered—in layers of doctrinal gauze.

The nearest we have to contemporary portrayals of the life of Jesus comes, of course, from the New Testament gospels, each of which told the story of his life from a slightly different perspective. These accounts, written one or two generations after the death of Jesus, may or may not have been the work of Matthew, Mark, Luke, and John; most are certainly compilations of various texts. The Catholic Church acknowledges that there are three stages of tradition within the Gospels that must be considered: first, the actual life of Jesus Christ, his actions and his words; second, the oral handing-down of the story of his life and ministry; and finally, the actual written word, which forms the basis of the New Testament as we know it today. So, each stage possesses its own reality—some of which we know, much of which we do not.

In his life, Jesus seemed to play many (often seemingly contradictory) roles. He was at once an obedient and divine Son to a heavenly Father, and a normal mortal pleading for an alternative to the bitter cup of death by crucifixion. He preached peace, yet angrily overturned the tables in the temple. He allowed the tax collector to continue his rounds, but demanded that the rich young man sell everything. Jesus is alternately teacher, ruler, judge, king, holy man, mystic, liberator, brother, apocalyptic prophet, social revolutionary, and healer. He is both peacemaker and the disrupter of peace. We see him today as a man who responded differently in different situations, sometimes surprisingly so.

Confronting such a multifaceted individual, it is little wonder that the church attempted, over the centuries, to interpret the words of Scripture so that the faithful not be led astray. Many Catholics can remember the days when simply reading the Bible was discouraged, on the belief that the ordinary faithful did not possess the knowledge or erudition to understand the reality of the man upon whose life their own religious life was based. Instead, we were served up tiny dollops of Scripture each Sunday and immediately told exactly what they meant.

Much debate throughout church history has centered on questions concerning, on the one hand, the "person" of Jesus Christ, and, on the other, the "work" he performed. In other words, this debate sought somehow to distinguish between what about Jesus was human and what was divine. The early church struggled to construct a body of teachings about Jesus that stressed his divine nature, and overlooked, if not ignored, his human side, as well as the historical era in which he lived. By the Middle Ages, culminating in the work of Thomas Aquinas (d. 1274), the distinctions became even more marked; Jesus Christ the human being was deemed too immediate, too lowly, for inclusion in teachings about Jesus Christ the Son of the Most High.

With the dawning of the Enlightenment in the eighteenth century, as political upheavals, philosophical skepticism, and scientific discoveries challenged what had become the church's unquestioned religious authority, new approaches to understanding Jesus Christ were born. These ideas were opposed bitterly by the church for over a century, which maintained that it alone—not human reason, historical research, or scientific fact—could plumb the depths of the mystery of Jesus Christ.

It was not until the Second Vatican Council (1962–1965) that Jesus Christ was "released" from the shrouds of mystery and doctrinal exactitude imposed by centuries of church intervention, and a new appreciation—indeed, a reintegration—of the historical and divine man begun. Even so, many Catholics alive today—myself among them—were taught to set Jesus Christ apart from and above them, convinced that it was nothing short of sacrilegious to bid him come down from a tabernacle on an altar, or a throne in heaven, and into our lives.

The past twenty-five years have dramatically changed how we regard Jesus Christ. As the theologian David Tracy notes, more has been written about Jesus in that comparatively short period than had been written in the 1,975 years preceding them.[2] Archaeological discoveries in the cities and villages where Jesus preached and lived, interpreted by a new generation of biblical scholars, have given us a much clearer understanding of this man—placing him not only in a historical and cultural context, but in an even more accurate religious one. Where once this field of "Jesus studies" was the domain of a small group of academics and theologians, many of today's Catholic seekers, struggling with their own religious beliefs, are hungry to understand who Jesus really was in hopes of making him an integral and active part of their lives. Marcus J. Borg, a leading Jesus scholar, observes of these seekers, "For them, their childhood understanding of Jesus and the Bible at some point stopped working, but their religious interest remains."[3]

We Good Enough Catholic lay people are not alone on the path of discovering who Jesus was and is. The majority of Catholic priests and nuns were themselves schooled in the same limited view. "I love that experience of these different parts of Jesus that seem strange to me for long periods, and then all of a sudden become familiar," says Father William Kenneally,[4] the pastor of St. Gertrude's, one of Chicago's most vibrant parishes.

# FORMED TO FIT

Whether our Jesus resides on the altar or sits next to us as we drive to work, we may discover that our own idea of the Savior is sometimes born of convenient choice.

"Too often the Christ of our personal faith bears little resemblance to the Jesus of history or the Christ of the church's faith," advises Richard P. McBrien in his comprehensive and readable volume, *Catholicism*. "We make of Jesus Christ what *we* would like him to be for us. Consequently, he no longer challenges us from the outside to conform to him, but rather we project on him all that we are or would like to be. The affirmation of the Lordship of Jesus becomes, then, a form of self-affirmation."[5]

To stubbornly make only one of the characteristics of Jesus your definitive statement about him and the measure of how he should influence your life is much the same as quoting from the Bible to prove a point. Through skilled and selective use of Holy Scripture, it is possible to support an argument for unrelenting warfare or for absolute pacifism, for resisting authority or yielding to it, for turning a cheek or standing pat. Such arguments are not necessarily wrong—but by reducing the message of the Bible to a few favorite phrases, the result is likely to be far from right. No less the same is true of the complex character of Jesus of Nazareth.

If Catholicism is to be the truly rich, life-enhancing experience we expect it to be (or else why pursue the Good Enough Catholic life at all?), we need to find in Jesus Christ a model to challenge and inspire us, not merely an empty vessel to fill with lukewarm self-affirmation. We need a divine presence, here and now, in our present condition. We need a Jesus in the home, on the street, on the job, in the community and world—as well as a Jesus in church or private prayer. We need a Jesus who is consistent, and yet able—and who can help *us* to be able—to deal with the inconsistencies and ever-changing circumstances of life.

Moreover, we will find that we need a *different* Jesus Christ at different points in our lives. If there are stages of emotional growth, are there not stages of spiritual growth? The Jesus of our childhood is not the Jesus of our adult life.

What stops many of us Catholics from really drawing on Jesus Christ's example and power is that our Jesus quite literally never got past grade school. We grew up, but somehow he didn't. The Jesus that many of us learned about was a superhuman being possessed of divine qualities and miraculous powers. He could turn water into wine, produce a net full of fish, heal a leper, even raise the dead. He seemed to know exactly what his mission was, and he fulfilled it to perfection. He was profoundly other-worldly. Yes, we were taught that he was "like us in all things yet without sin," but few really believed it. Jesus was to be honored and revered—and therefore, in deference to his overwhelming holiness, most of us kept our distance.

We could hardly imagine a Jesus who cried as a baby, didn't want to do his household chores as a teenager, or wondered (and perhaps worried) as an adult where his next meal would come from. In the pre–Vatican II church, theology was more dogmatic than pastoral, more interested in defending the "one, true faith" through the development of apologetics than inspiring people to live that faith as best they could. The theology of that era was selective, effectively cutting Jesus off from his time and place in history. As Catholics we were to adore, but never to befriend; to have a personal relationship with Jesus seemed too Protestant for most of us. "Jesus Christ, the same yesterday, today, and tomorrow," resounds through the corridors of our minds. Ultimately, that distant, unchangeable Jesus was not much of a help to us as we grew—and indeed, often more of a problem.

The idea of an unchangeable Jesus Christ simply hasn't proven true in my life, and perhaps not in yours either. The Jesus I prayed to for a new electric train, or to help me penetrate the mysteries of algebra, is not the Jesus I call out to in the dark nights of the life of a writer or parent. Yes, a childlike faith can remain with us; I hope it never leaves me. But as we understand more about ourselves and experience more of life, our relationship to Jesus can also change.

"I knew who Christ was theologically, historically, doctrinally from my seminary training, that I was supposed to bring the message of the incardinated Christ into the world. But what did all that mean to a living, breathing human being? Ah, my youthful, intellectual, and sure approach to Christ! What I didn't understand was that the Gospels are living, being borne out in each generation, that Christ is alive in a different way every day of my life."

—MARTY HEGARTY

> "I listened to high school kids—rough-looking kids you would
> be afraid of on the street—and heard them talk about Jesus as their
> 'Walk boy,' their best friend. They had faith, they really *knew* him;
> he was a part of their lives."
>
> —JOHN BUTLER

# THE "CORE" OF JESUS CHRIST

Accepting that the words of the New Testament can neither be taken completely at face value, nor are completely accurate historically, might at first seem an insurmountable impediment to understanding Jesus as a man, and as God's son. But getting past such literal restrictions actually frees the Good Enough Catholic to better understand, and then embrace, Jesus' message.

Indeed, stripped of our selective readings and the church's sometimes self-serving interpretations, the message of Jesus is startlingly clear. There is a sturdy consistency in what he said, did, and stood for that has not materially changed. Four threads, woven through his life, underscore this consistency: Jesus' dealings with religious authority; the audience he chose to speak to; the new commandment, love, that he stressed; and the way he never shied from being tested. These "attitudes" of Jesus show us the essence of his life and message, and create a foundation upon which the Good Enough Catholic can build a life.

In attempting to understand the man regarded as the founder of Christianity, we must remember that Jesus was a traditional, law-abiding Jew—and not the first Christian. He worshiped and taught in a synagogue, prayed as a Jew, and performed Jewish rituals. Modern scholarship has concluded that it was never Jesus' intention to start a new religion, but instead to reform and humanize Judaism as it was practiced in his day. He said he came not to abolish Jewish law, but to make it a means both to salvation and to a good and peaceful life on earth.

It is when Jesus confronts religious authorities (notably, he never advocated revolution against the Roman occupation) that the first key aspect of his ministry becomes apparent. At a time when ritual observance was central to Jewish religious life, Jesus was calling for something far deeper: an inner, personal transformation. Circumcision marked the Jewish male; Jesus was calling for a circumcision of every heart, male and female. External observances, while they could help to enrich one's faith, were hollow without a proper inner disposition.

Again and again, Jesus found himself in opposition to the clerical hierarchy and teachers of the law—the Judaic "magisterium," if you will. He exasperated the religious authorities of the day by proclaiming that not every law was of equal importance, and that no law could be uniformly enforced in all situations. Food was not impure; it was what came *out* of one's mouth that mattered, not what went in. He pointed out that Judaism's leaders had fashioned an oppressive yoke, rather than a means to salvation; they had strayed from God's intent. Yes, the sabbath should be kept holy—but not if a person was in need of healing, or a donkey required a lift out of a ditch. Jesus challenged traditional beliefs, proclaiming that it was not only acceptable, but sometimes *necessary*, to disobey religious edicts in order to obey God.

And so, Jesus Christ's teachings regarding religious practice were object lessons in divine common sense, not slavish adherence to a given set of rules.

"The Jesus that I know is a Jesus who works with people nobody else wanted to deal with. I want to walk in Jesus' shoes and do what he would have done with these kids. They're dangerous, they're drug addicts, they are hard to handle. But what do we do, just leave them to die on the street? Would Jesus have turned his back?"

—DOROTHY PAPACHRISTOS

"I don't think Jesus ever asked of people if they were good or bad, law-abiding or law-breaking—straight or gay. He confronted them with the Beatitudes. 'Did you feed the hungry; did you clothe the naked? Did you take care of the person right in front of you?' That's the measure of Jesus, the Jesus I follow."

—TOM EAKINS*

Jesus' presence among the socially marginalized and politically disenfranchised demonstrated that, while they might be outside what was a relatively small privileged class, they were never outside God's concern. The New Testament stories remind us continually that Jesus spent most of his time with the poor, the sick, and the ritually unclean, with outcasts, lepers, and prostitutes; it was upon the neglected and ignored that he chose to shower his teachings and miracles. As though to underscore the point, he chose illiterate fishermen and others of questionable repute for his companions. Jesus showed over and over that he had come to save all people, not just those regarded by society or themselves as holy. He constantly preached that every man and woman stood equal before God as his created beings.

But for all this, Jesus seems to have been completely uninterested in creating any kind of formal structure, or in writing a new set of laws. He was hardly an organization man; he wrote not one word. He simply lived what he believed.

## WHAT IS THIS THING CALLED LOVE?

By the time Jesus Christ was born in Roman Palestine, human communities had fashioned and fought over a number of different systems to run their affairs. Raw power exerted by the strongest was one way, Roman law another, Jewish law still another. Jesus astounded and enraged the vested powers of the day by claiming that something quite different from any power previously called upon, any system previously attempted, was needed. There was a better foundation for human interaction; love was the answer, Jesus said. Love of God, love of neighbor as oneself.

The mere mention of that word—love—conjures in some minds the image of a bearded Jesus clad in a flowing robe, two fingers raised in a peace sign, with a dreamy smile on his face. As Good Enough Catholics face the complexities of their lives in today's world, this image of Jesus Christ is hardly the kind of inspiration we are looking for.

> "My Christ is a *strong* Christ. At the crucifixion he showed great strength and courage. Yes, I believe the words about turning the other cheek, but I also believe we are temples of God and not doormats. Yes, be kind and compassionate, but you must also respect yourself—Christ wants that of us, too."
>
> —MAGALIE SALAS

The love that Jesus spoke of and lived was certainly not sentimental mush, accepting every action. His was not an "I'm okay, you're okay" approach. Dostoevsky spoke of a "harsh and dreadful love"; and sometimes Christian love is exactly that. "Tough love," a term that has entered our lexicon recently, seems a contradiction in terms, but it is often the sort of love we are challenged to offer. Saying "no," turning our back—real love at times requires such acts of toughness. At other times, gentleness is the only loving response. The love that Jesus embodied had many, many expressions. Again, it depended on the circumstances, the people involved—balancing the need of the moment against longer-term needs.

Love wasn't easy for Jesus to put into practice; after all, he inhabited a human body and was subject to normal human emotions. How well we Good Enough Catholics know that living up to the best that is in us isn't easy in our everyday lives. But it is upon this cornerstone of love that his life was built, and it can be our foundation as well. This need not be a hair-shirt denial of self, giving no place to one's own needs and deferring to others in every situation; not at all. It is a love—while difficult to practice at times—at once practical, useful, and fulfilling. When do we feel better: loving or hating? Healing a wound or inflicting one? Indeed, love *is* the answer.

Paul's letter to the Colossians spells out clearly how Jesus lived and what he wanted of his followers: "Put on then . . . compassion, kindness, lowliness, meekness, and patience, forbearing one another and, if one has a complaint against another, forgiving each other; as the Lord has forgiven you, so you also must forgive. And above all these put on love, which binds everything together in perfect harmony."[6]

That is a daunting, lofty goal, and certainly we will fail in achieving it. But as Good Enough Catholics, not Perfect Catholics, applying, genuinely and sincerely, our best efforts, we will often—quite often—succeed.

Finally, what comes through strongly from the life of Jesus Christ is the way he constantly opened his principles and ideas to testing. Whether it was by the petty pharisaic priests, the devil in the wilderness, or the timidity of his own disciples, Jesus was regularly confronted with choices: accept the status quo, take the easier path, abandon those high ideals as unworkable, impractical. What is more, beyond the human capabilities we bring with us, Jesus had another option: He could act like the God he was, summoning the powers that were his to command.

Jesus never set aside the humanity he accepted by being born into this world. He seemed never to make up excuses, or to use an excuse readily at hand. Couldn't he, on Holy Thursday evening in the Garden of Gethsemane, have looked upon his sleeping disciples and complained (with some justification): "I'm going to die for the likes of *you*?" He saw beyond that moment, and measured up to the ultimate test.

"Christ to me is Nikos Kazantzakis's *Last Temptation of Christ.* He was someone who grew, who struggled, who made horrible mistakes. He was delighted by things he did well and appalled when he didn't do things well. Human, totally human; he could never escape that—and neither can any of us."

—PAT REARDON

"Christ was revealed to me in a strange way, when my teenage daughter played Christ in a Passion play. She yelled, she screamed, she stamped her feet. She was a Jesus who bowed to God, but not without a struggle, a man discovering his own destiny and trying to figure out his life. I believe in a divine Jesus as well as a human one, but I can't get close to the divine. I can always identify with a human Jesus. That wasn't my daughter up there. It was him!"

—NATASHA WITSCHY

Certainly Jesus flew into rages and sank into despondency; what human being doesn't? But he never gave up, sensing God's presence in his life, knowing that each test made him stronger, not weaker, forging a character that could stand up to anything. So will we be shaped by the tests that life presents to us; so can we be sure, with faith, that God seeks us as we seek him.

Ancient texts and modern research give us many pictures of Jesus. Similarly, individual believers experience Jesus in a variety of ways. In my travels through Catholic America, I was constantly amazed by the diversity and richness of this relationship. Catholics are struggling to understand the man Jesus Christ, to bring him down from the altar and into their lives.

"As a kid in Los Angeles, I remember the priest coming to bless the house," said David Suley, who works for a nonprofit organization in Washington. "We had the Sacred Heart enshrined in our house. *He was there.* God was present in our house, and I never felt religion was oppressive. I lived in one of the most conservative dioceses in America, one that fought Vatican II to the end; but I just don't have memories of Catholicism being harsh. I had that nice fuzzy feeling about Christ but it wasn't until high school that I realized 'Holy mackerel, this is really real!' It was a revelation, but it was built on a firm foundation. He's always been in my life, in one incarnation or another."

The Kustusch family in Chicago is one of the growing number of Catholic evangelicals, unabashedly conservative in their religious beliefs. Bob and Cappy Kustusch are home-schooling their five children, finding even the local Catholic school not up to their demanding moral standards. When I spent an evening in their neat home on the West Side of Chicago, it was soon apparent that being institutional Catholics is not what is important to them (although they are); "A relationship with Christ, that is what counts," Bob said. His words were echoed by his wife and children. "Every day, every action, every breath, he's here," Cappy said as she patted the cushion next to her.

Christopher Hebein, who is twenty years old and serves as an altar boy at St. Nicholas in Evanston, has Down's syndrome. When I asked him, point-blank, "Who is Jesus?" Chris smiled that wonderful smile that only Down's children are blessed with. "Jesus is a girl," he said definitively. "She's pretty. She would say to me, 'I love you very much, Chris, and I'm walking with you, wherever you go, every day.' " A thousand-page book of theology couldn't say it better.

At the end of this short discussion of the life and personhood of Jesus Christ—and at the beginning of our consideration of what a Good Enough Catholic life involves—must we now constantly confront authority, talk to the marginalized, love unabashedly, and never pass up a test?

No; that is not what is asked.

In Judaism there are 613 laws, or *mitzvot*. No Jew yet created has performed all of them. They are guidelines, targets of moral excellence to aim for. So, too, the life of Jesus Christ provides both example and inspiration. No Christian has yet replicated that life; the challenge is to be the best possible person we can be, given our own abilities and life circumstances. Not perfect—but Good Enough.

Jesus made it clear, through his own example and in his words that come down to us today: Ours is a forgiving, merciful God, a God who asks for our best effort, not a perfect performance, not absolute results.

## THE GOOD ENOUGH CATHOLIC CHALLENGE:
## DISCOVER THE SOURCE

It is no longer enough for modern-day Catholics to follow Jesus Christ without knowing who it is they are following—or simply because the church says to do so. A Christ mandated by doctrine, or peering down from a pious face in a painting, may or may not provide a starting point for a spiritual life; but he is assuredly not the Christ who can be taken into the world, a Christ who can be our confidant, a Christ who will be our model and trusted guide.

By honestly trying to know and understand him, however imperfect and tentative our efforts may be, the Good Enough Catholic shows Jesus great honor and respect. To limit him only to a place of reverence—in church, for instance—is to imprison and marginalize him, showing how irrelevant he is to our real day-to-day life.

It is time to discover the source.

How can this be done? Some of the answers are spelled out in this book, but they are fairly apparent. If you want to get to know someone, there is no better way than spending time together. Here are some possibilities, the first Good Enough Catholic challenge.

Read one page of the New Testament, or one page of a book about Jesus' life and message each day for one week. Pray a short daily prayer for one week. ("I want to know you," is prayer enough.) Be silent, and listen for his response.

When you attend mass, do so with heightened anticipation. *Want* to know him. That, amazingly, is enough—Good Enough.

Think about him. What would Jesus do in this situation in my life? It is not that you must do the same; that's more than most of us are able to do. For now, just think of Jesus and watch what he does and says.

Look for him. Your answer to the presence of Jesus Christ in the world may not be the televangelist with the 900 number whose every second word is "Jesus." Rather, it may be that person in a newspaper story caring for a parent with Alzheimer's, or someone you work with who quietly brings a sandwich each day for the homeless person who stands outside your office building. Jesus Christ is present in many ways: be open to seeing him in the people around you.

Finally, call upon him—yes, call upon him. This is sometimes hard for Catholics, oddly enough. Call it prayer, call it whatever you choose. If Jesus Christ is God and God created you and me, don't you think he's open to our needs?

If we begin to honestly seek the power and the presence of this man, something will begin to happen. It is mysterious, but it is inevitable. We will receive counsel to make wise decisions, strength to help us meet both daily trials and major adversities; a new patience will be ours.

The Good Enough Catholic we want to be will begin to emerge.

## SELECTED READINGS

Raymond E. Brown, *An Introduction to New Testament Christology*. New York: Paulist Press, 1994.

Joseph A. Fitzmyer, *A Christological Cathechism* (revised edition). New York: Paulist Press, 1991.

Elizabeth Johnson, *Consider Jesus: Waves of Renewal in Christology*. New York: Crossroad, 1990.

Luke Timothy Johnson, *The Real Jesus: The Misguided Quest for the Historical Jesus and the Truth of the Traditional Gospels*. New York: HarperCollins, 1995.

Thomas Keating, *The Mystery of Christ: The Liturgy as Spiritual Experience.* Rockport, Mass.: Element, 1991.

John P. Meier, *A Marginal Jew.* 2 vols. New York: Doubleday, 1994.

Gerard O'Collins, *Christology: A Biblical, Historical, and Systematic Study of Jesus.* New York: Oxford University Press, 1996.

# MASS AND THE EUCHARIST
## The Source

It may seem strange to pluck one of the sacraments—the Eucharist—out of the context of the seven sacraments, and to continue the discussion of the Good Enough Catholic's inner life here. Yet in certain ways, it makes perfect sense. For as Father Robert A. Wolfe, a pastor in Houston, succinctly sums it up, the Eucharist is "[t]he most direct way Catholics have of experiencing the presence of God. . . ."[1]

Today, while it may be called a liturgy, a celebration of the Eucharist, or the mass, and though its language and appearance may have dramatically changed, this cornerstone of Catholic belief has remained a constant source of spiritual nourishment throughout the centuries. It is at once ritual and rally, community gathering and private worship, a sign of unity and declaration of individuality. Ordinary people gather with the intent of calling God down into their midst and, in that process, bring him into their lives.

As I listened to how Good Enough Catholics are living out their religious beliefs today, I heard no more intimate and detailed stories about any aspect of Catholicism than those I heard about Holy Communion. Almost everyone can remember their First Communion: the clothes they wore, the procession, the first taste of that wafer of unleavened bread, the sensation that this moment was somehow like no other. Many others can recall especially poignant Eucharists—in a foreign country, at a wedding or funeral, at a particularly joyous or difficult time in life. Moreover, converts often point to the experience of the Eucharist as the reason they were first attracted to the faith.

"Here I was, a good Methodist from Iowa, at a bad time in my life—and for some reason I looked in the phone book to find when the Catholic church closest to me had its masses. I went when I was sure there would be no mass, because I just wanted to check out Catholicism in a quiet, empty church. But, why was it, the listing was wrong? Mass was going on, so I just stumbled in. It was strange; I felt both restless and at home—and yet it wasn't my home at all. Then I saw all the people going to communion. Tears started streaming down my face. I *had* come home."
—CAROLYN SWEERS

"I try to go to mass and take communion at noon whenever I can during the week—just so I touch base with Christ right in the middle of the day to see if David is doing okay. It's a status report to see how I've done in the first half of the day, and to give me strength to be a better man in the second half."
—DAVID SULEY

While other Christian faiths place primary emphasis on the words of Scripture or on a preacher's interpretation and insights (which, it should be noted, was neither Luther's nor Calvin's intent in breaking away from Rome during the Protestant Reformation), Catholicism has always maintained the primacy of the Eucharist. This was and is seen as *direct* access to God, through a sacrifice inaugurated by his son. It is because the Eucharist is so powerful and so central to Catholic identity that this part of our religious heritage and culture has set an indelible mark upon our consciousness. It will not leave us alone—regardless of how we might at times try to avoid it.

Within most Catholics' memories is a time when Sunday mass was so much a part of a Catholic upbringing that missing it was simply unthinkable. But those days are gone—a shift confirmed in a recent study. Only about 25 percent of all Catholics attend mass on a given Sunday. As for the other 75 percent—what of them? Can Sunday mass be set aside so easily?

I think not.

I have a sense that, all across America every Sunday morning, millions upon millions of Catholics wake up to experience a weekly itch they cannot scratch. They read the newspaper, pour another cup of coffee, turn on their favorite music; they go out to play golf or sail the boat, play with the kids, work in the yard. If only they can fill those hours before noon, the itch will subside; but those hours on Sunday morning are some of the most difficult lapsed Catholics face all week.

"I used to lie to my parents about going to church. I might stop by and bring home a bulletin, just to cover myself. It was a church where you never felt good enough; you were basically bad. And I hated it. This was in 1968 or so, and I just stopped all pretenses of going to church. But what eventually happened in my life is that I just felt this great urge and need to go to church. I reconverted to Catholicism. And it was tough, because I felt surrounded by all these righteous Catholics, who didn't believe what I did as a feminist on a lot of issues. But a friend said, 'Wait a minute. This is your church, too. Don't let those people push you out of it.' "

—MARY MURPHY ZASTROW

"Right after my marriage—and it was a beautiful Catholic ceremony—I purposefully missed mass the very next Sunday. I wasn't going every week; I wasn't going to feel obligated. That was the old church, and I wasn't buying into it. Then I went, and one of the parables really struck me. I found I needed this, every week. I need to be educated, I need to be reminded. Mass became, instead of an obligation, an education of how to be a good person in the world."

—GAIL SMITH

They know something is missing; they know they want to be, need to be, in a place where they can be with God. It is as simple— and profound—as that. Catholicism, faint though it might be in the recesses of their minds, will not let them rest on Sunday morning. They *want* to be in church, in a Catholic church, at mass; but for whatever reason, they are not. They may be angry about a certain church teaching, or incensed at church narrowness; they may still harbor resentment at a priest or nun who treated them cruelly in their impressionable youth.

At one time, they might have felt guilty for not going to mass. That subsided years ago; but the resulting emptiness has not gone away so easily.

A yearning to be in touch with God may ripple across their minds at other, less predictable, times throughout the week. It can occur simply walking by the front door of a Catholic chapel on a busy city street and, seeing people go in, feeling an almost overwhelming compulsion to follow them. That tiny Catholic voice within, at once so faint, is still so clear. "I remember what it was like," the voice might say, "and I want to feel that connection with God again." The ineffable hunger that humans have felt down through the ages still calls out to be satisfied.

# TRADITIONAL MEAL, UNCOMMON FOOD

The first Eucharist occurred in a most natural way; it was at a meal, a thoroughly Jewish meal. It was Passover; the time had come to commemorate and relive once again the miracle of God's "passing over" the firstborn of the Israelites as he killed the firstborn of the Egyptians who had refused to release his chosen people from bondage.

With Jesus at the seder table was a gathering of quite ordinary people; all of them were observant Jews. They came from varied backgrounds, and the depth of their commitment to him varied as well. Some were frankly confused about who he was and what he seemed to be asking of them. Then something happened at that Passover meal, a divine inspiration that inalterably changed human and religious history.

Jesus sensed that his time with his followers was limited, that he would soon no longer be physically among them. He knew well the difficulties of human life, for he had lived one—but he also knew the power and love of the father who had sent him. He wanted to bridge that gap, that chasm between heaven and earth, for all time. Reaching outside conventional Jewish ritual, he took two common elements of the meal—the loaf of unleavened bread and the cup of wine. He blessed the bread he held in his hand, saying that it was now his body. He blessed the cup; it was now his blood. In essence, he was prefiguring the sacrifice he would make the next day on Calvary; but he went further. He asked his friends to repeat his blessing over the bread and wine at future meals, and to do so remembering him.

"The Eucharist to me is a chance to be spiritually fed, and a chance—as Jesus did on Holy Thursday—to refocus the dream. The dream is to transform the world into a fitting place for people and for God. And so, there is nothing worse than a sloppy mass and I don't blame people for not coming back or leaving the church if that's all they experience. The mass must be done with great dignity, honor, and intelligence. And people will hunger for it."

—DICK WESTLY

"Instead of the standard words of the consecration about the body and blood being given up for me, I hear 'David, my body, my blood, everything, is for you. My power. My grace. My love. You have it all. I give it all to you.' Now, what can be more inspirational than that?"

—DAVID SULEY

The magnitude of this moment and this promise cannot be overstated. God had instituted many rituals for the Jews, so that they might acknowledge their special relationship to him and recall those signal events when he had interceded for them. But this was not symbol, commemoration, or ritual; this was a guarantee of the *actual presence of the Lord God of the Universe*.

Equally noteworthy is the humility, the understatement, of the Last Supper. Jesus gave the power to summon God's presence into our world to ordinary human beings, with no special training, lineage or qualifications. It was to be neither difficult nor complicated. He would readily come when beckoned.

So often we have heard the term "the word made flesh"; here it was lived out. God's word in the law had been the Jews' experience of their covenant with him; henceforth, his flesh, the body of his own son, would continually feed the people of the New Covenant.

Biblical scholars have determined that it is doubtful the disciples initially understood what Jesus was doing. But, after his death, resurrection, and the Pentecost experience, they—and an ever-growing number of converts—continued the tradition of blessing and sharing bread and wine at their common meals together, and not only at their annual seder tables. Confidence filled them, happiness swept over them as they repeated Christ's words and shared this holy remembrance. And, indeed, they *did* feel his presence among them. Something beyond the sensation of warm memory, something transcendent, was theirs for the summoning.

It was not a formalized ritual; no one in particular was commissioned to preside. These followers of Jesus Christ were simply doing as he had bidden them: to gather in small groups, take common food and drink, and bless it—doing so in memory of him.

By the second and third centuries, as the growing Christian community evolved, the meal gradually disappeared; the Eucharist became a central focus, embellished by a variety of prayers, responses, and readings from both the Old and the emerging New Testaments. Singing was added, most often hymns based on the Psalter. Incense,

candles, and other marks of solemnity gradually found their way into
the commemoration of the Eucharist, as the early Christians combined Christ's words and teachings with elements of their own religious tradition, both Jewish and pagan. Creeds, which summarized
the common beliefs, were formulated by the bishops of the fourth-
century church and memorized by the faithful, most of whom were
illiterate.

As the church spread to other parts of the world, the celebration
of mass and the Eucharist developed into richly diverse experiences.
In different geographical areas, cultures, and religious orders, the
masses were fashioned in keeping with local needs, customs, and
language. Liturgical standardization, beginning with the restriction
after the thirteenth century that only the officially ordained, and not
the community, could offer mass, was firmly set in place four centuries ago with the Council of Trent (1545–1563), which mandated
that Latin—and specific Latin prayers—be used for worship. This
move to make the mass the same throughout the universal church
also brought with it an increasingly reverential, as opposed to communitarian, form of worship.

The canon, or Eucharistic prayer, was eventually spoken only by
the priest, and in a tone inaudible to the congregants—a sign of the
holiness of the moment. His back was turned toward the worshipers; the sanctuary was set off from the body of the church by a
railing. Even the centrality of sharing in the Eucharistic meal was
undermined by the heresy of Jansenism (mid-seventeenth century),
because of which, considering themselves unworthy, many of the
faithful refrained from receiving communion. Jansenism generally
held a pessimistic view of human nature and demanded strict asceti-
cism. Only those who felt themselves sufficiently holy dared approach the altar. Certainly, the Good Enough Catholics of the era
were not among the chosen.

Nothing could have been farther from the spirit of the Eucharist
as it had been instituted at the Last Supper among that humble gathering of people with their varying levels of faith, commitment, and
understanding. Even Judas, it must be remembered, received the
bread and wine.

For centuries, the Eucharist was considered a sacred feast to be taken with great decorum, infrequently, and only by those untainted by even the slightest sin. It was only in the early twentieth century, under Pope Pius X (d. 1914), that early and frequent reception of the Eucharist was again advocated by the church. Pius X, otherwise a staunch traditionalist, concluded that the power of the Eucharist was simply too great to be so closely hoarded.

The Eucharist and mass have gone through many changes in style— and even content—as humans have attempted to fathom its meaning and experience its power. So it is important for the Good Enough Catholic to realize that the *essence* of the Eucharist is more important than its various liturgical forms. In fact, the "old," pre–Vatican II (or Tridentine) mass is hardly that old, and certainly was not the way mass had been celebrated through most of church history.

> "After a Baptist service, I might have felt pumped up, the adrenaline was flowing. But then I immediately began to feel empty. I need the mass to focus on Christ, not the individual at the front whose preaching might be good or bad that day. I found I need ritual in my life; I needed that kind of order in my life, and the Catholic Church gave it to me."
>
> —LEON ROBERTS

Happily for modern-day Catholics, the mass we attend today— and frequent reception of the Eucharist—has more in common with the communal gatherings of early Christians than with the Latin Mass that many of us knew as children. In these not-so-long-ago days, the congregation for the most part sat mute; the altar boy mouthed the responses in a language that probably he, like most of the congregation, did not understand; and the priest seemed to be performing a ritual of such secrecy that his words were not to be uttered by the likes of us. He *said* mass.

Today, *we*—now known as the priesthood of believers— communally *celebrate* the mass. *We*, responding to Christ's invitation, beckon to him to be present among us. The priest presides at this festive, holy occasion.

# THE OPPORTUNITY TO ATTEND MASS

The mass had changed dramatically in a single generation, and such change can be expected to bring a mixture of serendipity (for those who wanted to be more active participants, in a language they could understand) and loss (for those who treasured the richness of the old reverence). And what of those who have been away from the church for years, who may feel, upon returning to mass, rather as though they have come upon a new and strange sect?

"Where do I sit? What will I do? Like many immigrants, I was apprehensive about attending mass when I arrived in America. How should I behave? What will people say? And here I am, a—as you say—cradle Catholic. I was so amazed. I found the same God. The same Christ in this church as in Bangladesh. Different cultures, but here is a church that binds us together around the globe. The church is bigger and stronger than any nation or culture. What a wonderful feeling to have such a church."

—SHILPI D'COSTA

"I remember back to the days of bowing your head and worshiping in silence. I used to feel that's the way it would always be. Then, there I was, standing under the basketball hoop in a gymnasium for mass, a dialogue mass, and with a coffee hour afterward. The mass is people together, and that means more than individual piety. The first time I came to the gym mass I really wept, at the beauty of it, the closeness I felt."

—MARY ANNE BARRY

While some may have preferred the Latin cadences of the Tridentine Mass for its more devotional decorum, the rich diversity of liturgies today makes the mass both a more accessible and a more deeply spiritual experience for most people. In a sense, we have returned to a time before the Council of Trent, a time when the mass was more in tune with the diversity of the peoples who constituted the global church. Today, there are charismatic masses and African-American masses; there are masses chanted in the quiet of a Trappist monastery church, or accompanied with folk music in a gymnasium. At Weston Priory in Vermont, there is liturgical dance; at St. Mary Gate of Heaven in Hawaii, a blast on a conch shell summons worshipers, and drums are used for the processional. At a Tridentine Mass, Latin is the common language. At St. Mary's, my parish church in Wilmington, North Carolina, there are high-church masses, and masses with hand-clapping, foot-stomping accompaniment to the gospel choir.

In its many manifestations, the mass remains, as the Second Vatican Council proclaims, ". . . the summit toward which the activity of the church is directed; at the same time it is the fountain from which all its power flows."[2] And, in a revolutionary new understanding of the mass, the council taught that Christ is not *only* present in the consecrated bread and wine, but also in the biblical readings that are proclaimed, in the priest who presides, and—remarkably—in all of us assembled for worship. Christ had promised to be among those gathered in his name; now, finally, after centuries of theological and dogmatic encrustation, this gracious act has been returned to us in its majestic simplicity. We are there, seeking to be with Christ. Christ is there, seeking to be with us.

It is no wonder the mass has such a special place for Catholics. The Notre Dame study of Catholic parish life showed that we overwhelmingly *like* the mass. We treasure the ritual and the prayers, but are less enthusiastic about the quality of the sermons and music. The reality of God's presence transcends—whether you are surrounded by family and the like-minded, or among those with whom you have little in common, at home or far away, at peace or in conflict.

"At mass, I don't have to do anything but pray and be quiet. It's a real counterpoint to my week. No other time in my week is the power of faith so strong in my life, and without it, I really couldn't write the kinds of things I do, or live the kind of life I do."

—JOHN FIALKA

"When you have lost your country, you might be able to plant flowers to remember how you did it in Vietnam, but you really have no roots. We Vietnamese were frustrated and depressed and poor; we came with no more than we could carry. Many of us were Catholics, and we were used to a very serious mass, not like here in America. So the first thing we had to do was have our own mass, our own spiritual home so we could pray to God as a group. This, *this*, could not be taken from us."

—LE TRONG PHU

"The cocoon of the pre–Vatican II church is gone, of course. We realize the differences people had all along. But the idea is not to homogenize those differences. Respect them, even though there'll be friction."

—PAT REARDON

There are so many layers within the mass, so much richness proffered. In a single hour, the mass provides a time to focus on your inner self, to place the burdens of life before a loving father. It offers a pause from the hectic pace of life to see if the path we are on is the path to true happiness on this earth, and to eternal unity with God. Here is a chance to ask forgiveness, and to be assured it is forthcoming, to make requests and know they will be granted; here is a time for thanksgiving, for quiet meditation and communal prayer, an occasion to be guided and inspired by God's words. And, under-lying all this, the mass gives us a chance to be publicly surrounded, supported, and strengthened by a fellowship joined by a common belief—the haves and have nots, all equal in God's eyes.

The mass has two major divisions—the liturgy of the word, and the liturgy of Eucharist. In the liturgy of the word, we have time to clean the slate, make a confession, and open our minds to the words of Scripture and the homily. After this preparation, the liturgy of the Eucharist summons Christ into our midst so that we might share this holy meal. The mass also has a group of standard prayers, called the ordinary, and prayers and readings that change with the liturgical season, called the proper.

The beauty and genius of the mass is that different parts of it will speak to us at different times in our lives, in different ways. On some Sundays, it can be the time of confession that causes us to look deeply at something troubling us—and to see a better way. It might be the words of Scripture, calling down through the centuries to the circumstances of our lives; or the homily—by priest, deacon, or lay person—that gives us insight into our daily lives. It might be the consecration of the host, receiving the Eucharist, or sharing the sign of peace.

While some understanding of the mass is helpful, what is far more important is that you are there, open to its inspiration. Don't worry about theology or doctrine, or even the correct response to the prayers. Be an active participant, or be quiet. There is no *right* way to be at mass. This is the Lord's table; you are the invited guest. Speak with him at will. Or listen to him. Most important, take the holy food offered. Experience the actual presence of God in our midst, within us.

The mass is at once a spiritual and a sensual experience. Candles and incense set a certain mood, music enlivens our spirits. Kneeling at certain parts of mass is a sign of reverence; standing a sign of at-tention, sitting a contemplative statement.

And at mass you are not alone. All around you are people who have also brought their individual lives to this place. Everyone is an individual, all are joined together. It is a massive support group, with many Good Enough Catholics just like you nearby. Here, the values of the marketplace—speed, dominance, success—are set aside. Here your soul takes precedence. Introspection, sharing, and connectedness are the order of the hour. Here, you are the person you know you can be. Where else in the week does a person have this opportunity?

> "Transcendental meditation is a wonderful way to be in touch with that *thing* that is inside you. And I feel that way in church. I feel a great unity with God. I feel a force field. So many people believing in the same thing. When a lot of people are thinking of the same thing; this is very, very powerful. That's the beauty of Catholicism, because we are all there together and the force field is set up. Being in church will help you be better; everyone is believing in that. And I believe with that you cannot go astray."
>
> —STANLEY DEAN

Many Catholics—including Good Enough Catholics—bridle at the *obligation* to attend mass weekly. This is not a word that sits well with people today. Yes, the requirement is still in place. But Vatican II theology views the mandate to go to weekly mass not as an act for which a mortal sin will be etched upon our souls if we do not comply, but as an acknowledgment of a need. "Good laws do not create obligations as much as they express them and make them specific," is the way Cardinal Joseph Bernardin articulated it some years ago.[3]

For the Good Enough Catholic, perhaps a word substitution might be helpful. Substitute the word "opportunity" for "obligation." You have an *opportunity* to attend mass on Sunday. So, the Good Enough Catholic does not attend mass because the Great Scorekeeper in the sky is ready to mark down those present or absent; the Good Enough Catholic does so because of a simple, ever-present desire to go. You care to go. You, quite frankly, know you sense a *need* to go. To fulfill an ecclesiastical requirement is a worthy act in itself; but such motivation pales in significance next to our primal and deep desire to be close to God.

"I feel the transformation every time I go to mass. I can always change my life, and I know God is always there to pick me up no matter what I do. Look, I'm a sinful person. But I'm not a bad person. There's something about just walking into church with rich and poor, gays, prostitutes, black and white—and know I have come to the right place to begin that transformation."

—VANESSA COOKE

"Mass, to me, is getting a charge for the week. The message of the media is hate; the message of Christ is love. I need to hear that. I need to hear it every week. I feel worn down at the end of the week and it becomes increasingly difficult to be patient with my children. After I go to mass, because I've developed this relationship with Christ through the Eucharist, I'm stronger, renewed, fresher—and, thank God, more patient."

—BEATA WELSH

"In RCIA instruction they told me to focus on one part of the mass that had special meaning for me. For me, it was right after communion, when I had Christ in my body and I could really talk to him about my triumphs and my kids and my week. So much was concentrated in that short period of time and I felt very, very connected to God. I grew to need it; I had to have it. Even when I was sick, when I went through my back surgery, I always had communion, because without that, my week was not complete."

—NATASHA WITSCHY

# WHO CAN RECEIVE THE EUCHARIST?

In the pre–Vatican II Catholic Church, only baptized Catholics, in good standing with the church, and "in the state of grace" were judged worthy to receive the Eucharist. This state of grace implied that there was no mortal sin, unconfessed in a formal visit to the confessional, upon our souls. As for the "good standing" requirement, this usually meant that if you were married, it was within the Catholic Church—and that you had not remarried, unless you had first obtained, through proper church procedures, an annulment of the previous marriage.

Both conditions—state of grace and church standing—have caused enormous confusion, and perhaps more heartbreak, than any other issues among Catholics in the modern church, barring perhaps the Vatican's stand on birth control. Who doesn't know perfectly good people who feel so guilty about some past act, or who have been away from the church for so long, that they judge themselves unworthy to approach the altar to receive Christ's body and blood at mass? Or wonderful, loving couples, now remarried, who could not or would not go through the annulment process? A good number of them wouldn't think of missing Sunday mass; they sit faithfully, week after week, as others partake of the Eucharist.

Are these unforgiven sinners and the improperly married couples invited to the table?

For those who aspire to be Good Enough Catholics, this is not a matter to be treated or judged lightly. On the one hand, here is the presence of God, offered for human partaking. On the other, without thoughtful reception the Eucharist would be rendered a meaningless act. An examination of conscience is in order.

First of all, if there is some conscious act you have done—or continue to do—which you consider grievously and morally wrong (more on this in chapter 5, Morality, Conscience, and Sin), and you have the ability to correct it or make amends, you must earnestly attempt to do so. This you already know in your heart, and indeed the mass is the perfect place to receive the strength to change your life.

If there are other situations in your life in which you feel you are compromising your human dignity or moral code, but which are difficult to extract yourself from immediately or change completely (for instance, troubles within your family or on the job), are you trying to do what you can to alleviate the situation? Barring that, are you working to remove yourself from these troubling circumstances as best you can?

As for the rest of your shortcomings, will you try to do better in the future? This is a simple, but very important question to ask yourself. For Catholics, a "firm purpose of amendment," the desire to improve yourself, is *in itself* an improvement. Just keep in mind another well-known Catholic phrase, sadly used more to telegraph our sins than our saintlessness: "Intention equals the act." If you intend to be better, you are already better.

Does God expect you to absolutely control your temper? Or your tendency to gossip about co-workers? The unkind words, looks, and actions directed toward your spouse or children? Addiction in your body, or lust in your heart? No sensible earthly father asks for perfection—only a sincere and honest effort to be the best person you can, given the circumstances in which you find yourself. How much more understanding is the perfect father of us all? And remember the words of the mass: God is "full of gentleness and compassion." This father is ready to forgive, ready for you to go on with your life with the burden of guilt and remorse lifted from your heart.

Of course, the sacrament of reconciliation is available, and many people find this traditional form of confessing sin rewarding (more about this in chapter 3). But many churches offer periodic, group penitential services, with priests then available for one-on-one reconciliation. Also, at the beginning of every mass, there is a time for a personal examination of conscience, when all are asked to call to mind sins and shortcomings. This reflection on "what we have done and what we have failed to do" is a straightforward, brief, and healthy weekly review of our lives.

But Good Enough Catholics should know this: No human law, no public or private sin—*nothing* can prevent you from receiving the Eucharist if you earnestly desire this communion with God. If you can approach the altar with those wonderfully cleansing words on your lips and in your heart, the words that everyone says just before receiving the Eucharist—"Lord, I am not worthy to receive you, but only say the word and my soul shall be healed"—you are assured that indeed the invitation has been offered to you. Our Catholic faith guarantees this healing.

As for those who might be considered ineligible to receive the Eucharist because of where the church now draws the line concerning marriage and divorce, realize that there is an intense debate going on within the church about this issue. There are bishops who say that divorce does not prohibit a person from receiving; there is an official church teaching that claims the opposite. You, Good Enough Catholic, vested in the priesthood of the believers, guarding against both self-deception and therapeutic feel-goodism, can make that decision.

Vatican II places your informed conscience as the highest moral guide. Listen to it thoughtfully, prayerfully, honestly.

The divorced must take church law into consideration, and perhaps you will want to seek a formal church annulment. Many do, and find it enormously gratifying. But you must always know you are never outside God's love or mercy because of the circumstances or the specific acts that caused your marriage to fail. Even if you were the cause of that failure, you are not condemned to live the rest of your life in a horrible limbo, sent away permanently from the Lord's table without the sustenance you need for your life's journey. Who needs this divine meal more than the spiritually and morally hungry? Who needs encouragement more than those who consider themselves unworthy?

And what of another vexing question for Catholics: Can non-Catholics receive the Eucharist? We now have ecumenical services, where Christians—and even non-Christians—stand together before God. Should the Eucharist, which we believe to be sustenance for the journey through life, be shared? Or should this food be exclusively ours? Might it not be the more powerful Catholic witness to share something we regard as precious and absolutely necessary for our lives?

A look back to the Last Supper and Christ's actions might help shed light on our current questions of who is worthy to receive the Eucharist. Recall the words of Jesus that Passover night in Jerusalem. He had said again and again that he had come not for the righteous, but for sinners. But did he then look around the table and enumerate the failures of his disciples, pointing out their unworthiness? Did he evaluate the quality of their Jewish ritual observance? Or did he denounce the one who would deny him, the one who would betray him, and with a sweep of his hand condemn the rest who would abandon him? Did he welcome only the worthy and faithful to partake of this meal, and ask the others to stand aside as the loaf and the cup were passed?

Had he done so, Jesus would have taken the first Eucharist alone.

## THE GOOD ENOUGH CATHOLIC CHALLENGE: TASTE AND SEE THE GOODNESS OF THE LORD

The mass and Eucharist are avenues to God. They are rich and varied experiences at the very center of Catholic belief. We are invited to a mystical intimacy unrivaled in any spirituality.

To capture that power and be infused with that grace, go to mass this Sunday in a new and open way. You may be a regular; you may be a sporadic attendee or a nonchurchgoer. Allow this Sunday—this one Sunday—to be different. When you enter, realize you are in your Father's house. You are gathering with people whose lives are a mixture of wonders and mistakes—like yours. Here is an opportunity to lay down the baggage of your life, letting go, allowing the infusion of spiritual healing. What we Good Enough Catholics have in common is not holiness, but the *desire* to be holy.

Expect an intimate encounter with God. Open yourself to all the possibilities: words and silence, intellectual and emotional, sensual and spiritual. For the mass is a call not just to adoration but to intimacy. You are a Catholic, one person in a rich, long line that spans the centuries—and you have gathered as Christ bid you to do. Remember that when people encountered Jesus, they came away different. Anticipate that the you who enters the church will not be the you who walks out into the world and the rest of the week; you will have been refashioned as one of the "people of God." Let the mass set the tone for your week. Look for signs of God's presence in the world—and *expect* to find them.

The words of Scripture, which have inspired generations upon generations of people, are new and fresh in our day. Allow these words to speak to your life. Let the Scripture readings enlighten—or overcome—what you consider the most important issues in your life. Let Scripture draw a bead on the very problems you try to hide from yourself—pride, anger, complacency, moral laziness.

Or, try this variation: attend a daily mass. Just one. There is an entirely different and more intimate feeling in a church with just a handful of people. I used to go to a Trappist monastery; you might find that city chapel just right, or even your own parish church. Without the embellishments of choir and crowd, the mass often reveals itself to us in ways we could never have anticipated. You might close your eyes and imagine the Last Supper taking place. And that you are there, around the table.

You are exactly right.

## SELECTED READINGS

Raniero Cantalamessa (Frances E. Lonergan Villa, trans.), *The Eucharist, Our Sanctification*. Collegeville, Minn.: Liturgical Press, 1993.

Aidan Nichols, *The Holy Eucharist: From the New Testament to John Paul II.* Dublin: Veritas, 1991.

David N. Power, *The Eucharistic Mystery: Revitalizing the Tradition*. New York: Crossroad, 1994.

Second Vatican Council, *Constitution on the Sacred Liturgy*. Glen Rock, N.J.: Paulist Press, 1964.

Robert Sokolowski, *Eucharistic Presence: A Study in the Theology of Disclosure*. Washington, D.C.: Catholic University of America Press, 1994.

# CHAPTER THREE

# THE SACRAMENTS

## Divine Interventions

The infinite reality of God reaches us through finite things—and it is through those same paths that we, in turn, seek God. It is not uncommon to feel the overwhelming presence of God while gazing at a spectacular sunset or into a baby's smiling face; while looking at a picture of galaxies in outer space, or observing the intricate patterns of life on Earth revealed by a microscope. Art, a well-turned phrase, a huge gathering of people standing together for the common good—indeed, all things potentially show God's presence. For some people, that is enough; they may say they need no formal religion to enhance their perception of the mystery that is God.

Catholicism—which affirms the mystery and holiness of all things in the universe—has a specific and unique response to our human condition. These are the sacraments, seven in number, holy rituals that transcend and transform the ordinary, infusing natural things and natural events with the divine. Once understood for what they provide, how they are intricately interwoven one with another, and how they speak to us both at the turning points and in the everyday challenges of our lives, the sacraments can occupy their proper place as central to Catholic belief. Indeed, without the sacraments, there would be no Catholic Church; the sacraments make Catholicism what it is. Sacraments are living signs that God seeks continually to enter the world, to provide the sustenance, healing, or strength a particular moment requires. This is mysticism, Catholic mysticism, in its richest form.

Like the church, sacraments were not explicitly instituted by Christ. As Christ never said that there should be a new church, that it should be called Catholic, or that it should have as its head a pope in Rome, he never specified seven sacraments. In fact, in the Middle Ages there were literally hundreds of pious practices and sacred rites that were considered "sacramental." But naturally, organically, seven emerged as crucial landmarks in the Catholic spiritual landscape— social expressions of an inner need for God's presence. Each has its unique place and purpose.

Before embarking on a broader discussion of spirituality and prayer (chapter 4), I think it's important first to see the sacraments as a group, for they can be the building blocks of the Good Enough Catholic's spiritual life. It is equally important to understand how the sacraments "work," how they have evolved through the years, and what the revolutionary thinking of Vatican II has revealed about them. In the sacraments we discover, once again, that Catholicism is a dynamic, ever-changing religion, based in the life of Jesus Christ, but constantly adapted to current needs and open to new insights.

There are three groups of sacraments among the seven: sacraments of initiation, of healing, and of vocation.

The *sacraments of initiation*, which mark a person's entrance and eventual full membership in the church, are baptism, confirmation, and the Eucharist. As an infant, older child, or adult, a person is first brought into the Catholic community through the sacrament of baptism, given the grace and power to live a moral life through the sacrament of confirmation, and offered continued and immediate access to Christ's presence through the sacrament of the Eucharist. The process of becoming sons and daughters of God has begun— but, of course, we are human, not divine. Good Enough, yes; but inevitably, the perfection of these signal days in our life fade. Even moments after receiving the Eucharist we may forget its power. We will falter, spiritually and physically.

Our souls become morally sick through sin, and our bodies beset by physical illness—each rendering us less and less able to continue on the path toward God, and to carry out our responsibilities to our communities and ourselves. The next group, the *sacraments of healing*, stand ready with divine assistance. The sacrament of penance—or reconciliation, as it is currently known—wipes our sins away, enabling us to begin life anew, refreshed, and unburdened by our past shortcomings. The sacrament of the sick calls down God's regenerative power upon our bodies so that we might be renewed, ready once more for our life's journey.

Finally, the third group, the *sacraments of vocation*, infuse our lives at that crucial juncture when couples join together, or a man dedicates himself to the service of the church. The sacrament of matrimony blesses the tender and separate shoots of a man and a woman embarking on a life intertwined as husband and wife. The sacrament of holy orders consecrates a man to God and the service of others as an ordained priest.

## HOW SACRAMENTS WORK

At various times in the church's history (the years just preceding Vatican II included), the proper procedure for the administration of the sacraments was actually considered more important than the disposition of the people receiving them. Form ruled over content. It was as if the spiritual effect of the sacrament depended on the precision with which the ritual was performed, rather than on an interchange between a God offering grace and a human desiring to receive it. This emphasis on ritual harkened back to the days of the Pharisees—whose attention to strict adherence to law and ritual had come to take precedence over the human needs of the Jewish people they were supposed to lead.

Vatican II clarified that the sacraments are not some act of magic performed by a priest or bishop *upon* us. Sacraments are not ways to enforce proper church behavior, or to socialize church members. Sacraments are potentially blinding moments of God's grace, which work because we who participate *in* them bring the interior disposition, the desire, the faith *to* them. Each sacrament requires our co-operation. We make a statement—perhaps with misgivings and down-right doubt, but a statement nonetheless—that we want God's grace to be with us. And, the church teaches, that power *is* with us.

An elementary teaching about the sacraments is that they are "outward and physical symbols of inward and spiritual realities." Water in baptism cleanses. Hands laid upon our heads, a cross of oil on our foreheads—these give the power to carry out the responsi-bilities of an adult. Bread and wine of the Eucharist nourish and strengthen. Words of reconciliation release us from our sins. Oil upon our extremities and senses in the anointing of the sick brings healing. Vows of matrimony and holy orders bind us to a commit-ment for life.

"In the old days, I bought the magic part, novenas and all; it was a religion close to superstition. Now the sacraments are full of grace and goodness. I can't put God in a little box and have him in the same way I did as a child. God's changing and I'm changing. We discover each other anew through the sacraments."

—MARY ANNE BARRY

"The sacramental system in the church is not unlike the signs and symbols we see in Jung. They are wonderful, vibrant ways to bring people to a better understanding of what the church is and who Christ is."

—MARTY HEGARTY

"I love the peacefulness of meditation, the quietness of Quaker meetings, but I need living signs of God's presence in my life. In the Eucharist, I encounter Christ on a regular basis. In reconciliation this sinner is transformed into a saint. The beauty is that you don't have to step outside your life to express the presence of God. The sacra-ments are so basic to me now, moments of real empowerment."

—CAROLYN SWEERS

# THE SACRAMENTS OF INITIATION
## Baptism

Three moments in life absolutely *demand* religious symbol and ritual: birth, the taking of lifetime vows, and death. Acknowledging the miracle of new life, what can parents, family, and friends do but turn to God and give thanks—and, as they do, ask for the strength and wisdom to form that child? Equally, don't all of us wish for children a spiritual presence—a guardian angel, it might be called—to protect and sustain them?

Baptism is a formal welcoming, a celebration, a moment when God's grace is almost palpable as a new and unblemished soul is brought into the church community. The world begins anew; all is promise and hope. It is at once an age-old ritual and a modern-day encounter with the presence of God.

In ancient Judaism, there were different kinds of purification rituals—ceremonies used (for example) to prepare food, or to make a person worthy to stand in the presence of God. Water was central to these rituals, signifying cleansing, a washing away of impurities, a fresh start. In baptism, a symbolic cleansing takes place, so that an individual begins life in the church absolutely pure and without the blemish of original sin.

The story of Jesus being baptized by John the Baptist is well known, but it was only after Pentecost and the outpouring of the Holy Spirit upon the apostles that the early church began to see baptism as crucial to entrance into the Christian faith. In the ancient church it was a time when people—usually converts from Judaism—stood before God in the midst of their community and declared their desire to follow in the way of Christ. Infant baptism was not practiced in those days. Because it was not only a life-changing statement but a dangerous one as well, baptism had to be freely chosen by a person old enough to understand both the commitment and the risk involved.

Over the centuries, with the development of the concept of original sin, it came to be thought necessary for newborns to be baptized as soon as feasible, lest they risk being denied entrance into heaven. In addition to the wonderful symbolism of welcoming an infant into the community of faith, baptism speaks far more eloquently to those gathered around the baptismal font and in the body of the church. It could be said that infant baptism isn't for the baby at all—it is for the community in attendance. For baptism is a chance for all present to be reborn, to feel the presence and the power of the good news of Christ's life in their own life once more. No one looking upon the innocence and vulnerability of a baby can fail to see the need to protect a small child from harm, to want to be a model of good behavior.

"At the baptism of my first child I wasn't really prepared for what a powerful moment this would be for me. I wanted to offer other people the opportunity to experience that moment so I started a baptism class in my parish. Of course the baby doesn't know what's going on, but I found this is a great time to enter into the parents' lives, to let them know what baptism can mean. You can get down on the world, but when you see that little face, it's a vote of confidence that the human race isn't going to hell in a handbasket. It is a time to see God."

—SUZANNE LEFEVRE

In some parishes, marginal or lapsed Catholics are turned away when they bring their child for baptism by priests who say—perhaps with some justification—that, as they are not living as Catholics, don't attend mass or participate in parish life, the sacrament is therefore meaningless to them. If it will not be brought up Catholic, why initiate a child into the church? Other priests, like Father Brian Jordan of Silver Spring, Maryland, have a different view. "I wouldn't deny entry into the church to anyone. I wouldn't deny God an opportunity to enter into a family's life. It is not my place to say no to God's graces."

# Confirmation

The purposes of baptism and confirmation are deeply interrelated, so much so that in Eastern-rite churches, the two are administered as one sacrament. In Western churches, confirmation signifies the adult acceptance of baptismal responsibilities. It has much in common with the ceremony of bar mitzvah for Jewish boys (and bat mitzvah for Jewish girls) when they reach the age of thirteen. It is a rite of passage, an event in which young people, at the dawn of adulthood, stand before their religious community to demonstrate that they have been schooled in the rudiments of their faith, and are ready to make their own public promise to live out, and pass on, that faith.

Confirmation recalls Pentecost, a seminal event in church history. The followers of Jesus, at once confused by his death yet wanting to believe in his resurrection, wondered how they, simple men and women, were going to live out the mandates that Christ had asked of them. Then, in a moment of divine intercession, God came to be among and upon them in a completely new way. The comforter promised by the resurrected Christ, a "holy spirit"—a new, spiritual presence of God on Earth—would now walk with them, inspire them, sustain them. From that day forward, they would never be alone; they would never be more than a prayer away from the Christ who had inflamed their hearts.

> "My confirmation as an adult was one of the most dramatic moments in my life. When the hands were laid on me, I trembled. It was like electricity going through me."
>
> —ALLEN STRYCZEK

Confirmation is a day to be remembered and treasured. It comes at an extraordinarily impressionable age for most confirmands, when they yearn for a challenge to test their bold young hearts—while the world dismisses them as not yet ready. What a genuine, profound thrill—the first moment when we are taken seriously as young adults. It is the first day as a true man or woman. No longer is a parent or godparent needed to answer for us; a new voice will be heard.

## Eucharist

As discussed in chapter 2, there is nothing more central, more basic, to Catholic belief than the Eucharist. It is "the sacrament of sacraments," as the new catechism of the church proclaims. And here, in the context of the other sacraments of initiation, Eucharist presents itself in still another light.

Baptism and confirmation—one marking the welcoming of an infant into the Catholic community, and the other signifying a mature assent to a choice made by others for that person's benefit—happen but once. Each are needed at the junctures at which they occur; birth makes real to new parents the hope that their child will receive spiritual guidance and protection, while the onset of adulthood brings a new level of introspection, as some paths are chosen and others bypassed. But after these signal moments, we need continual sustenance—we need reinforcement to continue along our chosen path, to live out the promise those important days symbolize. We need to know we are not alone in our quest for God.

Eucharist is not so much a call to adoration as to intimacy. Heads bowed in awe, yes—but hearts and arms open to God's love and influence are what this sacrament is truly about. Eucharist is an opportunity to take God's very presence into our bodies, a virtual spiritual transplant. It is the most powerful sacrament Catholics have—and it is comfortingly available to all: those whose lives are worthy, as well as those who have lost their way.

"After my divorce, I felt decidedly unworthy to receive, a failure. But as I sat in a pew at my parents' fortieth-anniversary mass, something happened, something that miraculously healed me, summoned me. God was so viscerally present. He wanted me to receive. I knew that. After that, regardless of what was going on in my life, if I felt worthy or unworthy, I never again denied myself communion."

—JOAN SULLIVAN

"The incredible diversity of those who come to the Eucharist; I don't find that kind of community anywhere else in my life. We have the least class-connected church there is. In the breaking of bread I am one with people who may absolutely disagree with me on just about everything else. In this, we are unified."

—DANA GREEN

# THE SACRAMENTS OF HEALING
## Penance/Reconciliation

The dynamism and common sense of Catholic sacraments are perhaps nowhere more evident—and nowhere more misunderstood—than in the two sacraments of healing. Before the scientific study of psychology, before the realization that the mind had great power to cure the body, before wellness and spiritual healing were the hot topics they are today, the church in its wisdom recognized that when life took its inevitable toll, souls and bodies would be in need of healing, both symbolic and actual.

Certainly there is a continuing need to acknowledge failures and be done with them. No one lives in the past, only the present; but when the memory of bad judgments and improper actions linger, it is difficult to change our ways. The grip of these memories can become an imprisonment, from which we can imagine no escape. The sacrament of penance (or reconciliation) addresses the spiritual sickness we encounter when we sin. It is a release from that prison. (We will look more closely at sin in chapter 5.)

This sacrament—based on Christ's charge to his disciples that if they forgave sins, those sins would indeed be forgiven—has taken a circuitous path through church history. In the early church, penance was received only once, usually on the deathbed, as a preparation for the final judgment. Later, public confession and public penance became customary, with the sinner required to show that his or her life would be changed from that day forward. Eventually, confession became less a public act, and was instead done face-to-face with a monk. This intimate approach to confessing and absolving sins marked the early stages of what we now know as spiritual direction.

As the sacrament evolved, intricate codes were formulated defining exactly what a sin was, how grievous it was, and what type of penance should be performed by the penitent. Of course, this was a movement away from the compassion and ready forgiveness that marked Jesus' life and ministry. He had said to sin no more, and go forth in faith. Instead, confession was used by the church as a control mechanism to keep the ever-errant faithful in line. Many Catholics still recall the rigors of weekly confession: the long lines, the stiff penances, and the horror of dying with a mortal sin staining their souls—which meant, they feared, a direct plunge into the eternal fires of hell.

But even in those days, the purifying effect of confession could be quite beneficial. There was nothing like unburdening yourself of your guilt, even if it had to transpire in those stuffy little confessionals. How relieving, how refreshing it was to walk out of church knowing everything was once again right with God. The slate was wiped clean. You were resanctified; you could almost feel the grace flowing, savor the purity and liberation.

But for many—too many—those sensations were often drowned in the raging seas of negativity and guilt.

Vatican II recaptured the spirit of the sacrament that had been corrupted over the centuries. And while some bemoan the downturn in individual confessions, perhaps this is actually a good sign. We may have rediscovered what Christ intended: that we are already forgiven the moment we ask in sincerity for forgiveness. No longer are we to mechanically prepare our laundry list of wrongs, in exact number, kind, and circumstance. What is emphasized instead is a conversion of heart, an inner disposition to do better in the future.

Sin ruptures our relationships with both God and other human beings. Reconciliation repairs.

"Reconciliation makes me feel fresh again, like a young girl. I feel so good about it."

—BETTY TORRES

"I rediscovered the sacrament when my children were being taught the new approach in CCD classes. It's not about getting through the five Hail Marys for a penance; this is true reconciliation—a much better idea."

—MARY MURPHY ZASTROW

"Catholics and non-Catholics ask me why I need to tell my sins to another person. It's simple. As human beings, we need signs, we need someone to tell us we're all right. We need validation that we are trying hard to be good people. The priest is an instrument. I can almost envision Christ talking to me."

—MAGALIE SALAS

Although personal confession to an individual priest is still readily available (and, for some, is a grace-filled, enlightening interchange), there are other ways to make peace with God—and with yourself. The new understanding of the sacrament of reconciliation emphasizes the individual's return to the church community as a value in itself. Today, entire parishes participate in penance services. The word of God is heard, quietness allows each individual to focus on personal shortcomings, and forgiveness is asked from God and others. A sense of being made whole pervades.

At St. Nicholas's Church in Evanston, Illinois, twice-yearly parish reconciliation services—before Christmas and Easter—address not only personal reconciliation, but reconciliation with others, with God—even with nature, against which we may have sinned through acts of irresponsibility or arrogance. While these are dignified liturgical services, they are equally happy occasions at St. Nicholas's, where children and parents alike have a communal and individual opportunity to admit to their shortcomings. Smiles radiate throughout the church in recognition of God's forgiveness.

Each mass we attend offers a time for contrition. This happens to be my personal choice for reflection on my own faults and sins. At a minimum, it is a weekly examination of conscience, a reckoning that I need. Beyond this, I find it helps to open myself to the words of Scripture that will follow, and to prepare for reception of the Eucharist.

In some parts of the country, reconciliation comes before a child's First Communion; in other areas, it comes when the child is more mature and can better comprehend sin and its consequences. Not a few Catholics wonder which is better and which is correct. The placement isn't important. What is important is that the child be guided at an appropriate age to the understanding that there certainly is right and wrong, and that he or she must struggle to be the best, holiest, and most Christ-like person possible—in every situation. That is the goal. But the child must also know that the Jesus they receive in the Eucharist believes in forgiveness. They must understand that we all make mistakes and fall into sin—and that God is always ready to forgive us when we ask sincerely.

Many returning or recovering Catholics who have been away from the church for extended periods have mixed feelings about this sacrament. At once they want to clear the slate and start afresh; and yet they may have painful, negative memories of confession. They know the distance that exists between themselves and God, and crave to be delivered from the bondage of sin. Deep within them, there is a sense that there is only one way to make things right with God. But they fear the process of confessing their sins to a priest and asking forgiveness.

If this is you, all I can say is that you should give grace a chance—give God a chance. That leap of faith might prove to be one of the most rewarding risks you ever take. The resulting peace is beyond measure. Reconciliation can occur in the anonymity of a confessional booth, or in a face-to-face encounter—whichever you feel would be best for you.

"When I hear confessions, I will always end, 'Well, you're a good man, aren't you?' 'You're a fine woman,' " says Father William J. O'Malley, S.J., who teaches at Fordham Preparatory School in the Bronx. "Invariably, the penitent blushes and says, 'I hope so,' or 'I try,' or 'You don't really know me.' I have to tell them that bad people don't confess, only good people do."[1]

The Good Enough Catholic is not, as we said early on, the Perfect Catholic. But we try. For the Good Enough Catholic, the sacrament of reconciliation, in one of its many forms, is the perfect place to lay down the burdens of our failures and move on.

## Anointing of the Sick

Here again is a sacrament that may have two very different meanings for Catholics of different generations. As with other sacraments, the anointing of the sick performed today is certainly more in keeping with the original intent of this ritual. Although there is no formal sacrament at the death of a Catholic—theologically, the soul has already left the body—we'll also deal with the last rites, funeral, and burial in this section, as they are often linked in people's minds with the sacrament of anointing of the sick.

In the early church, when a member fell ill, it was customary to pray over the person. Eventually the practice of anointing with oil became part of the ritual. Medicine was little known at the time, and the spiritual healing of physical ailments and diseases was sought through the symbol of what were believed to be curative agents.

Originally, this ritual was meant to assist in healing; but as with penance, the changing ideas of the church brought about a change in the purpose behind this sacrament of healing. The sacrament eventually became an acknowledgment that death was near—and that a believer needed to prepare to meet God. Signifying this change of view, the sacrament was called extreme unction for many centuries.

Today's anointing of the sick is a beautiful reclamation of Christ's healing power. No longer does a person have to be at death's door to receive this sacramental support; to the contrary, it is a bold statement for life. Yes, medical science has advanced dramatically in 2,000 years; wonders are performed every day. But the power of the Almighty remains mysterious and unparalleled; it is here that true miracles are seen. In the creative, complicated feat that is our body, this sacrament stakes its claim that the God who made us is a God who can heal us—specifically and directly.

Catholic last rites, funeral, and burial can also be powerful religious experiences—a true manifestation that life in God triumphs over the death of the body. The last rites often include the sacrament of the anointing of the sick, in addition to the reception of the viaticum ("food for the journey"). No longer are Catholic funerals and burials impersonal, sad, standardized rites; readings, songs, and a eulogy can specifically speak to the life of each individual during a Mass of the Resurrection.

"AIDS cut a wide swath through my community at St. Augustine's in Washington, D.C. Too many friends and choir members. Each death was a loss; but each burial was a triumph of that person's spirit. I remember Tucker's funeral so vividly. He often came to rehearsals drunk; he didn't lead the most virtuous life, but he had a gorgeous, gorgeous voice. When the choir surrounded his coffin and sang 'Alleluia, Salvation in Glory,' there wasn't a dry eye in the place. We were drug addicts and government bureaucrats, pimps, lawyers, hustlers, and professional people with heavy incomes—and we all knew our Tucker was right up there at the throne of God."

—LEON ROBERTS

"When my brother, a suicide, was buried in the Catholic church in our hometown, I looked back on the funeral procession to see a line of cars, snaking through town. I realized how many people loved him; I thought about how life can be pretty harsh, and how I needed the support of the Catholic church right then."

—TOM LENZ

"A well-liked young man in our town of Hardwick, Massachusetts, died in a freak automobile accident. I guess I'm like a lot of
Catholics, I've had a love-hate relationship with the church
throughout my life; but when I went to the funeral, I was so
proud, so happy to be a Catholic. It was a beautiful and fitting way
to face this tragedy and let that wonderful guy go."

—PAULA DAWSON

As Jacqueline Kennedy Onassis—a lifelong practicing Catholic—
said after Robert Kennedy's assassination: "The church is . . . at its
best only at the time of death. The rest of the time it's often rather
silly little men running around in their black suits. But the Catholic
Church understands death. We know death. . . ."[2]

# THE SACRAMENTS OF
# VOCATION AND COMMITMENT
## Matrimony

From the book of Genesis—with God's charge, "be fruitful and
multiply"—to the pages of the New Testament—where the union
of man and woman is extolled (with venerable St. Paul presenting
his own slant, decidedly more focused on the Second Coming than
the advantages of the married state)—humankind has faced the complex issue of how the species is to be perpetuated, how man and
woman are to coexist in this world, and exactly what a "marriage" is
to be.

To make the issue even more confusing, the Catholic Church has
traditionally put a high premium on virginity and celibacy, at times
elevating these above the married state. Somehow, if people could
go through life unencumbered by the requirements of an intimate
human relationship and the distractions of carnality, the thinking
seemed to go, they would somehow be holier.

If people did find the need to marry, the church taught for centuries, there could be only one sanctioned purpose: the procreation of children. Large Catholic families were the norm for many generations, a sign of God's blessing—and of the couple's forgoing any form of birth control.

Much has changed within the past few decades.

Modern psychology and ancient wisdom concur that, for most of us, it is better to join with another person than to go through life alone. Now that marriage is more often based on attraction and love than on family ties or the number of sheep that will change hands, it is generally agreed that having children is but one consideration of a marriage. Similarly, it is no longer an article of faith that more children are necessarily better than a more modest number.

Additionally, Vatican II rescued the married state from the concept of being a contract, viewing it instead as a covenant. The words are important: "contract" seems to imply a legalistic undertaking, while "covenant" connotes an agreement entered into freely that constantly needs recommitment to keep it alive.

The sacrament of matrimony makes a definitive statement in this age of broken promises. Two people announce to the world that they are in love, and ask God's blessing upon their hope in, and commitment to, their love for each other. This is a beautiful, stupendous, and scary commitment in a day when so many marriages—Catholic marriages included—end in divorce. As fraught with improbability as matrimony is, it is also absolutely necessary.

"I was living with my boyfriend when we decided the time had come to get married. Although we were both Catholic, neither of us was practicing at the time. But if I was going to make this kind of commitment, I had to be married in a Catholic church if I was going to keep my integrity. My idea about the sacraments is that you don't have to feel worthy of them. Not at all. God made them to strengthen us. Here I was, the Woodstock generation, but I wasn't going to be married at sunset on a beach with some non-

denominational minister. I wanted standard Catholic vows, nothing fancy or different. It gave me this great feeling of unity with
the rest of the church throughout the world. It marked a turning
point in my religious life. I came home with my wedding; I started
an entirely new life on that day."

—MIRIAM WEILER*

"Suzanne and I couldn't have gone to a justice of the peace any
more than we could have flown to the moon. We designed our
ceremony. We clipped away all the encrustations that had been
piled on over the centuries. We greeted people when they came
into the church. We faced the congregation when we said our
vows. We had the great sense of marrying each other, with the
priest being there as only a witness. It was our commitment, and it
had to happen in church."

—TOM LENZ

Even with the euphoria that love and a wedding can engender,
there are few couples who stand before a priest absolutely certain
that they will stay together until death do they part. As blissful and
invigorating as love is, most couples come to discover the truth of
an old bit of wisdom: "Love in action is a harsh and dreadful thing
compared to love in dreams."

What is crucially important for a man and woman considering
marriage in the Catholic Church is that their intentions are in line
with the church's perception of the married state. The desire to
make the marriage work, and to stay with a chosen partner a lifetime, must be present; so, too, must be the desire to be a friend in
good times and bad, and the desire to rear children—if God so
blesses the marriage. If these desires are not mutually held, it seems
fair to ask: Why be married in the Catholic Church, which stands
for the permanence of marriage?

Oftentimes, as nonpracticing Catholics approach marriage, they
want it be in a church, so that this important day might have the

beauty and pageantry of a Catholic service. Every parish priest has a hundred stories on this theme: the prospective couple comes to the rectory as if visiting the florist shop or caterer, another item on their check-off list of details to be arranged. Not infrequently, such couples are discouraged by priests who see this approach as regarding the church as little more than window dressing.

At Old St. Patrick's Church in downtown Chicago, which has attracted thousands of young, urban professionals, Father John Cusick explained his parish's philosophy. "Do we want to be Catholic, or do we want to be parochial? Do we want to check if the couples are registered in the parish, or offer them an opportunity for a sacramental encounter with the mystery of God? The place where you marry is your religious home, at least for a while. People who are ready to get married know they are in love. They just don't know they are *in God*. It's our job to show them, and this is our chance."

One of the finest parish priests I've ever known, Father Joseph Greer of Natick, Massachusetts, asked couples who might be similarly casual about their church relationship to think about why they were inviting God to their wedding when they had no other relationship with him. If the couple were living together before the wedding, Father Greer asked them to spend some period of time before the wedding living apart—so that their wedding day might have a special meaning of new intimacy.

However the priest measures the sincerity of prospective brides and grooms, all that can be said is that the church offers a luminous sacrament to those whose hearts and souls are open to receive it. It is a time of enormous blessings; it is a time to chart a new life. It is, in essence, the baptism of the couple. And, like baptism, matrimony is only a beginning. Love must grow from the wedding day on for this sacrament to be fully realized in the lives of the couple.

Of course, there is understandable concern over the church's teaching about the indissolubility of Catholic marriage. There should be. We will discuss this further in chapter 7; here it will suffice to say that in the imperfection that is the human condition, no one is expected to be perfect—just Good Enough. But this is no easy way out; being Good Enough will require more than you possibly thought you could ever give, in all areas of your life. Marriage is no exception.

## Holy Orders

These days, the concept of a lifetime, celibate commitment—exclusively male—to the priesthood is one that certainly and properly occasions a lot of debate. In the years ahead, I sense this debate will persist and intensify, clarifying even further who will serve as Catholicism's ordained ministers.

Vatican II tells us that there is a "priesthood of all believers." Yet it would be foolish to say that a person who embarks upon the years of training leading to ordination has not chosen a quite different—and remarkable—path to God. Unlike the teaching that many Catholics grew up with, with its implication that the priesthood (and other lives of celibacy and exclusive church-related service) was somehow a *better* path than ordinary secular lives (whether single or married), today no such claim is made or received seriously. Each of us, in our own uniqueness, has a way to God. God, in his graciousness and mercy, is ready to receive each of us, regardless of the way we have chosen—or that circumstances have chosen for us.

Looking back to the history of the priesthood, we see that the early church relied more upon elders, or presbyters—respected, but ordinary people chosen from within their communities, earning their living through normal occupations—to oversee or administer ritual, maintain church order, assure religious instruction, and provide care to the sick and needy. There was a reluctance on the part of the early Christians to institute a caste of priests, remembering, as they did, that Judaism's high priests at the time of Christ often abused their prerogatives terribly. Actually, it wasn't until the thirteenth century that priestly ordination was required to celebrate the Eucharist—surely the most important and frequent Christian ritual. Since Vatican II, the church has reinstituted the order of the permanent deaconate, which is open to both married and single men. By the year 2005, it is predicted, there will be more ordained deacons in the United States than ordained priests. With the shortage of priests, and priestless masses becoming increasingly frequent, who knows what additional changes or permutations in the sacrament of holy orders the future will hold?

For now it is enough to say that, as matrimony commits woman to man and man to woman so that they might sustain each other and grow together through the joys and storms of life, holy orders grandly and heroically commits a man to the service of the church. Holy orders is a sacrament to be cherished; those who choose it are rightly to be applauded for their courage in making such a commitment in this time of religious and societal transition.

Current theological thinking on the priesthood places far more emphasis on the priesthood as ministry, rather than as a state in life that sanctions a man to perform Catholic rituals. It is an honor to be called to this vocation, and we have an enormous and special need for priests in our lives. If you, Good Enough Catholic, have the opportunity to attend a priest's ordination, do so with the happiness you would bring to any wedding. Go despite any contrary personal feelings or opinions you might have on celibacy or the ordination of women. Grant that priest his day. There are many days ahead for you to work for needed changes in our church.

I have known many excellent priests in my life—as I'm sure you have. My favorite was a priest I mentioned earlier, Father Joseph Greer. I was so taken with him that I wrote about him both in the *New Yorker* magazine and in a book, *In Mysterious Ways: The Death and Life of a Parish Priest*. Father Greer was a man who genuinely enjoyed helping people and viewed the priesthood as his entree into their lives. He was saintly in his fortitude as he faced a terminal disease; but he was also a sinner who publicly admitted he had violated his vow of chastity. He loved people; he loved Catholic ritual; he loved Christ. All in all, he was a Good Enough Catholic— who happened to be a priest.

❁

# THE GOOD ENOUGH CATHOLIC CHALLENGE: SEIZE THE MYSTICAL POWER

Look upon the seven sacraments as opportunities to be filled with the divine, for these visible signs of an invisible God are always invitations to grace. Sacraments are mysterious, mystical moments that transcend mere human reason or knowledge. Think of them as flights of God's imagination, a God who so desperately loves us he wants to be present every day—and especially at the turning points in all our lives when we triumph and celebrate, as well as when we stumble and fall.

Catholicism is the "church of the sacraments," with a built-in system of profound symbolism, rich ritual, and ready, available grace. In a day when secular men and women are confused and alienated by a world that seems to trample morality and values underfoot, and regard with suspicion anything religious offering transcendence, the sacraments offer a *guaranteed* encounter with God. So many spiritual avenues are offered to us, the array is dizzying. Some have proved helpful; most prove to be passing promises never realized. The sacraments stand ready, waiting for the Good Enough Catholic to summon their power.

At the next opportunity you have to participate in or witness a sacrament, be open to its power. Participate. Actively recall what the sacrament signifies; be ready to be cleansed, forgiven, fed, strengthened. Let your mind wander in the rich vineyard of the Lord. He wants to be present in your life. He is seeking to communicate with you. Only say the word, and he will.

# SELECTED READINGS

William Bausch, *A New Look at the Sacraments*. Mystic, Conn.: Twenty-Third Publications, 1983.

Bernard Cooke, *Sacraments and Sacramentality* (revised edition). Mystic, Conn.: Twenty-Third Publications, 1994.

Regis A. Duffy, *Real Presence: Worship, Sacraments, and Commitment*. San Francisco: Harper and Row, 1982.

Peter E. Fink, ed., *New Dictionary of Sacramental Worship*. Collegeville, Minn.: Liturgical Press, 1990.

Alexandre Ganoczy (William Thomas, trans.), *An Introduction to Catholic Sacramental Theology*. New York: Paulist Press, 1984.

Edward Schillebeeckx (Paul Barrett, trans.), *Christ: The Sacrament of Encounter with God*. New York: Sheed and Ward, 1963.

Herbert Vorgrimler (Linda M. Maloney, trans.), *Sacramental Theology*. Collegeville, Minn.: Liturgical Press, 1992.

# CHAPTER FOUR

# PRAYER AND SPIRITUALITY
## The True Path

Spirituality: Is there another word that evokes so many meanings? From the old pious practices like novenas, rosaries, and adoration of the Blessed Sacrament—shrouded in incense and ancient mystery—to the New Age methods that seem to crop up quicker than dandelions in spring, promising guaranteed bliss and lasting transcendence. With all the options available, spirituality is certainly one of the most confusing aspects of religious belief for today's Good Enough Catholic.

What is spirituality? Quite simply, it is the way we express our longing to somehow touch and be touched by God. It is our way of relating to that Being beyond all beings, that Power beyond all powers, that Cause beyond all causes. Is this a completely rational act, one that we can quantify, as we might state clearly why water seeks its own level or nature abhors a vacuum? It is not. And yet it is every bit as real as the most real things we touch, taste, hear, smell, and feel. This is the search for a God within our reach, but ever beyond our grasp.

Although this book is dedicated to a discussion of a specific religion—Catholicism—it is important to distinguish between spirituality and religion. Religion is form; spirituality is content. Religion is the institutional means used to learn, sustain, and spread beliefs. Spirituality is more elemental. Without a spiritual life—a life in touch with God in some way—there can be no truly religious life.

As spirituality is not religion, neither is spirituality the exclusive domain of Catholics. To be sure, there is a unique yet broadly diverse Catholic spirituality; but if ours were the only path to God, what could be said of the rich spiritual treasures of other religions? Catholicism once proclaimed itself the "one, true faith." Vatican II acknowledged that Almighty God was quite a bit more open-minded than that, welcoming all seekers after his truth.

## A NEW WAY OF HOLINESS

Catholicism's rich history of spirituality finds its roots in Judaism and the Old Testament struggles of the Israelites to understand the commanding physical and metaphysical presence of God in their lives. "I will be your God; and you shall be my people," God decreed. This relationship immediately created both a holy bond and a human dilemma. In the purely spiritual realm, what acts or actions should be performed so as to please God? In the real world, what should a person's posture be toward day-to-day life? In other words, should life be dedicated to basically giving homage to God and adhering to a set of rules, or to having some impact on the world? Adoration and obedience, or action and conversion? It's strangely comforting, somehow, to realize that the dialectic has continued down to our day.

After Christ's crucifixion, the disciples struggled with this problem. They had before them their own Jewish tradition—and they had the model of Christ, who had both conformed to, and contradicted, Judaic practice. Aflame as they were with the Holy Spirit after Pentecost, and eager to transmit what they had learned from Christ, the disciples naturally repeated Christ's words and taught the principles he espoused. They attempted to live as he had, with compassion and concern for all people, putting into practice the new covenant—a covenant that radically asked not for rote repetition of ritual, but the sweeping practice of mercy, forgiveness, and love. As the disciples believed that the world was soon coming to an end, they understandably advised that human needs be put aside; there was no place or time for

temporal concerns. The First Letter of Peter articulated the new community's mission: new Christians were to conduct themselves "so as
to live for the rest of the time in the flesh no longer by human pas-
sions but by the will of God. Let the time that is past suffice for doing
what the [nonbelievers] do. . . ."[1]

The early Christians knew human desires quite well, but this
"will of God" was far more difficult to discern. Most of them were
ordinary people, not saints. They understood that this "will" en-
joined them to proclaim and live the message of Jesus; but as for
their individual lives, some concluded that the most worthwhile
way they could emulate Christ was to suffer as he did. And so mar-
tyrdom and self-sacrifice were considered the paths to true holiness.
In a sense, these early Christians were offering themselves up as a
sacrifice, not unlike the sacrifices of animals of the Old Testament
that they were familiar with—nor unlike Christ's sacrifice on the
cross. A budding new spirituality, a new approach to God, was
forming. It was to be practiced in a wide variety of ways.

The early desert fathers and mothers of the third and fourth centuries, who turned their backs on the extraordinarily hedonistic civi-
lized world of their day, pointed to the need to subjugate bodily
desires if one were truly to know God. They purified themselves
through prayer, austere practices, and extreme living conditions. Although their lives appear to have been unbelievably difficult, they
were men and women filled with such unspeakable happiness and
peace that many joined them, forming the first communities of
monks. Even in the harshness of barren wastelands, existing on wild
plants and praying long hours, it was apparent that, whatever they
were doing, it was working.

In the fifth century, St. Augustine advanced the understanding of
Catholic spirituality by arguing that, as the knowledge of God was
important, so was *self*-knowledge. (The modern concept of self-
fulfillment was many, many centuries away.) Augustine taught that
these two—knowledge of God and knowledge of self—instead of
being at odds, were actually complementary, each enhancing the
other. So, holy though it may appear, a life of total self-abnegation,
exclusively devoted to seeking God while ignoring completely human

needs, was not necessarily or exclusively in keeping with Christ's spiritual legacy. The needs of soul and body grew a bit closer.

But Augustine's approach required reflection and direction; for the common Christian, who was more than likely an illiterate peasant, it was far too complicated. Various devotions grew up over the centuries, and pious practices—long hours in front of the Blessed Sacrament, pilgrimages to saints' tombs, the saying of the rosary—were considered propitious acts for the laity. These acts, the church taught, would forgive sins and assure a place in heaven. Such was everyday spirituality for the lay person—the performance of acts perceived as pleasing to God (which harkened back to pagan belief that the gods needed to be appeased), and designed to put the evil propensities of the flesh under control. The things of God and the things of the world were still at odds in much of Christian spirituality.

Throughout the Dark and Middle Ages, Catholic orders of men and women virtually preserved civilization and kept alight the light of human decency through their charitable work, evangelization, and heroic example. Their spirituality, lived out within monastic communities, was both admired and inaccessible to the vast majority of Christians.

Thomas Aquinas (d. 1274), that wise "Angelic Doctor," broadened Catholic spirituality by reiterating the much-needed balance between prayer and reflection—and the need to put into action the results of that contemplation. But there was still much of Catholic spirituality, well-intentioned though it was, that verged on superstition. The adoration of relics is a good example. Spirituality for the masses was really a kind of formulaic moralism that the church could easily teach, enforce, and reward.

After the Protestant Reformation proved Catholicism ripe for needed change, it was St. Ignatius (d. 1556) and his famous "Spiritual Exercises" that again called for a healthy balance in a Catholic's life. Ignatius believed in a both/and approach, not an either/or dichotomy. He taught that a combination of intense, regular prayer and liturgical life, along with a serious, effective, holy life *in* the world, was really what the life and message of Christ taught—and what needed to be put into practice.

This conflict between flight from the world and acceptance of the world continued to be at the heart of Catholic spirituality. Related, but at a deeper level, was the conflict between the view that all the temporal world was evil and should be avoided, and the belief that all creation was holy and should be embraced. There were saintly men and women who sought and felt the presence of God, and brought it into the world. Others separated themselves from the rest of humanity; still another group pursued the dramatically esoteric—visions, relic worship, pilgrimages to holy places—that to them seemed to offer not only the best way to God, but a guarantee that God would listen to their cries. But, by far, the vast majority of Christians went about their daily lives quietly seeking God through the most common ways: attendance at mass and individual prayers. The thought of a "spiritual life" was not even a consideration.

During the Enlightenment, a more discerning eye was cast on religious belief; and, with the continuing discoveries of science and human psychology, Catholic spirituality evolved still further, at its best embracing beneficial new insights while preserving Old Testament wisdom and the teachings and example of Jesus Christ.

Running through all these centuries of spiritual development had been something of a two-track system. Serious spiritual pursuit was really only for the formally religious, namely priests and religious. The ordinary lay person, considered somehow below spiritual or intellectual par, was expected to perform assigned, required rituals and generally to abide by the dictates of the church. Spirituality for this group was really moralism, a set of creeds and laws, rather than a relationship with God.

Even before Vatican II—which would crystallize and acknowledge an enormous spiritual yearning among all Catholics—it was becoming clear that seeking God was the right and responsibility of all men and women, whether in the workplace or a cloister, in a kitchen or at the altar, whatever their abilities or place in life. Would a God who created us all have it any other way? And what of the promise of Jesus Christ to be ever present to us, in every moment, in every situation? Is this not a promise we could rely on as we sought an authentic spirituality?

Vatican II made clear that there could be no place in an informed Catholicism for a spiritual caste system—one caste for priests and religious, and another for laity. Individuals, each in their own uniqueness, could chart their own paths to God. Their souls and bodies need not be at war, but instead were to be seen as equal parts, each at the service of the other, each needed by the other to complete a total being. Human spirituality was not something to be addressed only on Sunday morning. Believers were to bring their lives to church—and take church into their lives.

Traveling through the history of Catholic spirituality, we find both towering examples of true holiness and foolish excess. We find old ways being both reformed and stubbornly resisting change. We find innovation that worked and innovation that proved to be fleeting. All of this should be kept in mind as the Good Enough Catholic scans today's spiritual landscape. Spirituality is not an end point. It is an imperfect process of discovery that will witness false starts and true triumphs, moments of unspeakable joy and moments of utter despair. What is important to keep before us is the desire to seek God, and to discover our own truth.

## MANY VOICES

Thousands of books are written each year claiming to be about "spirituality." They promise to enhance your relationships with others, or with yourself. By reading them, you will be more successful—in business, in your sex life, with your pet, in the garden, on the golf course; the claims are dizzying. Some of these books find a wide audience; our best-seller lists and talk shows are filled with varied approaches to spirituality, often a sort of "spirituality by objective" (to slightly alter Harvard Business School's classic practice of "management by objective"). In other words, if you set your goal, and follow a list of prescribed steps, the goal will be yours.

But as these new methods flower and fade (it's always educational to look at what the "big" human improvement books were five or ten years ago, and see what sort of impact they made), Catholic spirituality endures. Not that Catholic spirituality isn't constantly changing, for it is. Not that it doesn't learn from other religions and cultures, psychology and science—sometimes reluctantly and begrudgingly—for it eventually does. But there is something deep at the core of Catholic spirituality that has stood the test of time, ready to reveal its truth in this day as well.

For there is an enormous difference between the authentic quest for kinship with God—which implies faith—and the "spirituality by objective" approach, which teaches that the individual, and not God, is the prime motivator. There is an enormous difference in a centuries-old spirituality that will see us through the peaks and valleys of life, and attend us in our weakness and our strength, and one that falls apart when we ourselves begin to falter. There is an enormous difference between role models of Ignatius and Thomas Merton, Aquinas and the Little Flower, of Dorothy Day and Charles de Foucauld and today's prophets of enlightenment.

"God speaks where he will—for me, I found a clear message for my spiritual life, oddly enough, in a management book I read. One of the *Seven Habits of Successful People* is to have a mission statement about your life. Being a methodical kind of guy, this appealed to me. So I made up a mission statement that really said who I am: 'I pray to be a wise, evangelical servant of Jesus Christ, complemented by and in union with my wife and supported by friends and family, using my time, talents, and treasure to help the urban poor to help themselves to improve and maintain their physical environment.' That drives me, focuses me, inspires me. I say it every day. And I revise it as necessary."

—ALLEN STRYCZEK

# THE POSSIBLE, IMPOSSIBLE QUEST

As a Good Enough Catholic embarking upon, or continuing, a spiritual quest, it's comforting to know that you are hardly alone in the hunger you feel, the questioning about how to satisfy that hunger—or the gnawing doubt it can *ever* be satisfied. What you feel is felt by others, a growing number of others. People may not be attending formal religious services in the same numbers they did a generation ago, but their spiritual selves still seek communion with that mysterious force outside them.

> "We are leaving individualist ways behind as we search for spiritual values. I hear street-wise teenagers talking about it; I hear it in federal offices—people aren't ashamed of their religious beliefs anymore. I see Bibles on people's desks. You wouldn't have seen that five years ago. Something is happening."
>
> —JOHN BUTLER

What we seek in a spiritual life is usually twofold. First, and most important, is to find ways to communicate with God—and have God communicate with us. In other words, in that once-feared Protestant idea, we seek to build a personal relationship with God. Second, we strive to make our spirituality the basis of our moral behavior, the framework by which we live our daily lives. Let's first deal with ways to start, build, or enrich a Good Enough Catholic spiritual life. Then we'll talk about how—or *whether*—to assess your spiritual progress, and whether God is indeed communicating with you.

# PRAYER

The most direct pathway to a spiritual life and to God is through prayer. In Catholicism there are essentially two kinds of prayer—formal and informal prayer. Formal prayer includes the mass and other liturgies, the Divine Office, the rosary, novenas, and devotions. As we explored in chapter 2, the mass is the most perfect prayer in Catholic practice and the place most Catholics meet and have a sense of the presence of God. The mass is our rich banquet of spirituality, a combination of individual and corporate prayer, scriptural readings, instruction, and inspiration; it balances time for silent reflection with time for group assent.

Informal prayer may either be the reflections of others or our personal prayers. A few minutes spent browsing in any serious bookstore will yield one or two books of prayerful meditations that will resonate with you, containing imagery that makes sense and inspires. There are spiritual classics; there are modern masters. (My favorite happens to be Thomas Merton's *New Seeds of Contemplation*.) You'll be surprised when you ask friends of yours—those whose spirituality seems to radiate in their lives—what books have touched them.

But it is personal prayer that most people find difficult to carry out. How do I start? What do I say? How do I know God listens? Don't feel embarrassed, Good Enough Catholic, that these questions are in your heart. Moses asked them, too.

A recent survey by the National Opinion Research Center found that over three-quarters of all Americans pray at least once a week; half said they prayed at least once a day. So, while we might agonize over its proper form and efficacy, prayer is more a part of this secular culture than we sometimes realize.

There is no *right* way to pray; that is the first point. This is *your* conversation with a friend, and you can use whatever means or aids you choose. What is important is that you make the attempt. Prayer does not happen in theory, it happens in practice. For too long, too many people have attempted to pray in some preordained way, as if their own insights, experiences, and circumstances were unimportant. You are the composite of those insights, experiences, and circumstances; why shouldn't they be employed in your prayer life? "Thou" and "Thee" are words of another era. If they are comforting, use them; but don't feel they are the only language of prayer.

Must we have faith before we begin to pray? Is this a precondition to a fruitful prayer life? "If you wait until you have enough faith, you'll never pray," says Richard Foster in a *U.S. Catholic* magazine interview.[2] Foster, who has guided many others in prayer, both in person and through his books, admits: "My prayer life began out of desperation. It started with . . . 'O, God, help.' "

The Good Enough Catholic might look at it this way: Would a loving, merciful God who wants to be close to us impose the precondition of a strong faith on those of us who find ourselves struggling to believe? For that matter, isn't the mere act of putting oneself in the presence of God itself a magnificent act of faith? Just in asking—Am I worthy to be praying? Am I in the right state of mind? Am I holy enough to even consider prayer?—the Good Enough Catholic has the answer. The answer is a resounding yes.

If you want to begin or return to a prayer life, it is important to take your impulse seriously. As tentative as you may feel, don't let your understandable ambivalence put you off. Set aside a special time and a special place to pray. Tell no one about your pursuit, at least at the beginning. Keep it between you and God, who understands completely. You may wish to be in a darkened room, with a candle and incense burning; you may choose to sit overlooking a lake or a field—or at the blank face of the next apartment building. Your best time may be morning or night. But, as with any pursuit you take seriously, you must be disciplined about it. You may find that setting aside five or ten minutes at a certain time of day—no more—is exactly right. Most of us can't pray much longer than that. When you need more time, you will know.

There are many techniques for praying. Centering prayer calls upon you to simply repeat a single, peaceful, meaningful word ("Abba," "Father," "grace," "love"—for example). In an excellent article in *America* magazine,[3] Dennis Hamm recommends another method: praying backward through the day, remembering both the good and bad events and always paying attention to the feelings they evoked, both positive and negative. You may want to read a paragraph of Scripture and meditate upon it, or you may want to picture yourself within a Bible story, talking to the people there, conversing with Christ himself. You may find that breathing exercises or a meditative technique (transcendental meditation, for example) naturally lead to prayer.

> "I'd been in a prayer group for twenty years, so prayer was hardly foreign to me. But, there I was, going through a long dry period in my spiritual life. Nothing seemed to work; I tried everything. Then I came across Al-Anon's twelve-step program. It was exactly right. I needed that kind of specific approach at that time in my life. It brought my spiritual life alive again."
>
> —DOROTHEA TOBIN

And, the most basic form of all—spontaneous prayer—can be amazingly accessible.

I am a person who resists prayer techniques. I find myself more inspired and heartened by the words of the Gospel of Matthew,[4] where Jesus, in teaching his followers the Lord's Prayer, says not to "heap up empty phrases" but to pray simply. I seek to be open and straightforward in my prayer life—the qualities I most enjoy in conversation with people. I imagine that God is no different, hoping for honest talk from this person who wants to be intimate with him.

A sketchy outline of my typical prayer might go something like this (although I'm sure my mind doesn't express itself in complete sentences): "Here I am, Lord. Here is what my life is about today. This is what I need. Here is where I need guidance; here is where I am confused and frightened. Here is where I am joyful and content; here is where I am at peace with myself; here is where I am at war. You know my needs better than I do. Please be with me and guide me in whatever I do. Thank you for your blessings; you've given me so much. Thanks, too, for the difficulties—they have formed me. Help me where I need help. Give me patience to know that my time is not always your time."

That would take about a minute or two.

I may ask for something specific. For instance, I may be seeking help in making a wise choice if a major decision is at hand. But more often I am praying for patience in dealing with my children and my wife; wisdom to see where I should be devoting my energies; the ability to in some small way alleviate the hurts my friends may be suffering, or my world may be experiencing; honesty in facing my own strengths and weaknesses. In essence, I am praying for virtue, because with virtue all the decisions I need to make will have a good foundation.

Do I ever pray for a specific *thing*? A good book idea? Friends for my sons at school? That my wife, a social worker, might pass her licensing exam? Yes, I do. But I always do so with a proviso: "Grant my prayer if it is best for me, or for them." I'm not wise enough to know if what I'm seeking is really right or good. I leave that up to God. Do my thoughts ever wander during prayer? All the time. As Thomas Merton says in *New Seeds of Contemplation*, "Our minds are like crows. They pick up everything that glitters, no matter how uncomfortable our nests get with all that metal in them."[5]

There is nothing wrong with your real life entering your prayer life, with your mind wandering from the sublime to the secular. So don't fight it. Our Buddhist friends, masters at meditation, learned long ago to allow such random thoughts to wander out of the mind as gently as they wandered in. Neither fight them nor hold on to them; do not regard them as your enemy or as your friend. If they return enough times, that is their own message to be taken more seriously. But most thoughts during prayer are just passing distractions, and should be granted safe and unencumbered passage on their way.

An authentic prayer life is really tailored to the person. Joan Sullivan, a single woman in Chicago who has been a foster mother to many troubled adolescents, confesses, "I don't have answers to many of the things I'm doing, so I just pray to be conscious of the decisions I make and how I treat these children whom nobody else wants. My kids need me to be spiritual. They sense it." For Minnie Diana prayer is hardly peaceful. "I cry. I kick. I scream. I argue. That is my relationship with God; I am honest with him." As a little girl, Shilpi D'Costa asked God to be with her on the dusty roads of the family farm in Bangladesh, "to keep me safe and help me to be a good person." And now that same prayer, bridging miles and cultures, is on her lips as she walks the streets of Washington a mature woman.

When Adela Torres's infant daughter contracted meningitis, her prayer was for a miraculous cure. The daughter lost most of her hearing; instead of a miracle, Adela found that she received what she would need: "The strength to go through this. It was at a time I didn't feel like praying, but I made myself. And with God in my heart, our life went on. We learned sign language together. Now, we have another beautiful bond between us."

# SPIRITUAL READING

The number of books published dedicated to spirituality has quadrupled over the past twenty years, a testament to how hungry we are for spiritual nourishment. Of course, not all these books are about spirituality. Many are simply thinly disguised invitations to ego enhancement. In other words, these are books about I and I, not I and Thou—books that glorify Me, rather than lead me to glorify God.

There is nothing wrong with recovering the child in you, learning how to deal with your anger, or discovering how to be a friend to yourself. And, sometimes, books on such subjects may even lead to deeper spiritual insights. But most of the time, by themselves, they do not—so don't kid yourself into thinking they will. These are not Good Enough Books on spirituality. They are Good Enough Books about Me—and, for most of us, while we surely want to be happy and self-actualized in life, we know that the relentless pursuit of well-being can be a dead-end street, spiritually speaking.

Let me state emphatically that reading books about psychological wellness, or undergoing therapy or analysis, can in themselves be very beneficial. I have read such books; I went through four years of psychoanalysis. Each was enormously important. Insightful books and guided introspection can clear the static from our minds, allowing us to deal more effectively with life. They can be holy pursuits in themselves—perhaps even needed conditioning for a spiritual journey. But they are not the same as the pursuit of an authentic spirituality.

We want to know God better. We want God to know *us* better. And so our spiritual reading must keep these goals in view.

The best and most time-tested spiritual reading is Holy Scripture. As London's Cardinal Basil Hume has written, "It is hard for us to realize that the words of Christ, spoken nearly 2,000 years ago, are contemporary in every age. Read the gospels and allow God to whisper in your minds and into your hearts words that can have a profound effect on the way we think and act. . . . He will find us if we listen to his voice calling to us through the fog that often surrounds us, a kind of cloud of unknowing, and above the noise that muffles his call."[6]

Biographies of heroic people, or autobiographical books that tell of noble pursuits, can be powerful spiritual reading; a few pages are just the way to begin or end your day. (When I was searching for guidance in my own life, I looked to the example of people with a moral imperative in their lives. The result was a collection of essays, collected in a book, *Companions Along the Way*.) You can reach back to the classics; you can get the latest by a contemporary author. Spiritual reading, an often underutilized asset in the ascent to a holy wholeness, stands ready to relax and ready your mind for inspiration.

In my own life, I have been inspired by Charles de Foucauld's desert experiences and Karen Horney's journeys into the unconscious. Formula books never worked for me. It is not that I didn't seek and devour them; I may have been momentarily filled, but the hunger that existed before soon returned.

# SILENCE

There is no more perfect prayer than silence, putting yourself in the presence of God and doing nothing more. For silence is the ultimate manifestation of respect for another. It is a sign the other has something to impart that is important, indeed essential, to you. Silence is often difficult for us, as we are more used to expressing our thoughts and desires in words. But it is in silence that we most clearly hear the voice of God. For God is *always* in communication with us. We just need to be aware of it. Silence is a gateway to that awareness.

Think of it this way: If prayer is a conversation, when do we give God the opportunity to speak back to us if we are talking all the time?

If you want your prayer to be silence, find a quiet place or a quiet time and go there, as though expecting to meet a friend. Present yourself, ready to hear that friend. There will be time enough for you to speak. Let the friend take the lead.

My own opportunities for silence occur in both predictable and strange places. In my travels, I love visiting churches and chapels in European cities or American hospitals. I just sit quietly to absorb the holiness of the place, to listen to the echoes of the thousands of prayers that have gone before mine—and to allow God time to communicate, if and as he wills. Also, after my short daily prayer each morning (I try to say the Divine Office, which takes about fifteen minutes) I always leave a quiet moment for reflection.

But, to be honest, one of my most fertile periods of silence occurs on weekday mornings in a local swimming pool. Once I am no longer aware of my stroke or breathing, and encased by the beautiful silence of water, I find myself in a state I rarely achieve throughout the rest of my day. If I have any insights into my life or my work, it is usually here. If there are intractable problems facing me, it is usually here that they are solved. Is this silence in the swimming pool a prayer? Or, is it a prayer when, caught in a traffic jam, I consciously do nothing at all, but open my mind and heart and life to God? I honestly don't know if these are times of prayer; but I do know that in times like these, God speaks most clearly to me.

# HEARING GOD, SEEING GOD

How do we know, people often ask, when God is talking to us? How do we hear the voice of God? And do we ever actually *see* him?

For the vast majority of us, God does not come in apparitions or make his presence known through audible communication. Rather, the voice of God is that nudge we feel to repair a relationship we have damaged—or it may be the equally insistent nudge to break off from a relationship that brings harm to our souls. To show kindness in a situation, or to find the strength to walk away; to take a risky path, or to wait. The voice of God might be sensed on a walk along a busy street, or on a lonesome beach; in a dream, or in another's face. Tom Eakins,* raised in a traditional Catholic family, had done everything to run from his homosexuality; for him, the voice of God came as he prayed before a statue of the Blessed Virgin. "I was horribly depressed; I hated myself. I felt I had done something terribly wrong to deserve this sexual orientation. In the quietness of that moment, my prayer was answered: I finally had the strength to face myself and my problem. I found a wonderful Jesuit psychologist who told me that I had to see whether this was who I am, and if I would ultimately find love as a gay person. An older Jesuit miraculously fell into my life and became my spiritual director. It all happened in a remarkably short period of time."

Darrell Colbert, strung out on alcohol and drugs, slit both his wrists in utter desperation after a friend died of an overdose. "I woke up, the blood had clotted, and I wasn't dead. My prayers, my family's prayers, the people of my parish who stayed with me when I was in the worst shape, all were answered in that moment. God showed me I was supposed to live." For Vanessa Cooke, who tries to penetrate the tough and confident facades of her high school students in Virginia, "Prayer is what allows me to see the big picture.

And that's the scariest gift of all—because then I have to use it to help them."

It is up to each of us to "test the spirits," by reflecting on our experiences (Does this leave me sad, or happy? Is this good for me, and for others?) and by prayerfully asking: "Is this from you or not?" The answer will come. God guarantees this.

Thomas Merton put it this way:

> How am I to know the will of God? . . . the very nature of each situation usually bears written into itself some indication of God's will. For whatever is demanded by truth, by justice, by mercy, or by love must surely be taken to be willed by God. To consent to his will is, then, to consent to be true, or to speak truth, or at least to seek it.[7]

In a fascinating survey published in *America*, "How Can I Find God," Peter-Hans Kolvenbach, S.J., superior-general of the Jesuits, notes that our desire to *see* God can be traced at least as far back as Moses. As God said to Moses in Exodus, "You cannot see my face,"[8] but assured him that "you will see me pass": so it is with us today. ". . . [I]t is less a matter of searching for God," Father Kolvenbach writes, "than of allowing oneself to be found by him in all of life's situations, where he does not cease to pass and where he allows himself to be recognized once he has really passed. 'You will see my back.' "[9]

# RETREATS, WORKSHOPS, ADULT CATHOLIC EDUCATION

Within Catholicism there is a remarkably wide range of opportunities to start, enhance, or expand a spiritual life. Often a concentrated period of time set aside is exactly what is needed by a person whose spiritual yearnings can no longer be denied. You may not know exactly what to do about these yearnings, but Catholicism offers many options among which at least a few will match your temperament, needs, and available time. From a silent retreat to a charismatic gathering; a Catholic/Zen sasheen to a traditionalist weekend anchored in a Latin Tridentine mass; ecoreligious outdoor treks to a marriage encounter—all are within the embrace of a church with a far greater reach than most of us imagine. The best of Eastern mysticism and New Age insights are incorporated somewhere under this sprawling tent called the Catholic Church.

> "When I was just a baby Catholic, right after my conversion, I opened a special section of the *National Catholic Reporter* and saw their retreat list. I felt like a kid on the farm getting a Sears catalogue. I was dying of spiritual malnutrition, and here was a cornucopia of great places to go."
>
> —CAROLYN SWEERS

My personal choice is to spend time periodically at a monastery of one of the contemplative orders (Trappist, Benedictine, Carmelite, Dominican, and Franciscan are perhaps the best known). Recently, an excellent directory of these places has been published; they are dotted all over the country.[10] There, in the quiet rhythms of monastic life, in the richness of their corporate prayer and worship, I have found peace, rejuvenation, and clarity. Too many people today go from guru to guru, from meditation center to encounter group, forever in pursuit of "it." After a long and fruitless search, I found there is no "it." Indeed, as most spiritual guides advise, if we find "it," we most probably have found a false god.

Another readily available spiritual resource are the adult religion classes offered at parishes and other Catholic religious centers. The range is enormously wide: from classical studies of Scripture to mini-courses dealing with stress, competition, unemployment, or parenthood from a religious perspective. Not being the Perfect Catholic—who would probably select a course because it sounds like something you *should* take—the Good Enough Catholic might do a little market research to find out the content, who's teaching the course, and how others have benefited in the past.

Or, take the opposite tack—equally the sign of the Good Enough Catholic—and leave the work up to God. Simply take a course and let the Lord work his way with you. Our intelligence can get in the way of something we have more need of in today's world—faith. Lead with your heart, not with your mind.

## OF WHAT MEASURE?

Once the Good Enough Catholic has begun the conscious pursuit of a spiritual life, it is not unreasonable to wonder whether or not it is being effective. In other words, is this working for me? Am I making progress?

As a person who shies away from the five- or eight- or twelve-step approaches to just about anything, I would be the last to offer a spirituality quotient check-off list providing some standard of measurement. Some who regularly counsel spiritual seekers, like Sister Mary Luke Tobin of Denver, call such evaluations a "false step." In Sr. Tobin's opinion, "You need to grow without observing yourself. . . . Ask yourself, 'Am I faithfully praying every day?' If you are, progress and growth will take care of themselves."[11]

And yet, without resorting to actual measurement, certain things can be said of a life that seeks union with God.

As with physical growth, spiritual growth comes in stages. The innocent spirituality of our First Communion day—wonderful though it was—is not the spirituality that we can take into adult life. What seemed perfect years ago will simply not do today, for our experiences have formed a much different person. All we have to do is look back to pre–Vatican II beliefs and practices to see how far we have already come.

When our lives are confusing, or it becomes clear that the next step in our inner growth will require pain before peace, we may want to cling to our youthful understanding of God, the sacraments, even life itself. Everything was so simple then; we wonder why we can't return. Why, in the midst of a tumultuous world, can we not reclaim these precious memories?

We cannot because we have grown beyond that. We are on the threshold of a faith based on personal choice and a mature spiritual awakening. We may go to the attic of our mind, and open the chest to touch and cherish those tiny garments; but we must then take on the faith that will clothe us as a mature man or woman.

A helpful parallel can be drawn between a spiritual life and a love life. We seek romantic intimacy and feel absolutely wonderful—invincible—when we fall in love. The feeling is so sublime we want it to go on forever. But experience proves that the initial bliss never lasts. Falling in love must eventually be replaced by *being* in love. It is here that love can be sustained, grow, and deepen, ready to weather the inevitable storms that sweep over every human relationship.

Spirituality is quite similar. When we experience God's transcendence, we may experience an all-encompassing sensation of power and love. We can see why the people of the Bible danced and sang to acknowledge the feeling of God's presence, why they were accused of being drunk. But this euphoria—while its memory may inspire us for a lifetime—does not last. At least not in that form.

Even the hermits who left the world to seek God in the deserts, or the later monks who gathered in monasteries, found that their spirituality, once so sure and sustaining, inevitably seemed to abandon them. This sensation—the feeling that prayer is hollow and meaningless, that God is absent, that the very efforts a person makes are foolish and ultimately useless—is called *acedia*. It is a word that encompasses boredom, depression, ennui, torpor, confusion.

Virtually everyone seeking a consequential life with God probably will experience *acedia*. It may happen more than once on the winding path of a spiritual life; but most often it appears first at exactly the wrong time, just when people feel they have successfully launched a spiritual life. They feel in touch with God; they can finally pray; they feel better about themselves and their lives—and, suddenly, the bottom drops out.

These "dark nights of the soul" are certainly not to be courted, but they should be seen for what they are. When they occur, the Good Enough Catholic's soul is usually receiving one of two messages. The first is that there is some obstacle blocking the way to real spiritual growth. Often this is sin or a sinful pattern, and it is necessary to look honestly at ourselves to discover whether we need to change something in our lives in order to move on, unencumbered. To what are we addicted? Are our inordinate attachments so powerful? Power, work, jealousy, hate? Are our hearts so hard God cannot break through?

The second and more usual message of *acedia* is actually an invitation. Your soul is seeking to grow, but an old shell must first be shed. A new space must be opened up in us so that God might fill it. A new path is being opened. Your new prayer life has quietly removed the clutter in your life; you are stripped back to the essentials of who you are. In this moment of spiritual trial you no longer have the defenses that so handily had kept God at bay.

Too many people earnestly embark upon a spiritual life of prayer, reading, or retreat, only to abandon their search when this moment of truth strikes them. Why am I doing this to myself? you might ask. My life wasn't *that* bad before—and this is truly horrible. What kind of God is God when I can be made to feel this awful trying to find him? Why shouldn't I listen to the promise of the latest best-seller, the surefire technique, the convincing talk-show hosts, the charismatic "spiritual master"?

The spiritual life requires patience and persistence if you expect lasting results. This is certainly not to say that such testing is some sort of divine punishment, retribution for our sins or the dues we must pay for the time we have stayed away from our faith. That is not in keeping with the message of Jesus. The pursuit of God—like the pursuit of any lover—can be exciting and it can be frustrating; it is nearly always mysterious. And the Good Enough Catholic willing to engage in this mystical dance will find unimaginable rewards: joy, serenity, happiness, and the courage to face whatever may come our way.

The bliss will not last, and neither will the agony. What will last is a certain peace and confidence that we can carry throughout all our days.

## HELP ALONG THE WAY

As we try to separate the wheat from the chaff of spiritual approaches and disciplines, a few simple questions might help to clarify for the Good Enough Catholic which of them might be helpful to pursue—always being aware that the Holy Spirit will descend where it chooses, and not only in those ways that seem "right." Ask: Is a relationship with God crucial to the approach? Is the hoped-for end result not only to make us feel better, but to *be* better? Does our spirituality result in "fruits of the spirit"? In other words, do we have more peace, and less anxiety? Is it easier to both confront life's problems and leave some to take care of themselves? Am I more open, less judgmental? Pay attention to your experiences.

As Allen Stryczek's adaptation of a management principle helped focus his spiritual life, there are many other avenues to personal holiness for Catholics, if we are only able to see them. "For me, Buddhism provides the technology for nurturing the habits of service and spirit that Jesus taught and exemplified," says Carolyn Sweers. "For instance, Jesus said, 'Go into your room and shut the door and pray to your Father.' We can't always go into a room, so the job is to find a quiet space within your head. Buddhism provides that through meditation—and then you can truly pray always." When people talk to Marty Hegarty about their spiritual hunger, he never gives then anything Catholic, or even Christian to read. "I introduce them to Carl Jung. He speaks to people's soul more than most priests in the pulpit, and more than most books you can start with."

The Good Enough Catholic seeks an interior life—but not a spirituality of insularity. Spirituality is not an escape from the world, a safe refuge in which we can hide and hoard our newfound treasure. This link to the divine releases power, with the potential to transform us into the most complete, most fulfilled people we can possibly be. It gives us the opportunity to bring that power into the world. It helps us resist the temptation to seek escape from an increasingly technological society by becoming so inner-focused that we shut out the needs of the society around us.

We must always remember that this is God's world, too. Our task is no different from that of the Israelites or the Apostles: to make the Earth a place where God's presence is alive.

# SPIRITUAL DIRECTION

One of the surest ways to stay on track spiritually is to seek the guidance of a spiritual director. Here, the Catholic Church uniquely has a long and proven tradition that is ours to build upon. The spiritual director—many today are trained lay people, while others are priests and nuns—can suggest reading that might be helpful, and generally serve as a guide along the individual's spiritual path. Such a person can help in discerning what methods or disciplines to undertake that are most in keeping with the individual's personality, lifestyle, and needs, and suggest what to do during the dry periods as well.

Discernment is an extraordinarily important regulator of a spiritual life. Usually, when a person makes the decision to establish a relationship with God—whether this is a conscious choice, the result of some major outside event, or just that awful feeling of emptiness—it is often difficult for us to see whether we are being helped or hurt, advanced or hindered by the myriad people and situations in our lives. Is God speaking, or our own self-will? A spiritual director with a gift for discernment can literally work miracles in guiding us through the maze.

At one of the driest periods in my personal and spiritual life— which lasted several years—I found a wonderful spiritual director in a Trappist monk. As I look back on the experience, he did not so much give me advice as listen intently to me and allow me—with God's help—to work out my difficulties. Our conversations were not usually about spiritual classics (although I did read some), not about the state of my soul (although I inevitably began our sessions with a white-knuckled assessment), not about how Catholic I was (although this was a Catholic monastery, for sure); it was more about books I was reading, what was in the news that day, how my work was going. Somehow, through the real and immediate—not the transcendent—he could see my struggle and, while gently moving me along, stood beside me so I knew I was not alone.

The Good Enough Catholic in search of a spiritual director might look in a variety of places. Your parish priest, religious education director, or diocesan spirituality office are all good places to start. Often, the chaplain at the Newman Center on a local college campus will have names of qualified spiritual directors. Members of any religious order (for instance, Benedictines, Dominicans, Jesuits) who teach at a nearby college or who have a community house in your area can be helpful. Then, there is the Good Enough Catholic grapevine—don't be shy about asking others if they know of a good spiritual director. Often Catholic therapists can recommend someone.

## THE GOOD ENOUGH CATHOLIC CHALLENGE: OPEN YOUR HEART TO GOD

You, Good Enough Catholic, sense a void unfilled by the many wonderful things already in your life—family, friends, accomplishment. You seek a way to cope with the disappointments, the hurts, and the failures. You also seek a way to celebrate more deeply the good times, the happiness, the good fortune you experience. There is no better time than right now to embark—or reembark—on your spiritual journey to true human fulfillment. Make a commitment to hold open your hands to God, to unlock your heart, to be at once insistent and patient.

You seek God's graces; you are ready to be surprised. You are ready to come humbly into God's presence.

Choose a way, or a combination of ways, that can help you—

whether it be silent meditation, spontaneous or formal prayer, reading the Scripture or a good spiritual book, attending a retreat, seeking a spiritual director. And persist. Set yourself a reasonable goal: a
certain amount of time each day for a week, let's say. Perhaps instead you want to dedicate a full day or a weekend to a retreat—
either at an established retreat house or monastery. Or you might do
a private retreat with the aid of a spiritual director.

Your way may be through a prayer group like the one that meets
in the early morning at St. Gertrude's in Chicago—where priest and
men are going through the reading of the Bible, stopping when they
want, lingering as long as they need. It may be through that person
who radiates a certain grounded spirituality; ask him or her what
book has inspired them. It may be through attendance at noontime
mass in the middle of your day, or in a few minutes of silence before
your family rises.

Don't give up when a highly recommended book doesn't speak
to you, when prayer is barren, or when your mind wanders in
meditation. In your heart you know that this is something you want
as much as anything in your life. It is worth your effort. Pursue a
spiritual life that will at once enrich your soul and spill over into
your relationships with loved ones, into the workplace, into the
community at large. If you meditate three hours a day and then are a
horrible worker or boss, what can be said of the state of your soul,
the fruits of your spirit?

Whatever your way, God will not deny you access. The time is
now. A divine friend awaits you.

# SELECTED READINGS

Karen Armstrong, *Visions of God: Four Medieval Mystics and Their Writings*.
New York: Bantam Books, 1994.
William A. Barry, *Spiritual Direction and the Encounter with God: A Theological
Inquiry*. Mahwah, N.J.: Paulist Press, 1992.

Peter L. Berger, *A Rumor of Angels: Modern Society and the Rediscovery of the Supernatural*. New York: Doubleday Anchor, 1970.

Frederich Buechner, *The Sacred Journey*. San Francisco: Harper and Row, 1965.

Michael Downey, ed., *New Dictionary of Catholic Spirituality*. Collegeville, Minn.: Liturgical Press, 1993.

Louis Dupre and James Wiseman, eds., *Light from Light: An Anthology of Christian Mysticism*. New York: Paulist Press, 1988.

Thomas Keating, *Open Mind, Open Heart: The Contemplative Dimension of the Gospel*. New York: Continuum, 1995.

Robert E. Kennedy, *Zen Spirit, Christian Spirit: The Place of Zen in Christian Life*. New York: Continuum, 1995.

Jack Kornfield, *A Path with Heart: A Guide Through the Perils and Promise of Spiritual Life*. New York: Bantam Books, 1993.

C. S. Lewis, *Surprised by Joy: The Shape of My Early Life*. London: Geoffrey Bles, 1955.

Shawn Madigan, *Spirituality Rooted in Liturgy*. Washington, D.C.: The Pastoral Press, 1988.

Thomas Merton, *New Seeds of Contemplation*. New York: New Directions Press, 1961.

Michael F. Pennock, *The Ways of Prayer: An Introduction*. Notre Dame, Ind.: Ave Maria, 1987.

Michael Ramsey, *Be Still and Know: A Study in the Life of Prayer*. Boston: Cowley Publications, 1993.

(Various authors.) *A Retreat With . . .* (series). Cincinnati: St. Anthony Messenger Press.

# CHAPTER FIVE

# MORALITY, CONSCIENCE, AND SIN

## The Architecture of Character

Sin—never the most popular of subjects—is having an especially tough time of it these days.

It's a word that has drifted to the outer edges of our consciousness, relegated to the dustbin of another, less-enlightened era. *Sin*. Too punitive. Too negative. Too dreary. Too judgmental. And certainly, too specific.

After all, who can say what is right and wrong? In our modern-day search to understand ourselves and what motivates us, we have conveniently assigned more and more weight to the many variables that shape our decisions, pointing to everything from hormones to history, birth order to world order. We have been less eager to discuss how we exercise our own free will. And, as a by-product, we may find that we have smudged the moral boundaries of our own words and deeds into a hopeless blur of relativism.

But sin, that most inconvenient of realities, hasn't gone away. We may not be able to pin it down as decisively as we once could in the old Catholic Church, but sin is still very much with us. And, deep inside, we know we do not want to be under its command.

An interesting public debate on the state of our souls recently took place—quite inadvertently—when the *New York Times* and the cable channel MTV each looked at what sin means today. As high culture met pop culture, a curious mélange of vaunted literati struggled valiantly (and with noticeable discomfort) to say something original about our basest potential, while, with a greater measure of charity (but rather more languor) youthful cyber-philosophers mused over the contemporary human condition.

With our current low-fat, low-conscience aversion to facing up to our shortcomings, little wonder that sin's co-relative, morality—both public and private—is having an equally difficult time. Without some barometer of whether our actions are good and beneficial, or bad and detrimental, to ourselves and others—a simple definition of sin—how is a person supposed to know how to make a sensible decision, how to live a decent life? For morality—as guided by that mysterious inner compass called conscience—is the code of ethics that informs our judgment each day. Without morality, individuals who no longer trust others find they cannot even trust themselves; families crumble; and society collapses into chaos.

Thus we can look at sin as a concept to be avoided, or, as one writer observes, a ". . . considerable treasure. If we squander or lose it, we also lose the capacity to speak with accuracy and depth of our humanity."[1]

Catholicism, properly understood, offers a way to face sinfulness directly—and to be rescued from its grasp, over and over again, for we will sin in various ways throughout our lives. As Catholicism acknowledges that there is a path to sin, Catholicism also charts a path *from* sin. Catholicism offers redemption—not only in an eternal world, but in this world, here, now, and today. Without redemption, the moral life becomes an eternal dusk; no new day can ever break, even after the pain of the dark night of remorse. Without redemption, how can we go forth to embody, to enjoy, and to spread the love taught by Jesus Christ?

# HISTORY: THE CODES WE LIVE BY

When the Code of Hammurabi ("an eye for an eye, a tooth for a tooth") was replaced by the Ten Commandments, humankind took a great step away from the justification of vengeance. In the Ten

Commandments, human actions were regulated in a new way; a blueprint was provided for the way God wanted people to interact. A moral baseline was drawn.

With Jesus Christ, God's interest in the human race widened; his covenant was no longer only with the Jews, but with all people of the world. A new kind of moral life—with a new kind of divine presence—was now at hand. For God had entered the world and promised never to leave it, opening his arms equally to the righteous and the sinners, both the chosen and unchosen. The Kingdom of God was at hand, and it was to be a kingdom built not only upon laws; as summed up in Christ's own profound synthesis, it would be based upon love of God, and love of one's neighbor as one's self.

The Ten Commandments—which were repeated aloud during early Christian services—provided a simple, straightforward foundation for the moral life. The moral mandate was complete and all encompassing. It was also impossible.

Humans were not angels. Conversion did not strip a person of greed or lust or envy. Recognizing this, Jesus preached again and again that a new means of moral cleansing was offered by God to ameliorate the inevitable human failure to meet this high goal. People would go astray, but through an acknowledgment of their failures—their sins—the slate could be wiped clean. Sin was not a burden to be built up and borne through life; sin was meant to be forgiven. As the father in the parable of the prodigal son welcomed back his errant child, God signaled his eagerness to embrace anyone who wanted to return to him. The gospels are filled with stories and words of mercy. Little is said of condemnation for sinful acts.

Throughout its 2,000-year history, the church has tried different approaches in dealing with sin. St. Augustine (d. 430) and St. Thomas Aquinas both saw sin as corrupting human nature, alienating the person not only from God, but from themselves and other human beings. At times, Catholic teaching attempted to quantify sin with such precision that you practically needed a canon lawyer to know exactly *how* wrong you were. The emphasis was more on avoiding evil, with short shrift given to the other half of the equation, doing good. There have been theological battles over whether each moral decision was unique—that an array of factors had to be considered concerning the good, evil, or neutrality of each given act—or, alternatively, whether some acts were categorically right or wrong.

It's interesting to realize that one of the key reasons the Council of Trent brought seminaries into being when it was convened in the sixteenth century was to ensure priests would be trained as confessors—people skilled at precisely assaying moral wrongs, and leading the sinner back to spiritual wholeness.

Judgment and legalism were thus key elements in Catholic morality for many centuries, and the foundation of pre–Vatican II codes of Catholic behavior. Obedience to divine law, natural law, and even human law was the standard. If you obeyed these laws, you were good. Of course, this invested enormous authority into the hands of the church hierarchy and civil officials; it also regarded the individual as incapable of making personal moral decisions.

Vatican II began a movement to right the balance and bring Catholicism back to the moral dynamism exemplified by Jesus Christ. We needed clear guidelines, and the church would continue to provide them; but merely living according to the letter of any law was not enough. Jesus' transforming message of love and forgiveness rang across the centuries once more.

The vocation of the People of God—as all Catholics, pope to pew dweller, were called by Vatican II—was to live the mystery of Christ, to be inspired by his life, and, encouraged by the Scripture, to live and spread the power of the Good News. It was a call back to the basics: a call for a morality at once freed from Pharisaic adherence to written norms, and imbued with an awesome measure of personal responsibility. Morality was no longer fixed; history could change circumstances. An individual's own human growth and understanding dictated changing personal standards.

A new era in Catholic morality was upon us.

"This is seen so clearly in the example of the Pharisee, who was so meticulous about observing the letter of the law while evading

> the spirit of the law. . . . Jesus attempts to present two laws—the
> higher and the lower. The higher, more exalted, is the law of
> love—the law where enough is always enough. The lower, the
> letter of the law, never touches the heart. Although worthy, it will
> never be quite enough."
>
> —LENA SHIPLEY as quoted by Gregory F. Augustine Pierce,
> "The Spirituality of Lay Life," *Catholic Courier*
> (Rochester, New York), 13 April 1995

# WHAT IS SIN?

There are basically two kinds of sin in Catholic teaching, original
and actual. Original sin was long viewed as a sort of biologically
transmitted stain that marked us down through human history because of Adam and Eve's disobedience in the Garden of Eden. More
recently—and more usefully—original sin has been understood as a
given predisposition of our humanity, the capacity for evil, something we must battle with all the time.

The other category of sin, actual sin, is the only kind we actually
have some control over committing or refusing. What then is actual sin?

If deepening and strengthening our relationships with God, our
neighbor, and ourselves is the goal we assume as Good Enough
Catholics, then whatever we do to injure or break those relationships can be categorized as actual sin. If that short definition sounds a
bit too trendy or *au courant*, it's consoling to look back through the
centuries to the time of St. Basil the Great (d. 379) and his *Detailed
Rules for Monks* to find this definition of sin: "The misuse of the
powers given to us by God for doing good."[2] The more punitive,
hellfire-and-brimstone (and mechanical) renditions of sin that many
of us learned as children present a decidedly narrow view.

Of course, sin covers a wide range of possibilities—both in what
role we play in sinful acts, and in the danger of our ability to over-

come sin immediately or to remove ourselves from a situation likely to lead to sin. A practical way for the Good Enough Catholic to look at sin is to break it down into three different types, each of which requires a different—yet similar—remedy.

The first kind of sin we perhaps know best, for these are acts we do that *we know are wrong*. We have taken something that does not belong to us; we have lied; we have been unfaithful. We had other choices, but we chose to act in a certain, detrimental way. We feel guilty for these acts, and we seek to be *forgiven*.

The second kind of sin is less an act than a *condition that infects our moral system*. We are estranged from our loved ones; we find it easy and convenient to criticize rather than console; we have walled ourselves off in our righteousness, our pain, or our guilt so thoroughly that no one can reach us, and we can reach no one. In fact, we daily choose not to reach or be reached. More than individual acts, these conditions prevent a certain honesty and forthrightness in our lives, preventing the native goodness we have in us to emerge. Sometimes this condition seems out of our control and may not appear to be anyone's fault. But a pall is cast over us. We seek not so much forgiveness, but *healing*.

The third way that sin is experienced is when *we feel trapped by an evil over which we seemingly have no control*. This may be the demands of our competitive world to succeed at any cost, the call of a peer group to act in a certain way, the sanction of the secular culture to live by today's—and not timeless—standards. Many objects, pleasures, and possibilities beckon to us from the media and advertising, proclaiming their worth and their ready availability. While in our most honest moments we know we ultimately have power to make choices, it is almost as if we are powerless against these forces. From them we seek *deliverance*.

We can see that the range of sinful behavior is wide and varied. Sometimes there is a simple, individual choice between an obvious good and an obvious evil. More often, there are complex factors present, shades of good and evil. But whatever the considerations— our own nature and abilities, or the situations in which we find ourselves—sin boils down to a simple fact: we are failing to live up to the high standards we deeply want for ourselves. We are disappointed in ourselves.

Yet, when we look at the words "forgiveness," "healing," and "deliverance," we readily see a commonality: all are forms of redemption. It is *redemption* we seek as sinful Good Enough Catholics. And, consolingly, it is redemption that is at the heart of the teachings of Jesus Christ, and available to us in Catholicism.

"Sin is something that dulls my senses. It's a cumulative thing so that I'm less and less able to say when I'm really going wrong."

—GAIL SMITH

"Sin is the rupture of my relationship with God or with other people because of what I do. What I mean is that sins are the choices I make that hurt myself and other people."

—DICK WESTLY

"Sin is my refusal to turn to God for grace. It is selfishness, cutting myself off."

—DOROTHEA TOBIN

"When I went to confession a while back, I found I had no mortal sins to confess. But my sin is my anger, my rage at my pastor when he preaches his liberal sermons and wants to circumvent what the pope teaches. I need to work on that."

—MARTY GERAGHTY

"I sin a lot in my mind. Yeah, about women, even though I never act on it. But I'm tempted all the time."

—DEE HARRIS

"When I yell at my kids."

—PAT REARDON

"When I'm not attentive. To myself or to others. When I'm just too tired to be attentive and give up."

—VANESSA COOKE

"When I was most irresponsible about my sex life."

—JOAN SULLIVAN

"Sex? No, I don't sin there. It's when I don't love the person who wants to do me wrong, a person so easy to hate. And I give in to that hate. Or when I gossip, saying ugly things—true or un-true—behind people's backs."

—MAGALIE SALAS

# CONSCIENCE AND THE ARCHITECTURE OF CHARACTER

What comes through in these reflections of Good Enough Catholics—and in our own experience as well—is that sin is not always the product of a single, wanton act. Just as often, sin is an attitude, a natural expression of the person we are when faced with a given situation. We could say it is a predictable manifestation of our character.

As Richard McBrien writes about the pursuit of a moral life in his book *Catholicism*, "The person does not set out to acquire and culti-vate moral goodness. The actions a person performs not only shape a particular situation, they also *form* the person who does them."[3] In other words, our everyday decisions create a momentum—not in-exorable, but certainly strong—that will likely carry through in our actions. If we tell the truth in seemingly insignificant matters, we will probably do the same in large matters; if we are dishonest with small change, we will be no different with large bills. Character might be summed up in the adage, "Plant an act, reap a habit."

Or, as Thomas Merton wrote in typically elegant bluntness:

We are at liberty to be real, or to be unreal. We may be true
or false, the choice is ours. We may wear now one mask and
now another, and never, if we so desire, appear with our own
true face. But we cannot make these choices with impunity.
Causes have effects, and if we lie to ourselves and to others,
then we cannot expect to find truth and reality whenever we
happen to want them. If we have chosen the way of falsity we
must not be surprised that truth eludes us when we finally
come to need it![4]

This mysterious presence that guides our judgment, that informs
us about the goodness or badness of our acts and in turn molds our
character, is our conscience. It is formed (and re-formed) throughout
the years of our lives by the morality—or lack of it—we witness in
our parents, family, community, relationships, and in our own experience. The teachings of the church and the words of Scripture also
have had their part in forming our conscience. So has our culture.

As conscience allows us to assess, judge, then act in specific cases,
here and now, it is important to see the conscience for what it is and
what it is not.

First of all, conscience is not a feeling. While feelings can and
should influence our behavior ("I don't feel good about this"), feelings in themselves are woefully inadequate and unreliable helpmates
in the moral life. You might feel guilty about not mowing the lawn,
but this is hardly a matter of conscience, and hardly a sin. You might
not feel guilty about cheating on taxes because you do not agree
with how the money is spent; but indeed this may be a sin.

Conscience is far deeper, far more complex than mere feeling or
emotion. Conscience is that quality in us that looks at ourselves as
moral people and takes into account as many elements of a decision
as can be grasped. Circumstances, cultural mores, our own moral
development, and self-knowledge constantly change, and the decisions shaped by our conscience also can change. What was wrong
for us as a fifteen-year-old may easily be right as a sixty-five-year-
old—and vice versa.

In the heady 1970s, Hal Gordon felt perfectly justified being an angry black man. His hate and rage at white institutions—especially those that dominated his hometown of Washington, D.C.—boiled inside him. "If I would have continued with that attitude without turning my anger into a positive force, I would have been sinning. It was all right—for a time. But you can't stay fixed in hate. It might start you on a path, but it is a dead-end street."

Because of our human frailty and limited knowledge, our conscience is not an infallible guide to the moral life. We will certainly make mistakes. But the conscience, informed by the moral teachings of the church, the instincts of our minds, and the stirrings of our hearts—and all utilized prayerfully—is the best buttress to personal responsibility we have. If we allow it to function properly and honestly, the conscience will always bring us back on track. A decision made in good conscience may indeed be wrong, but it can never be sinful.

In the pre–Vatican II church, conscience was almost regarded as a subversive force. The Catholicism of those days unequivocally stated a set of rules, and demanded obedience. In the years immediately preceding the council and afterward, other approaches to the moral life and formation of conscience were articulated. The principle of double effect—which sought to determine the morality of an action by delineating what was directly and indirectly willed—formed the basis of a new approach, called proportionalism. Proportionalism called for a thorough analysis of not only the act itself, and relevant church or secular laws, but the intention of the person, the possible consequences of the act, and the larger obligations to family, community, or society at large.

The Good Enough Catholic, faced with a difficult moral judgment and a possibly immoral (or sinful) option, may be required to consider all these external factors. Or, at times, it may be necessary to strip away all the intellectual arguments and cultural concerns, acting simply and bravely on a basic principle.

Some Good Enough Catholics, seeking to know how to act in a given situation, pose themselves a simple question: What would Christ do?

This need not be an act of hubris; it can be a moment of profound introspection. If we seek to know what Christ would have done when faced with an unethical boss or a dyspeptic teenager, a drug-crazed street person or an inflated repair bill, we must first know something of him and his life (chapter 1). In honestly squaring that template over our own moral decisions, we will more often than not end up with a good enough answer.

# MERCY WITHIN MERCY

Sinful acts in themselves undermine our spiritual selves, but these "little murders" we commit each day also cause a psychological disorientation. We are ashamed of what we have done, often unwilling consciously to admit our false steps to ourselves or to others. And this shame may be exactly why we continue to perform acts that we know are wrong. We feel so tarnished, so inadequate, so *bad* that, as we lurk in the shadows of our own deceit, we cannot summon the strength, the self-confidence to change our ways. We want to hide.

Many would call this old-fashioned Catholic guilt—and would quickly recoil, claiming guilt bad for personal development. Interestingly enough, two of the most dominant voices in modern psychology disagree. Abraham Maslow, who coined the term "self-actualization," saw the fully integrated person as one with a strong sense of right and wrong, and a desire to be virtuous. Such a person constantly held in view the impact of individual acts and deeds, and possessed the willingness to change destructive behavior. In other words, the self-actualized person is able to acknowledge guilt, and move on. Erik Erikson, who saw a person's lifetime as a series of stages of development, found that in the search for personal integrity, a healthy acknowledgment of inadequacy or failure was exactly what was needed to let go of one developmental stage and allow a new one, brimming with new opportunities for growth, to flower.

Spirituality and psychology are not at war. Spiritual wholeness is psychological wholeness; each seeks what is ultimately best for the individual. Guilt is only destructive when it is so pervasive and paralyzing that we are made to feel beyond forgiveness.

Often, when people feel the most sinful—usually when they are committing the same sin over and over, be it tied in with lust, greed, or dishonesty—they run from Catholicism, and from the church. The last thing they want to do is bring their sins and sinful selves before the presence of God.

"You should never leave the church because you're in the state of sin. That's absolutely the wrong way to look at it and one of the most misunderstood things in the church. The church is exactly the right place for sinners. We're all sinners and that's why we need to be together."

—GAIL SMITH

Catholicism's understanding of the truly (and rare) unforgivable sins can open us up to a new understanding of the futility of wallowing in an unhealthy, unproductive guilt about our moral failures—while at the same time offering a profound reflection on the life of Christ.

There are only two unforgivable sins, the church teaches—presumption and despair. Presumption means we claim not to need God in our lives. Despair is its opposite: we've absolutely given up that he can help us. While the lives of most Good Enough Catholics may have skirted on the edges of both sins, such arrogance and dejection are not our usual moral mode. More often, God simply seems far away from the circumstances of our lives, and we just don't how to make the divine connection—especially when we consider ourselves sinful.

While our church may have taken (and may still evince) a punitive stance toward us sinners, Jesus did just the opposite. He showed an unfailing empathy for human weakness. He seemed to love sinners. Their sheer humanity appealed to him. The New Testament is full of stories of forgiveness—from Peter's betrayal to the prodigal son, the woman caught in adultery to the Roman tax collector. Sex, greed, and betrayal were not very high on Jesus' list of sins. He even forgave those who crucified him.

It was not that Jesus was blasé about sin; he was not. He saw how sin ruptured human relationships and poisoned the soul. Once Jesus called a sin a sin, he told the sinner to sin no more—realizing, of course, that he or she might well commit the same sin again. Implicit was the promise that he would forgive again—as he said, seventy times seven times. "Let the dead bury their own dead" has for me always translated "Let bygones be bygones." Jesus' emphasis was not on justice, but mercy.

It seemed the only sinners who made Jesus fume were the hypocritical clergy of the day. These, who could claim to be sinless because they lived exactly by the letter of the law, had really missed the point of a moral life. Common decency, common sense had no place in their lives. Their nature—their character—was to be *right* rather than *good*.

So easily we forget that God is not only our Creator, Lord, and Savior but—in the words of the first prayer Jesus taught us—our Father. And, as any parent knows, children make dozens of wrong moves every day. But just one "I'm sorry" dissolves all of them. What parent can even remember the fault when faced with a child who wants to admit the misstep and get on with life? Does God have tougher standards for forgiveness than we do? It appears he is even more ready to forgive and forget than we are. Hellfire and brimstone—preached from too many pulpits—is not his way.

Since Vatican II, the church has rediscovered ways to rejoin us with God. No longer is the accent on imposing a penance or penalty for wrongs committed. Rather, the goal is reconciliation and redemption. No longer is it a case of somehow righting the balance, doing some penitential acts to atone for our sins. No longer do we dwell in the past; today, we look to the future. This is hardly new theology: the life of Christ stands as our truest example of how God really regards our sins.

Looking back to the most sinful period of my own life, I realize I had forgotten all this. (Perhaps sin is forgetting God's mercy.) I found myself in what therapists might call a fugue state—a thoughtless, inexorable condition in which I felt I had little control over what I was doing. The mere act of shaving each morning was an examination of conscience I didn't want to perform; I could hardly recognize the face in the mirror. There I was, in full-blown midlife crisis, acting out after my years of Catholic schooling, my years of observant Catholic life. But instead of happiness at my freedom, I was often pathetically sad.

Something else was working deeper in me than I really knew. For I found myself constantly drawn to churches, like a thirsting animal to water. My Saturday nights may have taken me on the dark side of town, but on Sunday morning I wanted to make contact with that force beyond, the force that kept me bound. It was difficult, for I knew my sinning days were not yet over. But somehow—and perhaps this is just the rationalization of a sinner—I wanted to bring myself, whoever I was, into the presence of God. I had little power over myself. Maybe he could help. It took years, but he did.

My favorite spiritual writer, Thomas Merton, who led a hedonistic life before he became a Trappist monk, described God as "mercy within mercy within mercy." Merton came to realize—which ultimately freed him to become a wonderful, happy monk and towering spiritual writer—that he could no longer do any wrong for which he would not be forgiven. And it was this merciful God who released Merton from a wayward life, whose powerful love so attracted him that he could not help longing to be closer.

## PEACE AFTER SIN

A recent headline in *America* magazine posed a curious possibility: "The Optimism of Sin."[5] Setting aside all the pessimistic portrayals of human beings—in the media as well as in some parts of church teaching—Joseph H. McKenna noted that our sinfulness constitutes a small part of who we are and what we do. The vast majority of human actions, McKenna argued, spoke of virtue, not vice; honesty, not duplicity. People are made in the image of God; if that means we are more disposed to evil than good, how would this reflect on the one who made us?

Acknowledging sin is additionally optimistic, I think, because with this avowal we are more than halfway to redemption. When a patient simply admits to having a problem in psychotherapy, the assumption is that they are already embarked on the path to recovery. It is the same with sin. For Good Enough Catholics, to call sin by name is to say we want to choose another way.

Once we realize that sin is ultimately conquerable and controllable, a sense of peace will be ours (even though we may commit the same sin again). For, with this realization, we have ready access to a greater power than the power sin can wield over us. We have encountered a God who will not coerce, but awaits our decision, patiently and lovingly, to change our ways.

James Healy, a Virginia priest, tells a poignant story about his father who, as an altar boy, failed to show up for his assigned mass. Even though the reason for his absence was the household chores the boy's father had asked him to perform, his pastor was furious. Determined to teach a lesson the boy would never forget, the pastor assigned him the penance of kneeling at the altar rail throughout a Sunday mass. The boy, his legs trembling, slowly walked to the front of the church and took his place, a public sinner. He was humiliated, ashamed. And then he felt a hand on his shoulder. It was his own father, who then knelt down beside him, ready to share his pain.[6]

So it is with Jesus. Jesus wants to take our failures upon himself, and set us free from their memory. He is with us as sinners, even more tenderly and intimately than when we are floating along in the state of grace. For it is when we are in trouble that we need our Father the most. It is in sin that his desire to heal us is strongest.

"As for alienating yourself from God? An impossibility. Sin is wrong because it makes *you* unhappy, it makes other people unhappy. God is always there for you."

—TOM EAKINS*

Shame or pathological guilt for our wrongdoing can never be looked upon as values in themselves. Humility, yes; humiliation, no. Focusing on the wrongs only heightens the conflict within us, making improvements in personal behavior that much more difficult. Fred Sontag, in the secular journal *Encounter*, nicely encapsulated the Good Enough Catholic approach to redemption from the effects of sin. Addressing the question of why people too often look to the past to solve present problems, Sontag writes, "Forgiveness, reconciliation are in fact the only avenues to improved relationships, new opportunities, since the tragedies of the past, singled out for emphasis, are unsolvable."[7]

"My formula is pretty simple and straightforward. Whenever I do something wrong, (1) I try to undo it if I can; (2) I tell God I'm sorry; and (3) I realize doing it made me feel uncomfortable and I don't want to do it again."

—MARY ANNE BARRY

# THE GOOD ENOUGH CATHOLIC CHALLENGE: A CERTAIN KIND OF PERSON

We grow in the moral life in the pursuit of righteousness; we gain strength with every decision to turn from the sins each of us commits. It may be a road less traveled, but the pursuit of a truly "good life" is the most exciting and rewarding opportunity we face as human beings. Confronting sin is true liberation.

There are so many voices in the world calling out to us to take moral shortcuts, to forget or at least relax our principles. There are conflicting priorities—family, job, community—each calling out to us. We must be aware of all those demands and needs, conflicting as they will often be; but we must also listen to that still, small voice within us. Our conscience guards what is best in us, and we want to respond to its gentle urges.

How badly we want the world to operate on moral principles! From an honest estimate on a roof repair to honesty in negotiating international treaties, respect among children in our families to respect for the fragility of our environment; if only people wouldn't lie or cheat or deceive. If only people would have character.

Of course, if there is to be a moral world, it must be composed of moral people. Enter the Good Enough Catholic.

For the Good Enough Catholic is summoned to a different level of consciousness—to be a certain kind of person; a person who struggles to do what is right, and in failure is ready to make reparation and try harder next time. This is true self-actualization. And everyone from the high priests of modern psychology to the saints of Catholic history would agree.

An impossible task? Yes, for the *Perfect* Catholic.

We are but Good Enough Catholics, given to good instincts yet lured by the bad. But we realize that even in our sinfulness, we are already forgiven—just for the asking.

There are enormous rewards for living the moral life, here and now; heaven can wait. The shadows of our sins lighten from the glow of God's love and forgiveness. We become different people, no longer ashamed of our failures. Our failures are part of us and we face them directly; but they are only *part* of us. God takes them together with the many good things we do, the good decisions we make.

For the next week, the challenge is to pause and reflect on one act that you do each day, an act that you are conflicted about. It may be a habitual act, or something unique with which you are presented. Think it through. Let your conscience speak to you. Consider all the elements of your decision. Think about who is affected and how. Think about your role and how much control you have over the situation.

Then act, always remembering that while God is perfect, we are simply Good Enough. Morality is not a state, it is a process. And we Good Enough Catholics commit to that process.

## SELECTED READINGS

Raymond F. Collins, *Christian Morality: Biblical Foundations*. Notre Dame, Ind.: University of Notre Dame Press, 1986.

Bernard Haring, *The Law of Christ: Moral Theology for Priests and Laity*. Westminster, Md.: Newman Press, 1961.

# ❧ PART II ❧

# DAILY LIFE

*Love and work. These are the very essence of our daily lives; a mixture of pleasure and pain, triumph and defeat, seeking and finding, alienation and intimacy. Too often we feel torn apart, that we somehow must be different people as we move through our different roles: worker, partner, lover. But for the Good Enough Catholic, this need not be so.*

*Work (chapter 6) provides the opportunity to make our working lives not only holy lives, but infinitely more rewarding and exciting lives as well. Most of us will marry, some of us will divorce (chapter 7); all of us seek companionship on our life's journey. The complex issues of sex, birth control, and abortion (chapter 8) set storms upon our Catholic minds and hearts; yet, we can allow love to flow through our most intimate relationships.*

# CHAPTER SIX

# WORK
## The Art of Co-Creation

We spend more of our waking hours in working than we do in any other earthly activity. Yet, for the most part, God is strangely absent from this part of our life. At best, we hold him on the periphery, to be summoned only in extreme moments of despair, failure, or panic. It is as if God doesn't have an appropriate place in this most worldly area of our lives.

We expect to encounter God at mass, in prayer, on a retreat, or while reading a book on spirituality. To invite him into the office or behind the wheel, onto the assembly line or the Internet, into the kitchen or the telemarketing cubicle—somehow it just doesn't seem appropriate. Or is it that we think he'd find it uncomfortable to see us at what we do, to hear how we talk, to watch how we behave?

At the same time, many of us want something else for our world of work. "Is this all there is to life?" is the murmur on the lips of the assembly-line worker, the newly appointed vice-president, or the young mother. Whether in pursuit of a goal or career, just eking out survival or performing normal domestic chores, we want our work to be more fulfilling than it is—to feed our souls as well as our bodies. But we don't know how. We may even intend to engage ourselves in something more than a practical, purely economic means of meeting human needs; but with downsizing, "lean and mean" philosophies, global competition, and the evaporation of so many well-paid blue-collar jobs, this seems a luxury we can ill afford even to consider. This era of uncertainty may not be the appropriate time to ask deep questions about work and our relationship to it.

It isn't that remedies haven't been offered to humanize and dignify work at the dawning of the twenty-first century, to make it more gratifying for the individual and more productive for the employer. Team management, total quality management, sensitivity training, and employee ownership are just some of the innovative approaches; and any of them can indeed contribute to a more contented and motivated employee.

But if your goal is to blend economic pursuits with authentic spiritual values, you will find that there is something fundamental missing in all of them.

Catholic thought and practice confront this dualism in a depth and breadth unparalleled in any religion or spirituality, offering a transcendent yet practical approach, one that upholds the dignity of both work and worker. Catholicism lays out a way of looking at work that fights compartmentalization, separating the person we are on Sunday from the person we are on Monday. It acknowledges that the entire world is God's concern—not just neat rows of worshiping Catholics in church, but everyone, in their every waking moment. We find a way to make the working lives of Good Enough Catholics holy lives as well. In the words of William J. Byron, priest, former college president, and management expert, we can be transformed from "human doings"[1] into human beings.

# THE CATHOLIC VIEW OF WORK

My personal reluctance to put too much weight on the concept of original sin—and the mass condemnation of humankind—can be traced to an oft-quoted biblical phrase attributed to God in the Garden of Eden. Addressing the man who was about to become the world's first breadwinner, God told Adam that only "by the sweat of your brow" would he survive in the world. It seemed, from that moment on, that work was to be considered a curse, a price extracted for disobedience.

Going farther in Scripture, there is a parable that, for me, suggests a more reasonable approach to work. It is the parable of the talents, where a master gives three of his servants varying numbers of talents to use as they chose until he returned. In those days, a talent was a measure of money, but certainly this metaphor stands for a broader range of human resources—financial, intellectual, emotional, and physical. As we know, the first two servants took the talents and built upon them, increasing their worth. The third, fearing the judgment of the master, whom he perceived to be a harsh man, timidly buried the single talent he had been given. On his day of accounting, he was able to give back exactly what he had received—no more, no less. At this, the master *was* angry. He took away even that one talent, and pronounced his unimaginative and timid servant "worthless."

God's message was clear: do something with the talents given to you, regardless of their number. Intention, effort, and inner disposition are the important criteria, not merely the results.

As Catholic thinking has developed over the centuries—and labor was no longer forced, but mutually contracted—the concept of work as some form of necessary evil or punishment has been gradually replaced by a far more enlightened vision, one that would once have verged on the heretical. Work has come to be seen as an act of co-creation.

"We are made in the image of God, the creator, I always remind myself. Whatever we do with our hands or minds is holy. If we do it with care or dignity, it enhances human grandeur."
—DICK WESTLY

The thinking goes like this: God made the universe, but it is only through the utilization of the earth's resources and the employment of individual talents—humankind shaping the created world—that the purpose of creation continues to unfold. Prayer, worship, good works are all part of God's divine plan—but so is work. Truly, the *building* of the Kingdom of God has taken on its own sacramentality. The social encyclicals of the past one hundred years have consistently upheld both the preciousness of work and the dignity of the worker.

Both the lilting strains of Gregorian chant from a monastic choir, and the dissonant clanging from a stamping plant sent heavenward, are pleasing to the ears of God. My father's hammer, and the computer I type on, are the holy implements with which we ply our respective trades.

In the ringing words of Vatican II's document on the church and the modern world (*Gaudium et Spes*) we are told that where man formerly ". . . looked especially to supernatural forces for blessings, he now secures many of these benefits for himself, thanks to his own efforts." The range of co-creative acts ". . . extends to even the most ordinary activities of everyday life . . . personal efforts promote the work of the Creator, confer benefits on [our] fellowmen, and help to realize God's plan in history."[2]

A ton of coal mined, a blouse sold, a form filled out, a software program developed—all can be part of that divine plan. Commerce and enterprise and innovation were hardly the enemy; in fact, they were potentially the sources of economic transformation, human liberation, and spiritual development.

Potentially.

# NOT WORK, A MISSION

Pope John Paul II's 1981 encyclical *Laborem Exercens* ("On Human Work") contained what would prove to be a revolutionary term, "the spirituality of work." Within a small but dynamic lay sector of the church, the concept took root. "Rather than implying overtly religious acts, spirituality should refer to the integration of faith into the concrete circumstances of a person's life,"[3] reads a line from one of the many excellent position papers of ACTA Publications, a leader in the spirituality of work movement.

Although "spirituality of work" had not been widely used before this time, Catholicism's view of work in fact had a strong—although not always properly understood—spiritual foundation. It was one that seemed to fly in the face of both American free-market capitalism and the socialist/communist utopianism that had swept the world in answer to Industrial Age economic inequity. Work had never been looked upon as a purely economic pursuit in modern Catholic thought—in fact, work was regarded as no less than a vocation. The worth and integrity of the individual were more important than the worth of product, the means of production, or the growth of a business venture. This was moral idealism on the highest level.

Although the term "vocation" was more often considered the domain of those who chose religious life, Catholicism taught that everyone had a "calling" and that to live it to the fullest was a source of holiness. Regardless of what a person did—from executive to floor sweeper—their work, paid or unpaid, held the possibility of grace and salvation, a kinship in co-creation with God. You may not always have control over the work you do, but you will always have control over the person you are as you go about that job. If you approach it as God's work as well as your own, you are as sanctified as when you kneel in church.

"My Catholic upbringing never left me, and because of it I have my own gyroscope so I don't have to take a poll about what's right or wrong. That upbringing fuels me to do the stories I do. I can expose the bad guys in an investigative piece or I can write about a great priest in a wretched slum area in Haiti who built a first-rate school to educate kids who live in packing crates. Both stories have to be told. No, this job isn't a job; it's a mission."

—JOHN FIALKA

Contrary to the point of view once held by some in Catholicism, the implication of Jesus' warning—"What shall it profit a man if he gain the whole world but lose his immortal soul?"—isn't that Catholics should simply accept menial work and never strive to build the biggest corporation. But it does mean that morality transcends economics, that monetary remuneration is not the goal; the building of the Kingdom of God is. While we must work to earn our daily bread, the work itself must be somehow worthwhile. So dominant is this theme in Catholic teaching that if the product we make or service we provide is in itself immoral, we are obliged to refrain from being a part of it.

Some would say that the honor Catholicism accords even the most menial jobs—and even the concept of vocation itself—has worked to our detriment, making for a group of workers willing to be exploited. They contend that such an outlook fosters a "keep your head down" mentality. And Catholicism's elevation of altruism far above economic success—hasn't it held Catholics back?

# THE MISSING PIECE

The rapid, post–World War II rise of American Catholics to positions of leadership in all walks of life disputes any claims that we are some sort of economic fatalists or underachievers. I would say instead that Catholic insights can bring a new sense of worth and purpose to the workplace. It is badly needed. The voices in Studs Terkel's memorable book *Working* cry out that their jobs are too small for their spirits. Surveys show that at least half of working people dislike their jobs, the way they are treated, and the workplace in which they spend their days or nights. Something essential is missing in many people's work lives.

What we are witnessing today in the workplace is a crisis of meaning. Michael Lerner, the editor of the Jewish magazine *Tikkun*, has written:

Many Americans are in deep pain and living in the midst of a profound ethical, spiritual and psychological crisis. . . . They feel frustrated in a world of work that often calls upon them to invest their full energies and much overtime, yet gives them little opportunity to feel that they are working for some higher good besides accumulating profits. . . . The more people learn to think of others as selfish and only out for themselves, the more they adopt a defensive selfishness themselves that tends to weaken family and friendships.[4]

Even those in such prestigious and time-honored professions as law, medicine, and clerical life, find themselves questioning their worth and place. Longtime workers and middle management executives, cavalierly discarded by companies in which they invested years of their lives, are devastated. Journalists find their profession trivialized and themselves suspect. Winning, succeeding—at whatever the personal or societal cost—are held up as the only realistic, measurable goals. The bottom line or the bread line.

To make matters even more confusing, there is a movement afoot that seeks to enfold economic pursuit in a thin bunting of religious beliefs. Central to this "gospel of wealth" is the claim that success is actually evidence of God's blessings. In other words, give obeisance to God and God will grant your material desires. There is a battalion of positive-thinking preachers who, while rarely mentioning God or Christ—and certainly never the Cross—proclaim a new gospel of "name it and claim it."

But if the measure of a person's worth was only prevailing and succeeding, then you would feel vindicated, fulfilled, and holy when you prevailed and succeeded. When you did not, failure would rightfully make you feel reprehensible, a sinner for sure. If the paycheck or size of corporate growth were the barometer, you would be able to judge quite exactly how worthwhile you are in God's eyes. And yet we know none of this is true.

On the other hand, the Good Enough Catholic, sure in the belief that God is with us through success and failure, can look upon any work, when done with integrity—the best he or she can muster with the tools and materials at hand—as that day's living out of the gospel message.

Let us not glorify the boring, unpleasant, underpaid, exhausting, frustrating jobs that will inevitably be a part of our working careers. Let us not stay in dead-end jobs, or meekly put up with oppressive bosses and bad working conditions. That would be like burying our talents. We are called to do all we can with what we have. That, too, is part of the gospel mandate.

The idea is to see that in whatever work the Good Enough Catholic does there is an opportunity for grace, and for closeness to God. To deny this is to shut God out of the very parts of our lives where we need him the most.

From a windswept parking lot behind a 7-Eleven convenience store in Washington, D.C., to a tastefully appointed conference room overlooking the Manhattan skyline, Good Enough Catholics attempt to do just that. Huddled against the bitter predawn cold in the 7-Eleven parking lot, Carlos Gutierrez and Ernesto Martinez are but two of dozens of Latin American immigrants offering themselves for day labor. They are carpenters. "If this work is good enough for Jesus, it is good enough for us," says Gutierrez. And, with that inner disposition, the tone is set for the day.

Emilie Griffin's alter ego in her novel-in-progress repeats a line from the Twenty-third Psalm as she darts from a New York advertising agency's creative department to the conference room: "Thou preparest a table before me in the presence of mine enemies." Griffin, herself an advertising executive, has experienced her share of tough meetings, but instead of going in girded, she enters each area of the workplace prayerfully—and well prepared.

The work of Gutierrez and Martinez, the decisions of Griffin—they are holy acts, because these workers made them holy.

"It's not a matter of when you pray, and certainly for most of us the admonition to 'pray always' is difficult. What matters is that

God is fundamental to your life, the tent pole. As Ignatius says, we need to see that God is present in all things."

—EMILIE GRIFFIN

So often our quest for spiritual experience accents the dramatic, the sensational; we forget the ordinary possibilities. So it is with work. At the end of nearly every day, it is not difficult to think back and see how some people make work holy—certainly in their own fashion, and with their own beliefs—while others make it hell.

One of ACTA's publications, *Of Human Hands: A Reader in the Spirituality of Work*, poignantly points up the opportunities in everyone's work. Three women in the book, from different walks of life, illustrate how any work can be elevated to a new level of holiness. Maxine F. Dennis is a Rhode Island supermarket cashier who tries to concentrate on every person she serves. A sad-faced senior citizen and a bag of birdseed leads to a brief, but compassionate, conversation about his parakeet—and his recently deceased wife of fifty years, who had loved the bird so much. Administrative law judge May Elizabeth Toomey Dunne, facing a staggering calendar of sixty-nine cases in Albany, New York, makes time to take the hand of an overwrought woman, marking a turning point in her life and the recognition that good can come out of "the system." Postal carrier Rose Mary Hart knows she is the only person shut-ins see along her West Virginia route, so she works in a few moments for each one—and still has time to slow her walk for the school kids who want to tag along.

Their attitude toward work—their attitude toward you—shows on their faces and can be heard in their voices. Regardless of what their work is, it is not a burden. They would echo Kahlil Gibran's definition of work in *The Prophet* as "love made visible."

And, of course, *you* are one of those people each working day. You—carpenter or judge, engineer or retail clerk, teacher or student—are no superhero. You are just a Good Enough Catholic who wants to experience the presence of God in the workplace.

# WHAT YOU WOULD BE

Few of us live where we were born, with the natural support system of family, neighborhood, parish, and familiar institutions. Instead, we find ourselves routinely uprooted, either from simple, unbending necessity or in pursuit of education, a job, a dream. Whatever the reason, practically all of us, at one time or another, are forced to remake our lives.

Our primary community of support—a spouse and children—may travel with us, but with the high rate of divorce and career-motivated singles delaying marriage and parenthood, that is less and less the case for more and more people. Where can we—where *do* we—find our community? Where do we hope to encounter people who will care enough about us to be interested in what is happening in our lives: people we can tell about a fish caught, a child's first tooth, or just the lonesomeness of a new town?

More often than not it will be where we work. In today's ever-more-mobile society, the workplace often becomes the primary support system, whether or not it functions successfully, for both single people and family members.

I recall a touching story about a successful young business-man from the Southwest who had just joined a competitive New York firm, and was asked to give a speech to his peers as part of a confidence-building program. Others had spoken of their various techniques for maximizing their potential or strategies for coming out on top, sharing their secrets to success. He faced the audience with something else on his mind. He had been estranged from his father for years, and hoped that the birth of his first child would bridge the gap. While his father battled cancer, his wife's pregnancy progressed. Cancer won. His father never saw his first grandchild. The young executive would never again wait; now was the time to do those things most important to him. The audience was speech-less; most were in tears. Applause was followed by warm embraces from the very people he was supposed to compete against.

What does the story tell us? That this young businessman with no church affiliation, who barely had time to nod to neighbors in his new suburban neighborhood, shared perhaps the most intimate story of his life with the only community outside his small family that he felt he had—his fellow workers. And they, given the opportunity to come to his support in a time of need, were ready to do so.

It also tells us that we do not need to tend the poorest of the poor in Calcutta or to preach the gospel on a St. Louis street corner; we need look no farther for a place to live out our Good Enough Catholicism than our place of work.

Now, what does this mean?

No, it does not mean that work becomes one long sensitivity session, or that we start our memos and presentations with "The Catholic Church teaches . . ." or "As a Catholic, I. . . ." No, we do not have to piously read a Bible at lunch, or punctuate the day with prayer meetings. What it means is that we look upon the work we do as something precious and worthwhile, something worthy of co-creation with God. It means that we look upon the people we work with—those above us and those below us, the people we compete against, the people that pass through our lives in only one interchange, or those we work with day after day—as members of this movable and ever-changing tribe with whom we are marching through life. Our circumstances can and will change, but the present moment is the only one in which we have the opportunity to live out our beliefs. In this moment, in this day, the gospel comes alive—or it does not. Either God is in the marketplace, or he is not.

It means that we show something about being a Good Enough Catholic by our performance and our attitude. We set an example. We don't have to *say* what being a Good Enough Catholic means; we *show* it. There is nothing outwardly obvious about being Catholic—we don't look alike, we don't speak with the same accent, we wear no distinctive clothing. And yet we are a people unified in that magnificent but certainly imperfect worldwide body called the Catholic Church, desiring to live as close as we can to the life of the man whom we see as God's inspiration for the way to be fully human.

John Driscoll is the perfect example of the hard-driving tough-talking newspaperman. He didn't rise to the editorship of the *Boston Globe* by being Caspar Milquetoast. He is a Catholic, but "in 30 years as an editor, I never mentioned God or had holy pictures in my office," he wrote recently in *Nieman Reports*. "In workplaces . . . it is my belief that what's implicit is more meaningful than what's explicit. Indeed, explicit discussions of religious matters often can trigger a turn-off."[5] On his wall is a haunting picture of an emaciated Ethiopian mother and her dying child—a statement about journalism's responsibility to report the world's suffering. Driscoll concluded a Valentine Day's news conference by telling his fellow editors how much he cared for them. In his busy day, Driscoll makes it a point to listen to the personal stories of those with whom he works: who has sick family members, who is going through a rough time and needs a show of support. Such is John Driscoll's implicit Catholicism.

People—our co-workers, and co-workers all across this country—are starving for examples of moral strength and common decency. They are looking to model themselves, not after those who cheat and deceive to get ahead, but after those whose honesty and forthrightness shines through. People want to take the higher road. They want a work climate that favors candor and motivates their best performance—not out of fear, but out of caring.

Study after study shows that the moral tone set by executives and managers is mirrored in their employees. If the company ethos is to win regardless of what needs to be done, to cut corners, to lie, to treat employees like so many dispensable pieces—that will, in turn, shape the employees' attitude. If the company believes in cheating to achieve its ends, what is wrong with me cheating to achieve mine?

"As a car salesman, I work in a business that is already highly suspect. On top of that, I handle customers even other car sales people don't want anything to do with—bad credit risks who have a record of defaulting on loans. But if people can't get to work because they don't have a car and I help them to get that car, isn't that a ministry, too? Even if I do make a buck at it? I'm not going to put them into a car they can't afford—that would be doing them an injustice. I'm helping them on the road to recovery; a car gives them dignity."

—DEE HARRIS

"Each day at work, I have twenty-eight men under my supervision at the Federal Communications Commission. Some of them hate me—not only because their boss is a woman, but a Hispanic woman as well. My job is to get our work done, but in the process to love them and care about them even though they would just as soon I wouldn't be there. That's tough, but that's what I have to do if my faith means anything to me at all."

—MAGALIE SALAS

The workplace has enormous potential for the spiritual development of the Good Enough Catholic. It provides the opportunity for an ongoing examination of conscience about what kind of people we are; it is a proving ground for our beliefs. Learning to deal with disappointment or humiliation, conflicting needs, and difficult situations builds spiritual character. Not ducking tough or enervating tasks—hoping that we could be elsewhere—is a path to truly actualizing your potential. You may have to move on to other work, find alternative ways to perform the work you do; but it is only in confronting each day's events on the job that we play our part in co-creation with God.

The anonymous author of the spiritual classic *The Cloud of Unknowing* speaks to us in comforting words about work: "Not what thou are but what thou wouldst be does God consider."

You will perform better and more successfully, you will have a more satisfying time at it, and the world of commerce can go about its divine function when, as a Good Enough Catholic, you take your principles to work.

# FOR EVERY THING, A SEASON?

Until quite recently, it was generally accepted that work life and family life were separate. Issues and concerns arising from one were not allowed to impinge upon or influence the other; each had its own rules, value systems, and territory. The classic example was the commuter on the train going into the office, turning on his corporate self, leaving wife and children behind, as if on another planet.

Of course, this separation—if it ever really existed—has proved to be a myth. Our work lives and our home lives intersect and influence each other every day. A father leaves work early to attend his child's recital, or to tend to a sick child. A SWOC—single, without children—is gone promptly at five for dinner with her aging parents, who can't wait to hear about her recent business trip.

Perpetuating the myth that the person you are in your personal life can be totally different from the person you are in the workplace, each neatly compartmentalized, is to court a kind of schizophrenia. A Good Enough Catholic's values and attitudes simply can't be turned off and on depending on the hour of the day, or because of the place in which you find yourself. A moral life is just too difficult to live part-time, or on command.

For instance, how can a manager who is ruthless with her subordinates, ready to criticize or fire those who don't measure up, then go home and show compassion to a son stumbling through some grade school math problems? How can a doctor come home with medical supplies stolen from the hospital expect his daughter to bring the correct amount of change back from the store?

What's more, if living out our moral code at work and at home is difficult, striking a balance between the time and energy put into each is positively daunting. It isn't easy for anyone, be it single parents or two-income families, those in pressure-filled, competitive positions or those who work a straight nine to five. The art for the Good Enough Catholic is to be neither a workaholic nor a "fami-holic"; to invest ourselves fully in each place as the situation and needs require. Nothing is more galling than the person who constantly proclaims "family first" or "family values," and leaves the work to others. Equally, when family members have to squeeze their way onto the frantic schedule of a busy mother or father, the balance has not been struck. Neither work nor family can be the excuse for starving the other part of our lives.

## OFTENTIMES, A MATTER OF CHOICE

Catholics of my father's generation got work where they could, considered job security a blessing, concentrated on providing for a family (often a large family), and relegated personal desires or ambition to the status of pipe dreams.

Catholics of my own and ensuing generations are far better educated than their parents. And, while succeeding in our various fields and earning a reasonable living are certainly important, we seek something from work that our parents never even considered: personal fulfillment.

It is not that my father was not gratified by the smooth line of the wall he built as a carpenter—he was. He was a gifted craftsman, and he knew it. Perhaps, while not even seeking it, he received more personal fulfillment than those of us in succeeding generations of American Catholics, who find ourselves dealing with less tangible challenges. Rather than the building of sound walls, we have to deal with a complex and confusing marketplace, ephemeral tastes, and faceless clients. We deal with communications networks that may bring the world to our fingertips, but bring no song to our hearts.

If Good Enough Catholics want to believe in the idea and the ideal of vocation—that the level of success we achieve, the amount of money we make, the car or house we can afford, or the education we can provide for our children is not our measure as people—how do we go about putting that into practice? How do we find work that will both bring us personal satisfaction and allow us to achieve spiritual wholeness?

Although we may plead the opposite, most of us have an enormous range of choices in deciding what we will do to provide for our material needs. It is we ourselves who often limit the choices, viewing our lives as an immutable economic chain of events that begins with a premise: To live the way I want to, I need to make this much money. The next step is logical: These jobs, for which I am or can be qualified, pay that kind of money. Finally comes the seemingly inescapable conclusion: I may or may not find in any of these jobs a purpose I want to give my energies to, but—out of a perceived necessity—I will choose one.

It is a case of the ends justifying the means—and while in most people's lives this does not lead to blatantly immoral work, the work they do is indeed too small for their souls. If we want true satisfaction and meaning from our work, we need to turn things around.

While I do not share all of Joseph Campbell's views of religious belief, his concept of "following your bliss" in seeking personal fulfillment has something to say to Good Enough Catholics contemplating what they want to do with their working lives. What excites you? What job or work have you done that you couldn't wait to get to? Where did you feel best about yourself, where your talents were being most fully utilized? What did you produce or do that gave you the greatest satisfaction? And my own litmus test: What work was the most fun?

"As an educated, presentable, black woman, I guess I could have taken many roads. I could have made more money in the corporate world, but for what? I guess I choose to work at a small, all-girls Catholic high school in Virginia because I knew here I could be the fullest person I could be. At Elizabeth Seton, I can make an enormous difference in a lot of lives as a guidance counselor. I can openly talk about morals, which I couldn't do in public schools. What can I say? This fits!"

—VANESSA COOKE

How many stories are there of people on the fast track who jumped off to take on a simpler life in tune with their own inner voices—raising organic herbs or opening a guest house? My own favorite story is of a friend who was rocketing through the ranks of a Florida insurance company, yet found himself dreadfully unhappy. Insurance didn't resonate in his soul. He had always wanted to be a doctor, but that was now impossible at his age.

Although he had five children, he finally quit the job, went back to earn a physician's assistant degree, and eventually set up a medical clinic in a remote African village. Amidst typhoid and malaria, poverty and malnutrition, he was never happier.

But if the work of co-creation is to be accomplished, all of us can't open medical clinics. As for the herb farmer, is the growing of organic basil morally superior to the production of an aluminum engine block for somebody's lawnmower? Not necessarily.

The idea is not for Good Enough Catholics to become a legion of social workers. No; we need people working in investment banking and advertising and manufacturing in order to make those and all other professions holy, too. In fact, it takes *more* of a person to bring Good Enough Catholic values into a brokerage trading room or a sales meeting than to that village medical clinic. We need people to bind up wounds; we also need those with the talent to create new jobs, to enlarge the marketplace. Small is beautiful, but large can be lovely if the workplace expands to include those who have a hard time finding decent work at a decent pay.

Some Good Enough Catholics like Tom Lenz have found they need to straddle two worlds to accomplish their ends. With his master's degree in urban planning, he is perfectly at home in the business community, searching for the money grassroots community groups so desperately need. Christ's message and the opportunities of the marketplace can complement each other. Allen Stryczek, a computer whiz at a huge Chicago bank, became the first male employee to take a cut in pay and work a shorter work week. He had invested his money wisely, but wasn't investing enough of himself in things he really cared about. Now he works three days at the bank each week, and gives one day to Habitat for Humanity and one day to his parish.

In my own working life, most of which has been spent writing, I try to apply a few simple rules. First, I always look at who signs the check I receive—in other words, who am I writing for? Where will my "product" appear? For instance, I could never write for one of the sexually explicit magazines. It's not that the nude female body isn't beautiful, and it's not because I don't have lust in my heart; it's just that the idea behind those magazines, for me, is plainly wrong. Portraying pornography as art, and trying to disguise the prurient purpose of a magazine with good writing, often by prominent authors—I don't need to think too long about it, or employ any measure of double effect or proportionalism, to realize I simply don't want the work of my hands to appear there. I'd be ashamed to have my friends or family or children see my name on that cover.

My other rule is that I carefully choose my subjects. While I do a lot of writing about religion and religious belief, I am certainly no apologist for the Catholic Church. I try to find and write about people who stand for the best in religion. Or, I write about current issues—hopefully in a balanced way—that impinge upon religious and spiritual concerns.

I imagine I could make better money if I took my writing talent and employed it in a more commercial way. But I don't see that as what I would call my vocation. Besides, it wouldn't be as much fun, and I don't think I would feel very satisfied. Work as a free-lance writer is a constant struggle to think of new ideas and then to write about them. But I have been able to take care of my own and my family's basic needs over the years by following a rather modest dream.

It would be naïve to say that any job will be rewarding every day, or that we will not be forced to take undesirable work at certain times in our lives just to provide for our needs. Sometimes I dislike my writing work enormously; there have been terribly lean years during which I would happily have signed any contract without reading it—even one presented by the devil. I have worked in factories and bars and grocery stores and classrooms to make money to live. But it has worked; somehow I've made a living, and haven't had to (or, maybe, never had the chance to) make any horrendous compromises along the way.

It is only by a conscious and continuing assessment of who we are and what we are doing each day that we can be assured of making our work life not only satisfying, but holy. It is not an impossible dream; it is really part of the divine plan. We are people with talents that God wants utilized. The Good Enough Catholic, who seeks an inward life with God, wants an outward, daily life in communion with him, too.

In the end, we will seek—and usually are given—what is most important to us. It may be status or wealth, security or challenge. It may be the satisfaction of work well done, or work that makes the world a better place. Each has its costs; each, its rewards.

---

# THE GOOD ENOUGH CATHOLIC CHALLENGE: A NEW WAY OF LOOKING AT WORK

Work comprises the major portion of our lives; yet often our work life has little to with our spiritual selves. Our beliefs as Good Enough Catholics seem so far away as to be nonapplicable to the competitive world of commerce. And yet we realize we do not have two separate identities—one as a working person, and the other simply as a person. How can we bring these two selves closer together, to be that "certain kind of person," not only in the pew, but behind a desk or on a production line? Deep in our hearts, in our souls, we want to be that kind of person; but it seems difficult, if not impossible.

I've always found small goals, rather than sweeping promises, ultimately more useful. So, as Good Enough Catholics, let us start with a modest trial. Consciously dedicate the first hour—or even half-hour—of your work day to being a Good Enough Catholic. Say nothing about it to anyone, not co-workers, not anyone at home. If it is helpful, envision yourself wearing a Roman collar, or some other distinctive sign or symbol that people should expect the best from you.

Try to look at your fellow employees in a new way, realizing they have a range of emotions, that they want to be praised and appreciated—just as you do. But also remember that you still have to get your job done; this is not an invitation for a sappy smile and a ready "yes" on your lips.

This may sound a bit like play-acting, but give it a try. It is designed to put you in a frame of mind—the frame of mind of "a certain kind of person." After all, this *is* your parish, your community, for many hours each day. People are in search of support; they are looking for inspiration. Whether your job is a solitary one or one constantly in contact with people, make the effort in that first hour or half hour to do the best you can in producing whatever product you make or service you provide. Think of yourself as what you really are—a co-creator. There is no work so great or so humble that God is not with you.

Once your hour or half-hour is over, resume your usual "work" posture. At the end of the day, reflect back on how you felt in each role, and what you accomplished.

If you are doing work you dislike, but must continue to do it, find one part of the job that you can do really well and concentrate on it. A woman who arranges banquets at a hotel was asked to describe her work. "Dismal," she said, "drudgery." She was the one who "puts the cherry on the cake." But if she put that cherry on with pride and love, and with good wishes for her guests, I have a feeling that cherry would radiate throughout the banquet hall, spreading and multiplying the sentiment and effort that went into it. Certainly she would at least have the satisfaction of having done her absolute best.

And as for the type of work you do, gently take stock. Are you proud of what you do, or would you rather God not know the details? Do you look forward to doing your work, or is it a burden? What does your heart—not your bank account or your ego—tell you to do with your time and talents? What are your abilities? Are they being utilized? What does your soul yearn to impart to this world? What would make you proud to do?

Think of yourself as one of those servants in the parable, given a talent. Where do you want to invest it? Give God a chance to speak; have faith in new possibilities as yet unimagined. They can emerge out of the darkness if we are bold enough to ask real questions of ourselves. For such introspection is a prayer, a prayer for guidance in one of the most important parts of our lives.

God wants us, and needs us, in his divine plan of co-creation. Isn't he a good manager, the kind who listens attentively to his co-workers?

## SELECTED READINGS

William Diehl, *The Monday Connection: A Spirituality of Competence, Affirmation, and Support in the Workplace.* San Francisco: HarperSanFrancisco, 1991.

William L. Droel and Gregory F. Augustine Pierce, *Confident and Competent: A Challenge for the Lay Church.* Chicago: ACTA Publications, 1991.

Mark Gibbs, *Christians with Secular Power.* Minneapolis: Augsburg Fortress, 1981.

John Paul II, *Laborem Exercens* ("On Human Work"). Boston: St. Paul Editions, 1981.

Gregory F. Augustine Pierce, ed., *Of Human Hands: A Reader in the Spirituality of Work.* Chicago: ACTA Publications, 1991.

Thomas Smith, *God on the Job: Finding God Who Waits at Work.* New York and Mahwah, N.J.: Paulist Press, 1995.

Melvin Vos, *Seven Days a Week: Faith in Action.* Minneapolis: Augsburg Fortress, 1985.

# MARRIAGE (AND DIVORCE)
## The Moral Greenhouse

This chapter could easily—and beneficially—begin with a consideration of some of the valuable contemporary insights that have been offered on why certain marriages prosper, some merely survive, and others wither into divorce. Communication. Sensitivity. Honesty and fidelity. Openness. The need for a balance of dependence, independence, and interdependence. Surely a thoughtful discussion of how these concepts can be put to work would be helpful for anyone contemplating matrimony, as well as those who hope to enhance their marriage.

Instead I wanted to start on a different tack, one inspired by the words of a now-forgotten (and not oft-quoted) pope. His name was Pius XI, and he was writing in 1930—long before we had so many modern insights into marriage, and before we had witnessed the painful demise of so many of them. To me, his words succinctly summed up what this mysterious, alternately wonderful and perturbing state in life could be for the Good Enough Catholic.

> [The] mutual inward molding of husband and wife, this determined effort to perfect each other, can in a very real sense . . . be said to be the chief reason and purpose of matrimony. . . .[1]

I, the cradle Catholic, was so proud of my find that I read those words aloud to my wife.

She was hardly as impressed. "Determined effort?" "To perfect?" These words didn't sit as well with Tracy, born of a Jewish father and Episcopalian mother, who, raised as an Episcopalian, converted to Catholicism when we were married. She is now a social worker and child therapist, and the mother of our two young sons. "People change because they're loved and accepted—sins and all; not because of all that stuff," she said, in her usual blunt manner. "Marriage is the only place that you have the chance to love a person's weakest parts—because you make a promise not to walk away when you find out who you're really married to. And by the way—" she hesitated, perhaps not wanting to trample my ego any further, but inflamed with her own Good Enough Catholic vision, "Jesus never asked us to be perfect."

Thus was delivered to me a blinding lesson in why people get married. Not that I was wrong, but my ideas were woefully incomplete. I had resonated to one part of Christ's message, to seek only the highest ideals. But I had forgotten its counterpart—that Christ readily welcomed sinners and forgave shortcomings. And it was by that acceptance, by his showering of unequivocal affection and concern for them, that they were changed.

I was talking about the perfect Catholic marriage. Tracy was more sensible: she was advocating the Good Enough Catholic marriage.

The statistics on marriage today are a chilling reminder of the fragility of this state in life; for every two marriages entered into this year, there will be one divorce. This is sobering testimony indeed that the best of intentions (how many people marry expecting or *wanting* their marriage to fail?) can and do go awry in the face of the difficulties imposed upon us by the vagaries of life, and by ourselves as well.

Of course, there are many reasons for marital malaise and a rocketing divorce rate. And Catholics are certainly not immune from the dangers; we are not somehow inoculated at baptism from the stress of two-career households, the sexual revolution, the emancipation of women, the accelerating mobility of our society, and the inflated expectation that marriage should fulfill all our personal and emotional needs. In fact, Catholics divorce at about the same rate as the rest of Americans.

With such daunting prospects, it's a wonder men and women can still come before the altar, look in each other's eyes, and make a commitment to each other "until death do us part." Yet we do, and we will—simply because, for most people, there is no better way to go through life than with a trusted partner. Most of us know—and, as I can attest, are continually reminded—that we are incomplete alone.

Let's begin by taking a moment to look back to the basics of what a Catholic marriage partnership is founded upon. Perhaps, in the confusion of so many modern insights, Catholicism's message about marriage isn't being heard, properly understood, or taken seriously enough. We may be working hard to assemble the building blocks, but we may also be building without a cornerstone.

Marriage, like morality, is not so much a state or end point as it is a process—a process of continual self-reflection and adjustments, good moves and false ones. At its best, marriage is a testing ground for the rest of our relationships. For if we can encourage— and expect—the best of our spouse, and yet readily accept his or her shortcomings, we will take this attitude into all our other relationships.

As we speak of marriage in this chapter, we must also deal with the reality of divorce. On the one hand, divorce is a failure to live up to our marriage commitment; yet, like all our failures—if we believe in the redemption promised by Jesus—it holds the possibility of forgiveness, healing, and enhancement. When it happens, divorce marks an ending; it is also the beginning of the rest of our lives. It is the seed that must go into the ground and die in order to produce new life.

In talking as Catholics about divorce, we must also consider the whole issue of church annulments—and, for that matter, the possibility of a subsequent marriage. First, a look at how our ideas, ideals, and laws about marriage came to be.

# THE TIES THAT HAVE BOUND

The controversy over what is most important in marriage is hardly new. In fact, Genesis carries two accounts of creation's first recorded marriage. One stresses companionship, or support for the partner: "Therefore a man . . . clings to his wife and they become one flesh." In the other, procreation is central: "Be fruitful and multiply."

Actually, as history attests, both were practical and interwoven necessities for Adam and Eve. Soon, they would be living in a hostile, dangerous world; they would need each other's support to survive. What is more, their world would be abruptly devoid of human beings if they did not set about producing them. This small germ of creation history ingeniously contains two other key elements of married life: it would be monogamous, and—taking into account the stability needed both to nurture the relationship of the couple and to raise children responsibly—indissoluble.

With the benefit of a few thousand years of practical experience in the realm of love and marriage, the ancient Jews went on to embellish the marriage stories of the Garden of Eden. In the Book of Proverbs, a wife was idealized as a person of valor and dignity; in the Song of Songs, two lovers chart out the theology and the chemistry of the male-female relationship in their soaring dialogue. And in a number of the other books comprising the Bible's "Wisdom literature," marriage can be seen as symbolizing God's own unbreakable, fertile bond with Israel.

In the life of Christ, considerable weight has long been placed by Catholic tradition on the fact that Jesus' first formal appearance in John's gospel as a grown man—and the occasion for his first miracle, according to John—was at a Jewish wedding celebration. This dramatic intervention, helping to spare the newlywed couple the embarrassment of running out of wine—which would have abruptly curtailed the three- to seven-day-long festivities in first-century Cana—signifies the importance he placed on marriage.

As there would be a new covenant between Jesus and his followers, so the marriage covenant was confirmed in early Christianity as
an equally intimate and permanent religious bonding, prefigured in
Judaism, and a source of holiness for the couple. There were temporal and spiritual rewards promised for its fulfillment, and remon-
strance threatened for its default. Sex, intimacy, trust, exclusivity,
and children—as well as the land, animals, and family ties that were
all part of the marriage agreement—were too important to the social
fabric and the lives of the individuals concerned to be treated lightly,
or dispensed with easily.

While unions of man and woman were blessed and celebrated in
the first 1,000 years after Christ, the church exercised no actual jurisdiction over marriages. Only the impending breakdown of society
brought on by the Dark Ages called for ecclesiastical intervention—
the only recognized authority in this chaotic time. In the early thirteenth century, matrimony was elevated to the status of a sacrament;
later, in the sixteenth century, the Council of Trent declared that
marriages could take place only in the presence of a priest. The
church had decreed its stamp was needed to seal a marriage—and
that, because of its sacred nature, this pact could not to be broken or
abridged.

Consistently, throughout the centuries, Catholic teaching had
stressed the contractual element of marriage; it bound man to woman
and woman to man, giving them exclusive right to sexual intimacy
with each other for the divinely sanctioned purpose of procreation.

# FOUNTAIN OF GRACE

Vatican II took a fresh look at marriage, as it did at all the sacraments. The council stripped away the accretions that had encrusted
Catholic ideas of matrimony, demystifying the sacrament itself while
elevating in a new way the union of man and woman it had been
created to bless.

No, the council pronounced: matrimony was no longer to be considered an isolated burst of grace and blessings (like the reception of the Eucharist, for instance), but only the initial tapping of a continuing, renewing source. The marital relationship *itself* was an inexhaustible fountain of grace, not some magical act performed by a priest. In other words, God's assistance to those living as husband and wife did not abruptly cease at the end of the wedding service. Grace was available on a daily basis, in the very interactions of married couples. Each partner was, in essence, a source of grace to the other.

The council acknowledged that the world had changed dramatically since the Council of Trent had last spoken authoritatively of marriage four hundred years earlier. Marriage had then been looked on as a social and cultural convention, as well as a religious one. Love was hardly a consideration; marriage was a necessary, practical state in life, spent with a partner nearly always chosen by someone else. It was designed for the community's good and order, and to assure simple survival.

Vatican II was looking out upon the first generations of people who could marry someone they actually wanted to be with, someone they loved. The Catholic Church, the council wisely saw, had to change with this epochal shift in human relations. People expected more of marriage. The church would have to reach within its deep reservoir of wisdom, teachings, and tradition to reinterpret marriage for modern man and woman.

Vatican II struggled to put to rest long-held—and once vigorously advanced—views. The first was that a celibate religious life was somehow superior to married life. Pre–Vatican II Catholics had been raised to believe that being a priest, nun, or brother was by far the most meritorious path a person could take. Even in the post–Vatican II church, the consecrated religious life was still (erroneously) taught as the highest human calling. Gradually, Vatican II's thoroughgoing reappraisal of individual vocation became better and better known; giving up the use of one's sexuality could not be regarded as superior to its proper and fruitful use. Married life was its own holy calling, not merely a venal concession to concupiscence.

Another important new perspective opened by Vatican II concerned the very nature of marriage. Setting aside the term "contract," the council spoke instead of a "marriage covenant," showing a new sensitivity to the realization that men and women change throughout their lives. A truly healthy and productive human relationship, the council acknowledged, was one that called for continual and reflective recommitment, rather than begrudging assent to a pledge.

Perhaps the most important insight concerned the role of children. Before Vatican II, the procreation of children was held up as the highest ideal, the very reason for marriage. Now, there was a ". . . stress on the mutual exchange of love as constituting the sacrament of marriage, on the need for growth in this love in order to bring the sacrament to its full realization."[2]

Procreation and companionship—as in Genesis—had each been restored to its proper place.

Notably, one word in particular appeared in the council's documents on marriage that had appeared many times before, albeit with different emphases, in the writings of both church fathers and subsequent theologians on the subject. The word was *friendship*. In our own sex-sated times, friendship at first might appear too timid a hope for married couples. But the council saw friendship as the thread that could not only hold marriages together but enhance the love relationship of a man and a woman.

> For friendship, in its most authentic form, is an unselfish and mutual love persons have for each other, as each knows he or she is loved by the other. In sincere friendship the tie of love is enduring, for it is not based on the hope of gratification from the personal traits that can fade with time, but on the free and firm commitment of each *to pursue the good of the other, for the other's sake*.[3]

I've added the emphasis here to the words of a talk given by Archbishop Donald Wuerl on Catholic marriage—a talk given, interestingly enough, to a Jewish congregation in Pittsburgh.

# THE ART OF BEING MARRIED

There are many excellent books on marriage and love, many techniques to enhance what is our most intimate human relationship. For its own part, as the Catholic church has recognized the changing nature of married life, various approaches—dealing with spiritual, emotional, and practical aspects—have been employed through a number of marriage-preparation programs, weekend retreats, and mentoring by married couples.

I'll not presume to offer what specific strategies and approaches might be best for you, but rather concentrate on a few of the fundamental elements of a Good Enough Catholic married life. First of all, no, you do not have to agree on everything. Second of all, yes, you must simultaneously ask the best of yourself and your spouse, while maintaining the ability to accept, love, and respect who he or she—and yourself—actually is.

Married life provides a sort of moral greenhouse, a safe, yet dynamic testing ground for the rest of our lives. It is a place where we are encouraged to grow and blossom, even experiment. Yet it is also a place where we are always protected by, and provide protection to, our covenantal relationship; it is a place where we are daily, hourly, nourished by love. It is here, more than any other place in our lives, that we are in the hands of a keeper holding our own well-being in a heart that we, through marriage, have made whole.

It is not that couples need be absolutely in sync about everything in their lives; hardly. My own marriage is a perfect example (as I was reminded, with my wonderful quote from Pius XI). Without some brio in a marriage, neither partner is forced to reconsider what they stand for and why. Conflict is not bad; differences of opinion or style are not death knells. But if a couple does not have similar *values*, even the most ardent love will eventually show signs of wear caused by basic differences in their respective understanding of what the purpose of life is.

Speaking of basic differences, it is important to remember that

many Catholics are considering marrying non-Catholics, to say nothing of the millions of interfaith marriages that have already taken
place. What of their prospects?

The potential friction that can be caused by differences in religious cultures and beliefs should not be underestimated. But I don't
think it is a difference in religious belief that will ultimately matter
in married life; rather, it is the *lack* of religious belief as a basis for
values and goals by one partner or the other that points toward
trouble. If one person has, or seeks, a relationship with God—as interpreted by the Catholic Church or another religious body—and
the other does not, they enter marriage with incongruities far more
profound than a mere difference in denominational affiliation. Two
people fervent about their different faiths would each at least be
more likely to have a better understanding of something important
to their partner.

For in every marriage, *falling* in love—that wondrous state that
makes us ache with longing for one person—must eventually be replaced by *being* in love. And being in love involves a friendship and
bond that is at once patient, tough, and hopeful. Being in love allows you to be your real self, without pretenses or masks. Being in
love means falling in love over and over again, in different ways, for
different reasons, throughout a lifetime.

Falling in love again and again happens far more naturally when
you can honestly say that you support this man, or this woman, in
what he or she hopes for, or wants to achieve. It is far more difficult
if your values start out, or come to be, antithetical.

We said in chapter 6 that the Good Enough Catholic ideal of
work was not to transform everyone into a social worker. By the
same token, the Good Enough Catholic expectation for marriage is
not that every couple gets down on their knees and prays together
several times a day, listens attentively to each other's every murmur,
and responds immediately. Frankly, there is nothing wrong with
wanting to be the CEO of a major corporation, and having a summer house on the beach. Not everyone is destined to be a lily of the
field. But the upwardly mobile executive who climbs ruthlessly over
the backs of contemporaries may find difficult his married life with a

spouse who is trying to live a life—and raise children—imbued with a sense of compassion and fairness.

Being in love and staying in love requires many small, simple acts—and a profound commitment. Marriage, by virtue of joining together two unique people, is filled with compromises and ambivalence. The willingness to make adjustments as the years go by and new situations present themselves, and the ability to simply and readily forgive, are far more important than infrequent, extravagant acts of love. These are good, but they are not a substitute for daily human decency. In monastic life, it is not the monk who spends hours before the Blessed Sacrament, then retreats to his room to hoard his God, who is admired. It is the monk who passes the salt at silent meals with a smile.

Giving in and giving up, rather than staking out territory and jealously guarding our prerogatives. Being the person you want your spouse (or intended spouse) to be. Alternately ready with painful honesty and healing acceptance. Kissing your lover's lips; biting your own lip. These are the hallmarks of good marriages—and for the Good Enough Catholic, they are paths to holiness as well as happiness.

But be aware: this is not to say that, while seeking the good of the other, our own needs are never addressed. The always self-sacrificing spouse is a plant in the moral greenhouse of marriage that will wither and bear bitter fruit. Some needs your spouse will fulfill; others you must seek out for yourself.

"Your feelings change each day, and you have to work with those feelings in a marriage. You can't be in love the same way you were when you first met. You grow up and your love has to grow up, too."

—NUMA TORRES

"I really wasn't looking for a good Catholic girl, but when I found Theresa, I liked the fact that she was Catholic; we had so much in common. She taught me so much I didn't know, about holy days and Mary and the sacraments. I have a great sense of belonging to a church, even though I might disagree with it. I'm an all-American guy, but in the church—because of Theresa—I have traditions that mean a lot to me."

—JIM HELEIN

But, as those of us know who have seen a marriage die before us, life is not a fairy tale. Sometimes even the best efforts just aren't enough. Years ago, married people suffered through these agonies. That has changed—sometimes for the better, sometimes not.

# DIVORCE

In the history of both Judaism and Christianity, we see religious authority stoutly defending the sanctity and permanence of marriage. They could see that there was no other way to assure the stability of the partnership and assure a proper setting for raising children. More than a social contract between two people, marriage by extension wedded tribes, villages, societies, cultures, and economic holdings. Divorce was to be avoided at all costs. Only if that contract was breached by exceptional behavior that itself threatened the social fabric, was it judged advisable to dissolve a marital union.

The Jews, seeking to interpret the only passage of their Torah that spoke specifically of divorce, had taught that a man might divorce a woman ". . . because he has found something unseemly in her"—in other words, that she had committed adultery. The New Testament gives two very serious reasons to dissolve a Christian marriage: if the spouse was an unbeliever (and, it would be assumed, detrimental to the faith of a believing partner); or if the spouse was involved in serious sexual immorality. The use of the Greek word *porneia* in Matthew's gospel suggests that, in addition to marital infidelity, such conduct might also have included incest and other sexual taboos of the era.

But, with more experience in the human enterprise of marriage, both Judaism and Christianity began to reconsider their view of divorce. If marriage was a contract to link people as dutiful parents, a cohesive unit within their society, and observant people of faith, it could not be an anvil about the neck of foundering souls who simply should not remain together. While the sanctity and permanence of marriage was always upheld, Jewish law began to evolve toward a broader understanding, concluding that the separation of a man and woman was a lesser evil than their living a hateful or loveless life together. The unintended harshness of an otherwise good and just law was thus ameliorated.

In the Christian world, Origen, writing in the third century, forwarded an argument that was widely invoked: "The matter of divorce and remarriage was contrary to what has been handed down, but not entirely without reason." Divorce was an evil, Origen always maintained, and a regrettable—but necessary—alternative.

This was not to say that divorce dispensations were granted at all equitably or justly. Men were rarely held up as adulterers; women were more often accused, and nearly always proved guilty, of the sin. Hearsay and encouraged testimony allowed many a husband to be rid of a troublesome wife. Kingdoms and grain bins were shamelessly bartered with the dismissal of one spouse and the taking of another. These compromises with the strict rule of indissolubility provided a sometimes inequitable, but nonetheless necessary, escape valve—but only for men.

Judaism found a way to deal with bad marriages, as did the Eastern churches—who split from Rome in the eleventh century over, among other issues, the notion of papal supremacy. So also did the Anglicans, who were in nearly complete agreement with Catholic ideas of marriage. Each permitted divorce and remarriage, but only under certain, specific conditions; and these conditions changed as society was transformed from feudal to agrarian, agrarian to industrial, and industrial to the current postindustrial, information age.

Only Western Catholicism, its ecclesiastical power increasingly centered in Rome, actually became more strict on the question of divorce. The Council of Trent, clearly delineating between Catholic thought and the perceived heresies of the Reformers, reaffirmed the principle of indissolubility. What God had joined together in marriage, the church proclaimed stoutly, no man could put asunder. Origen's teaching, which had allowed for some flexibility, was discarded in favor of a categorical, dogmatic approach.

Although there were always voices of dissent within the church—chiefly from those who felt its laws on marriage were too inflexible and burdensome—Vatican II's new understanding of the sacrament of matrimony allowed both pastors and theologians ways to consider when and how it might be possible to dissolve a marriage bond. If the very relationship sanctified through the sacrament of matrimony—a mutual exchange of love, a freely chosen partnership—no longer existed, then, some concluded, the covenant had been breached, voided; it had lost its power. Grace could not flow into the marriage of two people who no longer had a lifelong commitment to each other.

Before Vatican II, sex was considered the very essence of the marriage contract. This free and exclusive use of sexual intimacy was a motivating factor that propelled people to be married and, in the church's eyes, was both a reward for their commitment and a sign of their state in life. But, of course, with the sustained marital discord and alienation that marked so many relationships, there was no thought of intimacy. Without a sustaining relationship, there was none of the bonding power of sexual activity.

Today, some six to eight million American Catholics are divorced. Regardless of the sternness of official church teaching, the Catholic divorce rate, as noted above, is little different from the divorce rate of the rest of America.

For some, the divorce came after a hasty marriage, perhaps because the young woman was pregnant. (Over 90 percent of all marriages of those under twenty and pregnant end in divorce.) Others have struggled to live with an abusive, unfaithful, or alcoholic spouse. Indifference, sickness, the lack (or presence) of children—

the reasons for divorce are many. Some marriages atrophy for lack of effort, others implode from conflict. That Eden-like garden of love and comradeship hoped for in married life becomes an arid desert of alienation and recrimination. Still others find that the man or woman they married is neither devil nor angel—nor the person with whom they want to spend the rest of their lives. Love simply dies.

Whatever the circumstances, there is always pain. A promise has been broken. There is a sense of failure, of profound disappointment. Often there are children involved.

## SEEKING A WAY

Within the Catholic Church, a new compassion for the plight of the divorced or those in irretrievably broken marriages has been increasingly evident over the past few decades. Groups of lay people continue to surface, and diocesan-sponsored programs for the divorced, separated, and remarried have helped to begin the healing and provide support for thousands upon thousands of Catholics. Moreover—and notwithstanding Vatican pronouncements that the divorced and remarried (the vast majority of all divorced *will* remarry) are living in a sinful state, rendering them unworthy of receiving Eucharist and precluding their full participation in the church—a significant movement is afoot to embrace them.

In 1993, three German bishops forwarded the argument that pastors should be allowed to make a judgment, depending on circumstances, that would allow the divorced and remarried to exercise full church membership and receive the Eucharist. In citing the many cases of emotional and spiritual hardship of those who were unable, or had not chosen, to pursue a formal church annulment, the German bishops observed that Jesus' words—an invitation to life—must not be made into "a crushing law."[4]

Commenting on the action of the German bishops (which was

later denounced by the Vatican's Congregation for the Doctrine of the Faith and the bishops were commanded to halt the practice), Catholic University theology professor John Grabowski observed:

> ... the church has always sought to exercise some pastoral flexibility, even while remaining faithful to Jesus' teaching. . . . After all, the witness of the church to the world cannot simply focus on a juridical notion of fidelity. It must also strive to be faithful to Jesus' ministry of reconciliation in the midst of human brokenness and sin. The credibility of the church as witness to the merciful love of God demands no less.[5]

In his article, Grabowski also quoted an earlier author who had advocated compassion for the divorced and remarried: "Whenever in a second marriage moral obligations have arisen toward the children and toward the woman, and not similar obligations from the first marriage exist, whenever also the giving up of the second marriage is not fitting on moral grounds . . . it seems that the granting of full communion . . . is nothing less than just, and is fully in harmony with our ecclesiastical traditions."[6]

We can only regard as ironic the fact that the author of this passage is Joseph Cardinal Ratzinger—expressing his theological opinion *before* he was elevated to become prefect of the very body, the Congregation for the Doctrine of the Faith, that condemned the German bishops' approach.

From the compassion of Christ's words to the sternness of that rebuke to the German bishops, from Origen to Vatican II, what we witness are examples of the continuing evolution of church tradition and practice. The current discussion about the status of the divorced and remarried is but the latest in a long series of such debates. Each has sought to discern the needs of the people of God *at a specific time in history*; and each has set those needs against the backdrop of centuries of church teaching, practice, and tradition. In the past, religious leaders were wise enough to understand the tenor of the times and care for their followers—without casting aside the very essence upon which religious belief must stand. Such wisdom is again in evidence today. Yes, it is difficult to see, especially if a person's divorce has been driven as a stake into the heart by an unyielding church pronouncement or uncaring pastor. But an evolutionary process is in motion that will inevitably lead to a more compassionate view of the divorced. For the nature of marriage has both remained constant and radically changed—all within our lifetime. The terms were altered by the first generations of people to have the freedom to enter into marriage because of mutual affection, not economic need or parental imperative. They will live longer, and their married lives will undergo a series of seismic changes.

Sexual infidelity or religious unbelief—once so destructive to a sacred marriage contract that the contract could be abrogated because of them—are certainly still key issues within a marriage; but they are hardly the only ones. Today's marriage covenant demands constant recommitment. Without it the covenant no longer holds its power, no longer serves as a channel of grace.

It is a difficult and dizzying time in which we try to figure out how to live together—a world so teeming with possibilities and so fraught with uncertainty. Taken to its absurd limits, a casual approach to marriage would seem to allow dissolution by divorce at the whim of either spouse. But, of course, the Good Enough Catholic knows this is not the case. Marriage is far too important for that. What the Good Enough Catholic must do in the matter of divorce is to look to the church for leadership, as well as to individual conscience for guidance.

The debate goes on. Meanwhile the divorced—once the exception to the rule, and pariahs within the Catholic community—are everywhere. They want to know that, as the German bishops proclaimed, ". . . whenever people fall short of the reality of redemption, Jesus meets them in mercy with understanding for their situation."[7] So many of them want to be Catholics, worship as Catholics, espouse a Catholic lifestyle. A failed marriage hasn't killed their desire to participate in parish life, to receive the sacraments, and to educate their children as Catholics. If anything, the experience of divorce has deepened their spirituality and intensified their awareness of the need for God's forgiveness and his grace.

"The church says that marriage cannot be dissolved. But all you have to do is live your life to know that not every marriage works out; some have to be dissolved. Marriage only has the potential to become a sacrament. Not all marriages make it to that level. When you see a divorced person enter a second marriage and it blossoms, you see the hand of God at work. Now, it can be a sacrament for them."

—DICK WESTLY

"When I told my kids we were getting a divorce, they went nuts. All their friends' parents were divorced. They felt they had something; they were special. But if you're not getting along and life is hell, you have to get out of the marriage. I tried. I taught CCD, I taught vacation Bible school. But my husband drifted farther and farther away. Playing rugby and going to a bar were more important for him. Then came his midlife crisis. And later, I found out another lady was involved. Why stay together if you're just hurting each other? It doesn't make any sense."

—LATICE NULAND*

"I believe in marriage, but not to kill two people's spirits by keeping them in a loveless marriage. I just don't think it's human. I don't think it's what Christ would have them do."

—MARTY HEGARTY

# FACING THE DEMON DIVORCE

What about Good Enough Catholics who are now contemplating a first—or subsequent—marriage? Must you consider divorce and its consequences? Is this any way to embark on such a marvelous part of your life? What of those who find themselves in a marriage that is so much less than they hoped it would be? Is divorce an option for you? And if you have already divorced, what of your life—both past and future?

For those considering marriage, to face divorce directly and understand its ramifications—almost as part of your premarital plans—is to care deeply about the marital relationship. Divorce is too much a reality to pretend it might not happen to *you*.

If you see divorce as a ready escape if marriage doesn't meet your expectations, you had best take a hard look at who you are marrying, what your common values are, and how honest you have been with one another. The pain of divorce can last longer, and cut deeper, than the sublime joy of a wedding. Make sure that you call the person you intend to marry a friend, and not only a lover.

On the other hand, if you intend to be married and can truthfully say—even with the normal misgivings that any Good Enough Catholic must have—that you are willing to make a permanent, for-better-and-for-worse commitment, you will go into marriage on the best possible footing.

Yes, you are fully aware divorce may present itself as an alternative; even in the best of marriages, the "D" word sometimes erupts in moments of anger or pain. But you vow, as you vow to be married, to resist the temptation of divorce. You will do anything to prevent the violation of this solemn pact you make before God and your spouse.

And yet the day might come when you will have to say you have done your best—and it was not enough.

For those Good Enough Catholics now married for whom divorce is no longer a word used in an irrational moment, but that points to an imminent or even certain outcome, you may be facing the most important examination of conscience in your life. You know better than anyone the height of your hopes and dreams when you married. You realize that the path you had hoped to travel is not, for so many reasons, the path you have trod. From the depths of what you are going through right now, those lofty hopes no longer seem attainable.

This is not a time to assess who is more to blame for the situation in which you find yourself. There is only one person you have any control over—and that is yourself. And that is the person who you will take into the days ahead, be those days together with, or apart from, your spouse. As someone who is not a perfect person, but simply a Good Enough Catholic, you want to walk on with all the dignity and integrity you can muster. That is within your grasp, when so many other things seem impossible.

A few questions might be appropriate for your reflection. Did you give this marriage your all, or was there a piece of yourself you held back? Were you more interested in being right than being a friend? Although you wanted your spouse to deliver you from times of irrationality or to forgive your sometimes foolish behavior, were you willing to do exactly those things? Have you reached outside for help—a counselor, a priest, a wise mutual friend? Have you prayed, offering your sadness and the possibility of a broken pledge to God— and then, in silence, opened yourself to divine urgings? Have you gone even farther—putting aside for the moment the hostility, the crushed feelings and the broken dreams—to pray *together* with your spouse, so that you both might be honestly guided to do what is best for each of you, your marriage, and your family?

Is there something, *anything* left undone? Have you been fair— even loving, remembering that this was a person you once promised to love for all your life—amidst the acrimony or the painful malaise that characterizes your relationship? Some modern prophets of self-fulfillment would say that looking out for another's interests rather than staking a claim for yourself—sacrifice, in a word—is destructive of the almighty *you*. Of course, taken to absurd lengths, this can re-sult. But isn't that kind of disinterested, loving concern exactly what you wanted from the other person in your marriage? Sacrifice is often the gateway to real happiness, as any spiritual seeker or parent will attest. The person who has not sacrificed mightily in a marriage has not given that marriage a chance to work.

If you have children, are you honestly addressing their needs and welfare? Are you able to refrain from using them as pawns to inflict pain on a spouse who has caused you pain, or as a means to have your way with a person who is determined to prevail?

Look deeply into yourself, your motives and your actions. And muster a smile at the twists and turns your life has taken. Laughter is often exactly what's needed in the midst of turmoil and pain.

In the end, whether you divorce or not, realize this: You are never outside God's love or mercy, regardless of what others may say about you, or some church teachings may seem to proclaim. You, Good Enough Catholic, know your own heart.

For those millions of already divorced Catholics, there may be a need to reflect on what went wrong with your marriage—so that you may not repeat behaviors or choices that were ultimately counter-productive. The sobering fact is that divorce and a subsequent marriage do not solve all problems. In fact, the divorce rate for second marriages is even higher than for first marriages.

But also remember what went right in your marriage. And, if you have children, give thanks for the lasting felicitous statement that union has made.

Settle those accounts that can be settled, and move on with the rest of your life. Forgive your former spouse; forgive yourself. Let the wisdom you have gained and the hurts you have endured continue to create in you the person you know you can be. It is easy to be hardened by a corrosive marriage. But what does it avail spending the rest of your life making those around you suffer for wounds inflicted by someone no longer there? There is love and there is friendship for those who can love and be friends, in turn.

This may be the very best time to reclaim your proper place, both in life and within the church. From a kind of death, resurrection is possible. The Christ who welcomed tax collectors, prostitutes, and all sorts of social outcasts must surely welcome you. You, who may feel a horrible failure; you, hardly a public sinner. You, a Good Enough Catholic who is ready to look ahead to a new life.

# ANNULMENTS

The issue of annulments may be the cause of more pain than any other Catholic procedure today. Few people are openly excommunicated these days, but there are millions of decent, otherwise-believing Catholics who feel they are outside the church because, while they have obtained a civil divorce from a marriage, they have not obtained an annulment.

Annulments have proved heartbreaking to many, while to others a sign of healing. There is a wide range of personal experience—and theological thought—about this controversial practice. Some see annulments as necessarily difficult, a bastion protecting family values. Others picture annulments as an ingenious and pastorally motivated device of an imperfect Church seeking to find a way to deal with inevitable human mistakes. Still others consider annulments little more than bureaucratic sophistry.

The Catholic Church, which does not claim authority over civil marriages, teaches that religiously sanctioned marriages take place with God as the unseen witness, and constitute a permanent, irrevocable bond. Therefore, what God joins together, no person can tear apart. But the key consideration—and the basis for annulment—is whether or not a valid marriage took place. This is where the confusion over what annulments are and are not often begins.

An annulment is the judgment of a church tribunal that a canonically valid marriage never occurred. It does not mean that there was never a loving relationship, that the couple did not truly intend to be married and felt married, or that the children of the marriage are illegitimate.

What the tribunal (customarily headed by a priest, but now more and more frequently by a nun, specifically trained in canon law) must ascertain is whether there was an impediment or a defect in the original marriage contract that, in effect, invalidated it. Such an impediment or defect could be anything from serious mental disease impairing judgment, a forced marriage, or a conscious decision not to have children.

The grounds most often invoked for an annulment are that the couple was not "emotionally mature" enough to make such a commitment and did not fully understand the ramifications of married life. Msgr. Joseph Champlin, a recognized expert on marriage, has expanded on this idea in a *U.S. Catholic* article. "I think priests can almost presume that the majority of marriages today are probably invalid . . . 50 percent of [those being married] are from divorced families. Their model has been divorce; it's a part of their unconscious psyche. . . . We live in a culture in which permanent commitments are no longer cherished nor the customary pattern."[8]

But such grounds—"emotional immaturity," a category to which most, if not all, of us, married in the Catholic Church or not, might legitimately lay claim—are why church annulments have gotten such a bad reputation. Many consider pursuing an annulment demeaning, jumping through false hoops to prove a false premise. They find themselves having to tailor or manufacture evidence to fit a pattern demanded by canon law and their diocesan tribunal.

On the other hand, many Catholics have found the annulment process a final and healing end to a marriage that had died and needed final interment. They married in the church; they wanted the church to acknowledge that their marriage, despite their efforts, was finally invalid. Most often, they wanted to be in good standing with the church, and to be able to marry again, in the church.

Still, a far larger number of Catholics say no to annulments. They wonder why the church cannot simply acknowledge that some marriages fail, and then assist people to go on with the rest of their lives. If they remarry, it will be outside the church. And they may or may not practice their Catholicism, held off at arm's length, as they are, by church teaching.

Some dioceses make annulments extremely difficult; others, because they do not maintain functioning tribunals, virtually impossible. Still others have introduced procedures to make the process less onerous. For instance, in my home diocese of Raleigh, North Carolina, boards of lay people are trained to assist those who want to obtain an annulment. Many of these volunteers have been through the annulment process themselves and are conversant not only with the technical aspects of ending a marriage, but the emotional aspects as well.

Regardless of what might seem an inequitable, expensive, time-consuming process, the divorced or divorcing Good Enough Catholic should make a decision based on his or her own particular needs and circumstances. But always bear in mind that annulment is a man-made procedure, created with both the best of intentions and a concern for institutional integrity. This is the judgment and work of man, not of God.

There is also another avenue. Formal annulments are referred to as "external forum," as tribunal proceedings are public. There is a body of theological thought, as well as pastoral practice (the German bishops in their letter called upon both), that provides for an "internal forum," whereby a remarried couple can return to the church and the sacraments. Many have found their peace in this manner after prayerful consultation with a sympathetic priest who can discern the state of their consciences far better in private conversation than in a court of canon law.

Some priests are openly welcoming to the divorced, regardless of formal annulment proceedings or "prayer consultations." Others make life uncomfortable for divorced folks, making them feel as though they will carry a certain stain of sin through life. Ultimately, it is incumbent upon divorced Good Enough Catholics not to let the rigid or insensitive deter them from their spiritual quest, or from their desire to find unity and wholeness in the sacraments and community for which they hunger.

"I heard this sermon in church about how horrible divorce was. My parents—who had five kids in six years; how much more Catholic can you be?—they were divorced, and they weren't horrible. They had to go through an annulment; it was so denigrating to both of them to have to dredge up all this stuff. I have this feeling that God up in heaven smacks his head in amazement at how we interpret his words and laws. 'They got *this* from *that?*' I can hear him saying."

—BILL MAJESKI★

"As much as I was against annulments, I found myself recommending them to people who are troubled about a first marriage. But my pain was too intense. I just couldn't go through an annulment. So I was sneaking around to other parishes so that no one would know this horrible, divorced woman was going to mass and receiving Eucharist. I had this dirty little secret. But I wanted this person, Christ, so much. I wanted to shout it to the world that I needed him. But until I had my annulment, I just couldn't do that. I'm so happy I did it."

—MAGALIE SALAS

"Married life is supposed to be the ultimate of God's love. My first marriage, unfortunately, was not and that is why I had to get an annulment. I wanted to be right with the Church."

—PETER DESFORGES★

# THE GOOD ENOUGH CATHOLIC CHALLENGE: SEVEN ACTS OF LOVE

It is a wondrous thing to share a married life with another person, filled as this relationship is with the promise of love and sensuality, friendship and companionship. There is the possibility of bringing children into the world. Marriage is equally intimidating, and frightfully uncertain—vowing to share that much intimacy for a lifetime, regardless of what emotional, economic, or societal storms sweep across your lives together.

But by its sacramental nature, the marriage covenant supplies us with the means and the grace to live up to the promise of those golden days of courtship, and high hopes of the wedding day itself.

Our actions, our intentions, our small, daily efforts to be a good friend and good spouse—all these can constantly enrich the most important relationship we will have in this life. We just need to be more conscious of how we can make that happen, for deep in our hearts we know that with each loving act, we are enriched, our partner is enriched, the marriage is enriched.

Marriage provides us with a protected and blessed testing area to share with a person who knows more about us—for better and for worse, to use words from the wedding vow—than anyone in the world. A person who really has our best interests at heart. Here is the place that love will prosper—or die.

So the challenge is this: Start with one small act, each day for a week, directed toward your spouse. It cannot be anything heroic or obvious. It might be something that we wish our partner would do for us. Do something before you are asked. Listen instead of talking. Your intention is to love your spouse through that one small act, to help your partner to be the best person possible, to care for them regardless of who they are at that particular moment. If your spouse lashes out angrily, let it pass instead of lashing back, meting out measure for measure. If your spouse is screaming at the children for something they have done, don't scream back, just occupy the children with something else. If getting out the door on time is an issue, have breakfast on the table a half-hour early. If you can do nothing more when a situation presents itself, your fleeting, silent prayer, while looking at your loved one, is enough.

Your one act a day for a week can fall under the category of sacrifice; or you can consider it something you've wanted to do anyhow, and now have the chance. Call no attention to what you are doing, as if this were a perfectly natural thing for one friend to do for another. Do not act as though your action requires anything in return; do not fix a saccharine smile on your face. And do not think you have to act like the perfect person the entire day. Remember, you are only a Good Enough Catholic.

Just one act a day, for one week. Each act is an occasion for an infusion of grace. See what happens.

# SELECTED READINGS

Patrick E. Brennan, ed., *Marriage Is More than You and Me*. Chicago: ACTA Publications, 1992.

Marie Theresa Coombs and Francis Kelly Nemeck, *Discerning Vocations to Marriage, Celibacy, and Singlehood*. Collegeville, Minn.: Michael Glazier (Liturgical Press), 1994.

Erich Fromm, *The Art of Loving*. New York: Bantam, 1963.

Ladislas Orsy, *Marriage and Canon Law*. Wilmington, Del.: Michael Glazier, 1986.

John L. Thomas (rev. ed. by David M. Thomas), *Beginning Your Marriage*. Chicago: ACTA Publications, 1994.

# CHAPTER EIGHT

# SEX, ABORTION, AND BIRTH CONTROL
## Of Life and of Love

A funny thing happened on America's way to a new sexuality. After eagerly embracing "free love" as a gateway to happiness and advocating "abortion on demand" as an inalienable right, a lot of people—Catholics surely among them—found that many of the tenets of the sexual revolution just didn't work for them. Despite their enticing appeal, casual sex, serial relationships, and childless marriages centered on material success weren't delivering the happiness they had promised. The senseless termination of pregnancies had caused a national heartache.

It isn't that the past few decades didn't help a lot of us Good Enough Catholics to regard and live out our sexuality in a more healthy fashion, to rid ourselves of the guilt that even something so simple as the mere mention of the word "sex" used to evoke. But then—when we saw the kind of society unbridled permissiveness would produce, the kind of family that would result, the kind of people we would become, the kind of children we would raise—even the most open-minded among us realized something was badly out of whack.

And there, during those same years, wafting across our consciousness were the church's teachings on the sacredness of sex and of human life, on the need for lasting commitments. In an age that accentuated the mandates of personal choice and personal fulfillment, when the ready availability of contraceptives took the lasting consequences out of sex and legal abortion became readily available, the Catholic Church defiantly stood its ground. Instead, the church offered its own unflinching testimony to what it perceived as true human dignity, restating what it saw as God's prescription for real and lasting happiness.

The church's stand has been admirable, even prophetic. But—the Good Enough Catholic might add—it has also been incomplete, unfinished.

Much of what the church has said about the human condition down through the centuries was right. And church teaching about sex still resonates with truth today. But the Good Enough Catholic knows instinctively and intellectually that the church has been slow indeed to give enough credence to what both our individual circumstances and the advances of science have discovered about human sexuality and reproduction. While the Catholic Church has produced documents on such varied subjects as the worth of human labor, on war and peace, and on the economy—all of which have inspired challenging and useful debates—its teachings on sex, birth control, and abortion are often dismissed as the heavy-handed edicts of a gathering of emotionally parsimonious celibate men. Through its teachings, the church seems to regard sexuality and our procreative abilities as being far more dangerous than, say, weapons of mass destruction. Most Good Enough Catholics would claim that they long ago stopped listening to the church's point of view on sex. And yet, strangely enough, we haven't.

In a time when Catholics appear to have lost the distinctive culture that once surrounded us, it is amazing—and, to me, heartening—to find that there persists a "Catholic ethic" about sex. Yes, even as a majority of the laity rejects church leadership on sexual matters, Catholics still hear the age-old message. Consider: young Catholic women are more likely to remain virgins and put off sexual activity until marriage than women in the rest of the population. And (which may be a corollary) while they, like the population at large, do not support the church's categorical opposition to any and all abortions, Catholics have fewer abortions themselves.

I, for one, believe in a distinctive Catholic sexual ethic. And, I believe, there is something precious to be preserved here—for our own good, for the good of our children, and, indeed, for the good of civilization. The young people I know are hungry for authentic moral guidelines. No, they will not abide imposed legalisms or the dictums of self-righteous authority; but give them rules and guidelines that are right and just and decent, and they will listen.

Not that we Catholics are better or stronger, or more or less sexed, than other Christians or non-Christians; but there is simply a Catholic way of looking at things. We know the ideal; Catholicism has never been a religious faith that has called for anything less than the best in people. There *is* such a thing as a Catholic ethic of sexual morality—and it makes sense, because it is based on the firm foundation of true love of self and true love of others, inspired by God's love for all. It is an ethic worth pursuing, a way of respecting sexuality that can last a lifetime, a legacy worth passing on to children who need a true and steady beacon by which to guide their lives.

But how to embrace the timeless wisdom replete in the teaching of the Catholic Church, while at the same time giving credence to the discoveries of modern science, and recognizing the real needs and capabilities of individual, flesh-and-blood human beings—without lapsing into hopeless relativism? As we discuss these three highly charged, interwoven, and complicated areas—sex, birth control, and abortion—it's important to remember one of the simplest, yet most profound concepts of Scripture, one that I find myself constantly resorting to as I try to sort out what it means to be a Good Enough Catholic. It is a concept repeated throughout the Old and New Testaments. And it is simply this: God wants a loving heart more than sacrifice. Love is always the answer; punishing ourselves by adhering with tortuous precision to institutional pronouncements never is. This is precisely what Jesus preached during his life on earth: God is not a stern bookkeeper, but a loving Father. God asks that we apply that divine love in our daily lives to the best of our ability. And no matter how unsuccessful we may be, we are never outside that love.

# SEX, THE MYSTERIOUS FORCE

Over the past century—and especially within the past fifty years—the Catholic Church has been struggling to come to grips with the fact that the divine law upon which it had structured an elaborate theology and code of behavior was neither completely adequate nor, in some cases, accurately conceived. Basically, the church had taught that divine law was ". . . eternal, objective, and universal—whereby God orders, directs and governs. . . ."[1] Or put another way, divine law was ". . . God's ordinances known through revelation,"[2] both in the Mosaic Law and the New Testament.

Divine law was a top-down way of looking at the world, a pyramid, with the pope at the pinnacle and lay Catholics forming the base. For centuries the Catholic faithful were regarded as so many weak-willed humans who needed a strict set of laws to live by. And the church magisterially handed down those laws to the members of the "one, true Church," so that they would know exactly what was right and what was wrong—and even *how* wrong.

But as an appreciation of historical consciousness grew, individual experience and the cultural realities of the time were also called upon to enlighten church doctrine. No longer were God's laws regarded as static laws; now, his unfolding plan for humankind was seen as including the revealed wisdom of human experience. This was a new approach; the pyramid had been turned upside down. The accent was on the rights of individuals, not on duties and obedience to a hierarchical structure. Scripture could no longer simply be repeated; it had to be recast in the realities of the present day.

During this recent period a new philosophical approach called personalism was being developed, further loosening the church's historical hold on the faithful. Among personalism's astonishing conclusions for Catholics was that they were self-creating beings first, and Catholics only second. They were beings who, as the authoritative *New Catholic Encyclopedia* put it, ". . . do not find fulfillment by passively accepting the facts of a situation, but by intelligently and aggressively shaping those facts and thus making them tools for the achievement of their own ends."[3]

It was a liberating and intoxicating twentieth-century idea, trusting people to make informed decisions, rather than demanding that they act only in obedience to a set of rigid codes. It harkened back to the very foundation of Christianity, when Christ instructed his first disciples to give precedence to the dictates of love and mutual respect over the myriad religious laws imposed by religious hierarchy. A new Catholic theology was in the process of being written, one open to insights from the actual life experiences of believing persons. Universal, abstract ideas like "the nature of things" or even "human nature" could no longer be wielded as a rigid template within which people would have to contain their lives. Catholic dogma, Catholic doctrine, and Catholic tradition still formed the basis for belief and action; but the days of the church as unequivocal lawgiver and arbiter of human experience seemed at an end. A new term—"creative fidelity"—came into wide usage.

Yet despite its new awareness of the potential of human beings to live moral lives through informed, rational decisions, one huge area of human experience continued, for the church, to remain outside the realm of reason. That area was sex.

The church's teaching on sexual matters was based on supposedly unalterable principles of natural law, which found their basis in Cicero (d. 43 B.C.) and Aristotle (d. 322 B.C.); were Christianized and expanded upon by Augustine (d. 430) and, later, Thomas Aquinas (d. 1274); and were forcefully defined by the Council of Trent (1545–1563). Personal morality was even more strictly codified over the ensuing years. There was a finite, objective moral order: the natural, which was holy, and the unnatural, which was sinful. There were no gray areas.

Sex was seen as a natural means to an end (procreation) and certainly not an end (pleasure, intimacy) in itself. So intricately interwoven was the fabric of divine and natural law on the issue of sex and sexual behavior, traditionalists argued, that if the church in any way altered its teaching on the role and use of sex, or admitted that it had erred in any way on this crucial matter, the very authority of the Catholic Church to speak on moral matters would unravel.

While Vatican II certainly acknowledged and extolled marital intimacy ("acts must be judged, not according to their merely biological aspect, but insofar as they refer to the human person integrally and adequately considered") the church held to its bedrock teaching concerning sex's procreative function. As the priest and sociologist Andrew Greeley has written, the stakes were perceived as high indeed:

> The institutional church has striven mightily during the last quarter century to protect the Catholic sexual ethic, an ethic which in effect it has interpreted to mean that sexual pleasure can be enjoyed only in marriage and then only with an openness to the possibility of the procreation of children. Authority and sex have been the two crucial issues, often combined into one: the church's claim to authority over the sexual lives of the faithful.[4]

Most Good Enough Catholics do not seek to undermine church authority on the issue of sexual behavior. (More on the Good Enough Catholic and church teachings in chapter 12.) Yet today's realities, and the experiences of our own lives, demand to be recognized and given credence. These, too, have to be part of our moral decision-making on issues of sexual behavior. And these real-life experiences, by the very nature of the corporate body that is the Catholic Church, are part of the body of truth that comprises authoritative Catholic teaching.

For the church's mandates on sex—while potentially saintly—are not only impossible for most of us to follow, they can be downright counterproductive and dehumanizing. We might be able to patiently wait for a new Catholic theology of marriage or the priesthood, but sex is too much a part of every person's life merely to look forward hopefully for changes that will surely come in the years ahead. The Good Enough Catholic, while honoring the church's unflinching disavowal of promiscuity and adultery, seeks in good conscience to make informed, prayerful, moral decisions about their sex lives now. After all, life is more than biology, and sex more than preservation of the species. We have come to understand that there is more involved than a lottery, capriciously matching up egg and sperm regardless of the ability or readiness of the individuals to welcome a new life into their world nine months later.

So let us consider this mysterious, powerful force, both for the married and the unmarried as well.

## SEX AND THE SINGLE CATHOLIC

Frankly and foremost, we must ask: Is there such a thing as a *moral* sex life for the single Catholic?

The only answer the church offers to the unmarried—those who have never married, as well as those who are divorced—is that they should practice abstinence. This is certainly a viable and moral option; a sound first alternative, and one certainly worth pondering.[5] Abstinence from sex—as mystics, monks, and such great leaders as Gandhi (later in his life) have proved—can unleash an energy and power that can compensate for the pleasure and satisfaction of sexual pursuit and sexual release. It is a certain form of fasting and, just as fasting from food or drink purifies the body, abstinence from sex brings with it its own liberation. Quite frankly, if you don't have to think about sex, you can focus your life on other pursuits—your work, service to others, spiritual development.

> "Abstinence as a single woman is just easier for me. Abstinence promotes the kind of contemplative life I feel drawn to. It frees me to a deeper spiritual life. I just couldn't have a casual sex life. It's not the kind of person I am."
>
> —CAROLYN SWEERS

For teenagers, over whom sexuality seems to sweep with the power of a typhoon, abstinence offers a sane alternative. In today's highly sexualized world—where sex saturates the media and the "everybody's doing it" mentality generates enormous peer pressure—a significant (and growing) number of teenagers are simply saying "no." Teenagers sign sexual abstinence pledges, and sport buttons saying "True love waits." Not that it's easy for them; but they have already seen the casualties of casual sex—unwanted pregnancies and broken relationships—littering the landscape of their young lives.

"Premature sexual acts can cripple and cut short the full development of love," Father Gerald D. Coleman, a seminary rector, advises in a *Church* magazine article. He continues:

> Teenagers should be taught that sex may be an obstacle to a genuine love relationship, that is, sex may make it impossible to distinguish the *presence* of human love from its mere *expression*. . . . Even later, when a relationship seems serious and is aimed toward marriage, every couple together must ascertain whether or not the dimension of an authentic love-project are truly present in their relationship.[6]

The venerable Catholic ideal was that men and women should practice abstinence until their marriage night, and then to be able to present themselves, virginal, to each other. That is still a wonderful aspiration. But for many—the majority, really—it will not be the case. A time comes—hopefully after both abstinence has been practiced and the ramifications of sexual activity have been thoughtfully confronted (at least, as thoughtfully as possible in the overheated circumstances that usually attend)—when a truly moral person is no longer able, or even wants to, abstain from sex. How can the Good Enough Catholic, in "creative fidelity" to the church's moral code, have a sex life?

Any of us who have led unchaste unmarried lives know that sex can have a wide range of meaning and fulfillment. There is the purely biological release; there are the experiences of tenderness and intimacy. A drunken grope in the dark after a long night at a singles bar is not the same as lying down beside a person you really know and care about. If we are honest with ourselves, it is not difficult to sense when we have been true to ourselves and our partner, and when we have cheated on both accounts. Once sex is over, do you want to do nothing more than escape? The next morning, as you think about the night before, do you feel good—or cheapened? Not that we won't do it again; but we *know*.

"My first marriage was perfect; I was the perfect husband, she was the perfect wife. But it was dead inside, selfish, childless by choice. And sex? Forget it. So after the divorce, I was like a kid in the candy store with a credit card. I had been a good guy all my life, a faithful husband; now I was going to make up for it. It was a time when a heterosexual male in New York, where I was living, could pretty much have what he wanted in terms of women. It became a game. I walked into a party, looked around the room, and decided who I would sleep with that night. I feigned intimacy and I faked tenderness. I really wanted a lasting relationship, but I kept jumping from bed to bed. I knew—oh, boy, I knew—that I was just being selfish, proving myself. But I wasn't satisfied. And once you prove you aren't so ugly or unappealing, that someone will make love with you, how many more times do you have to prove it?

"Finally, I got so sick of myself that I had to leave that life. It took a year. I lived almost like a hermit. And then it was clear. I married again, and today we have a great life and wonderful kids. I look back on those days, and I don't even know who that person was."

—BILL WILSON*

"It was the 1970s and the sexual revolution was at hand. At the beginning, when I became sexually active I felt guilty. I'm Catholic, after all. But I gradually became aware of both how powerful sex can be, and how a person can honor it or cheapen it, depending on the circumstances. Now that I have children, I want to tell them how precious it is, regardless of how powerful it is. I don't think you understand that when you're young."

—PRISCILLA RADEN★

"My marriage was over, and I found this wonderful boyfriend. We tried to hide our sex lives from my kids, shuttling back and forth. Finally, I took my kids aside and said, 'Is this going to be offensive to you?' And they asked, 'Is this going to make you happy?' I said yes, it would. They were great; they weren't casting a moral judgment. But I think it was a responsible act for me, reasonable and decent. He was the second man I had ever slept with in my life. I don't think that's a bad average. Even as I walked through the bedroom door with that man, I was still setting an example for my kids."

—LATICE NULAND★

Speaking for Generation X Catholics, now in their twenties and thirties, Catherine Walsh noted in *America* magazine that they were the first

". . . to experience full the freedom and the perils of the sexual revolution. The sexual repression of an earlier era, overthrown by the previous generation with abandon, has not been part of our experience. Our task has been learning to deal with sexual freedom, not repression. It's grappling with how and when to draw the line sexually. . . . We have some grounding in church teaching about what is right and wrong about sex. . . . But we're basically making up the script as we go along. . . . Is all premarital sex always a sin? Isn't there a difference in the morality of intercourse among uncommitted high school kids and a couple in their 30s who are engaged?"[7]

I wouldn't expect the single Good Enough Catholic to carry a checklist around, but let me offer for reflection seven values of human sexuality. This is not science. If life itself is sometimes a walk in the fog, finding our way along a moral path in our sex lives will require an ever stronger radar. These seven values are at least a start; they spring from a constantly developing Catholic position on sexuality, a Catholicism that has much to offer a culture whose outlook on sexual fulfillment too often results in hollow loneliness.

## Seven Values of the Creative and Integrative Sex Act

We can get at these core values by asking a series of questions about any given sexual act. Is it:

1. Self-liberating?
2. Other-enriching?
3. Honest?
4. Faithful?
5. Socially responsible?
6. Life-serving?
7. Joyous?

Those guidelines were drawn up by no less an authoritative body than the Catholic Theological Society of America.

Perhaps Julie Clague's words best sum up the Good Enough Catholic's approach: "Sexual relationships should be judged according to the same criteria as other human relationships. When our sex lives are dishonest, unloving, unfaithful or unforgiving, when we break our promises or do harm, we have failed. Our response should be to admit it, make reparation and start anew."[8]

# SEX WITHIN MARRIAGE

The seven points certainly speak to unmarried couples; but sex within marriage has many more implications and consequences. Sex in marriage provides moments of profound and precious intimacy within a life no longer adorned with the baubles and bangles of courting. Sex provides an opportunity for recommitment, to relive the excitement that first propelled you into marriage.

The church and marriage experts concur: sex must never be treated lightly or used to control. It is not a commodity to withhold or barter. Contrary to the way it was regarded (or disregarded) in the church not that long ago, sex need not be proceedings to hide away and be ashamed of. You are having an encounter with a lover who is your friend; you can talk about it. Contrary to what you may have been taught, this subject is not taboo. You can be playful. With matrimony, it is your right.

Married sex may not always be carried forth with the velocity and gnawing hunger of the days before a couple was pronounced husband and wife. But unlike sex with a person to whom you have not committed yourself and your life, it grows more intimate through the years. Intimacy with a person whose mind and heart you know as well as their body is just another one of the graces that radiate from the marriage commitment. It is sacred; it can be wonderful. Sexual urges that had to be controlled are, in marriage, given an opportunity for unfettered expression. Holy and healthy, this is exactly what the sex drive was meant to be. It was fashioned to overwhelm you, to be so powerful as to demand ocean voyages, precious spices, and perfumes; powerful enough to cause our hearts to be closed to all but one in all the human race.

# BIRTH CONTROL:
# REVELATIONS AND RESPONSIBILITY

In the afterglow of Vatican II—whose documents had, among other ground-breaking departures, elevated human intimacy between the married couple to co-equal status with the procreative aspects of sex—a much-heralded commission was called into being by Pope Paul VI. Called the Pontifical Commission for the Study of Population, Family, and Birth, one of its primary tasks was to take a comprehensive look at the church's stand on birth control in light of modern science and human experience. Birth control had been considered too complex and too volatile to be dealt with authoritatively during the council.

The commission itself was a model of new openness that Vatican II had fostered. Moral theologians and married couples, cardinals and gynecologists met in a series of closed sessions over eighteen months.

Married Catholics up to this time had been bound, under the pain of mortal sin, not to use any artificial means to thwart conception; they had been taught that *every* sex act had to be, in those unequivocal words of church doctrine, "open to the possibility of procreation." The "rhythm method," or (as it was eventually called) "natural family planning"—the only means of restricting family size or otherwise spacing the births of children the church recognized as morally acceptable—was predicated on intercourse being limited to the nonfertile times of the menstrual cycle. The bedside thermometer and a precisely kept calendar of menstruation were often the determinants of sexual activity. "Love by the calendar" was both the joke and the bane of Catholic married life as sincere, obedient couples tried to live by the teachings of the church.

Although St. Augustine, often cited to undergird church teachings about birth control, had actually rejected sexual abstinence in fertile periods as in itself immoral, twentieth-century Catholic theologians embraced such an approach as morally acceptable. But it was not only such theological inconsistencies in the church's stand on birth control that brought about the pontifical commission. Birth rates were exploding across the globe; medical advances were saving millions of lives that once would have been lost to disease; women were being emancipated; and the length and expense of children's formal education continued to grow. Reproductive biology was no longer the mystery it had so recently been. With healthy males producing billions of sperm in a lifetime and healthy women having to deal with the hundreds of viable eggs that would course through their reproductive systems, with huge families simply no longer sustainable in much of the world, the birth equation had changed, and changed drastically, in just a few generations.

It was my privilege to know one of the married couples who served on the pontifical commission. Pat and Patty Crowley of Chicago are extraordinary people and exemplary Catholics— joyous, generous, outgoing folks. They are the founders of the Christian Family Movement, the parents of five children, who gave generously of their time and resources to the church they loved. For the commission, they summarized the results of their survey of 3,000 devout Catholic couples from eighteen countries, all of whom had practiced the rhythm method. The Crowleys wanted to find out whether the church's teaching on birth control had hurt marriages, as they suspected, or enhanced them, as the Vatican maintained.

Here is their summary:

> *Does rhythm have a bad psychological effect?* Almost without exception, the responses were, yes, it does.
>
> *Does rhythm serve any useful purpose at all?* A few say it may be useful for developing discipline. Nobody says that it fosters married love.
>
> *Does it contribute to married unity?* No. That is the inescapable conclusion of the reports we have received. In marriage a husband and wife pledge themselves to become one in mind, heart, and affection. They are no longer two, but one flesh. Some wonder whether God would have us cultivate such unity by using what seems to them such an unnatural system. . . . Instead of love, rhythm tends to substitute tension, dissatisfaction, frustration, and disunity.
>
> *Is rhythm unnatural?* Yes—that's the conclusion of these reports. Over and over, directly and indirectly, men and women— and perhaps especially women—voice the conviction that the physical and psychological implications of rhythm are not understood by the male church.[9]

In a memorable exchange, a Spanish Jesuit, one Father Zalba, confronted Patty Crowley with the imbroglio that would result if her findings were allowed to alter church teaching. "What then with millions we have sent to hell, if these norms were not valid?" he fumed. Unfazed, Mrs. Crowley replied, "Father Zalba, do you really believe God has carried out all your orders?"[10]

Finally, the commission forwarded its report to the pope. Excitement within Catholicism grew when word leaked out that the vast majority of the commission's members—by a margin of fifty-four to four—were recommending that the church modify its strict ban against the use of such artificial birth control devices as the condom, the diaphragm, and the new, revolutionary oral contraceptive—the pill.

The long-awaited papal encyclical *Humanae Vitae* ("Of Human Life") was ultimately released in 1968. The document was almost lyrical in its affirmation of sexual intimacy as good and necessary to a happy married life. But as the text continued, it was soon evident that the pope and the drafters of the encyclical had disregarded the expert opinion of the commission—as well as the experience of most married couples. *Humanae Vitae* reconfirmed the church's stand, starkly condemning any means of artificial birth control as nothing less than acts "against the will of God." Those who used or advocated the use of such birth control methods committed such a grievous sin that they could be excommunicated and condemned to eternal damnation in hell.

It is church teaching that encyclicals are, in essence, the word of God. "He who hears you"—that is, the pope—"hears me," is the theological imperative of these documents. In the pre–Vatican II church, such a proclamation—regardless of the continuing difficulty Catholics might have in adhering to it—would have been either stoically obeyed or quietly disregarded. Instead, *Humanae Vitae* created a cataclysmic fault line in Catholicism, an open rebellion against papal authority that continues to this day.

If the intention among Vatican advisers who influenced Pope Paul VI's decree was to reassert papal authority and reaffirm the incontestability of the church's teaching magesterium over a morally rudderless flock, *Humanae Vitae* had precisely the opposite effect. A church that had not listened to its people on this crucial issue was not a church that millions of Catholics around the world would henceforth be willing to heed. Horror stories abounded: poverty-stricken mothers with already large families begging for a reprieve; women who had nearly died in childbirth being told they were forbidden to do anything that would prevent the next, almost certainly fatal, conception. Study after study has shown that *Humanae Vitae* stands as one of the least-obeyed church teachings of modern times—and possibly of all time. American Catholics went on to use artificial birth control measures, and today use them as frequently and as routinely as the population at large.

In the more than quarter century since *Humanae Vitae* reaffirmed the church's stand, those who have sought to defend its teachings have often linked birth control to irresponsible sexual behavior; contraception has been condemned as "monstrous selfishness." Most thinking Catholics, however, have come to hold a different view—that responsible birth control and responsible sexual behavior are really two separate issues.

# LIFE DECISIONS

It is logically true that both natural family planning (the rhythm method) and artificial birth control "directly intend to modify the statistical relationship nature places between insemination and conception."[11] The brilliant Jesuit theologian Bernard Longergan wrote those words in frustration some years after *Humanae Vitae*, to make the point that either a deliberate effort to interfere with the insemination process is moral, or it is not. If it is, the use of a thin membrane of latex is morally no different than the use of a thin piece of calendar paper on which the march of a menstrual cycle is recorded. If you agree with Aristotle, on the other hand, that each sperm is a tiny human being—and therefore must in no way be frustrated on its journey to the nutritive womb—you cannot believe in any form of controlling the process. You can even find yourself in the absurd position of arguing that masturbation is murder. The Good Enough Catholic—while perhaps not carrying a degree in reproductive biology, but knowing that insemination and conception are quite distinct, and that an egg is also part of the picture—must part company with the great philosopher on this one.

While I don't think it's necessary to belabor the point that the vast majority of Catholics do not abide by the Church's teaching on birth control, there are still a significant number who are haunted by their seeming disobedience. They ask the question: Can I still be in the church and receive the sacraments while practicing birth control?

There is a significant body of theological thought, as well as mountains of pastoral experience, to support you in a resounding "yes."

This said, the Good Enough Catholic must still regard every sexual act as having the *possibility* of procreation. This is not a return to old Catholic guilt, holding over your head the threat of an eternity roasting in hell. It is a practical consideration that cannot be avoided. Quite simply, every sexual act, barring true sterility, *could* lead to conception. And, as we will discuss in the next section, abortion cannot be regarded as a backstop for those who would treat this great power casually.

So it seems to me that if you are not married, and you have in good conscience made the decision to have sexual relations but do not want to have children, you must, both morally and practically, use some form of birth control. (In the age of AIDS, "safe sex" is also, of course, a real consideration; but an even larger issue is the potential that you are dealing with the possible creation of another life.) Birth control—the pill, a condom, contraceptive foam, whatever form it takes—says you respect life so much that you would not carelessly take the chance of creating a child you are not ready to nurture as a parent. Your sexual act remains an act of human intimacy—a value in itself—but not a pathway to procreation.

As for married couples, conscious use of birth control shows that both of you want to preserve and enhance the unifying power of a healthy and spontaneous sex life—without having to stingily apportion your love-making. Spacing your children shows that you look at your family as a whole. You realize that begetting a child is but one aspect of procreation. Raising a child goes on for years, not moments. You respect yourself and your spouse, as well as the children

THE GOOD ENOUGH CATHOLIC

you may already have. You want to be ready and able to care for each child you may be blessed with. You want to be as physically and mentally strong as you can be; you want to be able to give your spouse and your children what you can materially, emotionally, and spiritually. If there are circumstances in which conceiving another child would be detrimental to the good of the children already born, then you need to respect those lives already in existence.

Family planning has become an even more complicated situation today for the many two-career Catholic couples. But as discussed in chapter 6, although work is crucially important—after all, it is a vocation—it must not rule your life. Children planned to arrive merely at the convenience of their upwardly mobile parents indicate skewed priorities. If that happens, something is sadly missing in a marriage. If you must have the promotion, house, or sizable bank account first, if you must immediately return to work and subcontract the rearing of that infant to someone else, you have already made your priorities clear. If children, the sweetest fruit of married love, are instead only its side effect, the children will most likely be far from the center of their parents' minds as the years speed by.

After all this discussion about responsible birth control, let us end by reminding ourselves that the birth of a child is not always a matter of choice. The wind blows where it will, and sperm and egg conspire to meet up at what may seem some of the least opportune times in life. Even with all your conscious family planning, leave room for chance. My mother—decidedly a pre–Vatican II lady—had seven of us; she wouldn't have considered birth control. She always maintained that God will provide. She was right; he did, and he will. Faith plays a key role in conceiving and in raising children. But for Good Enough Catholics, common sense has a place, too.

"I believe in *life control*, as opposed to birth control. Abstinence is best, but some of my girls here in this Catholic high school aren't going to stay with that. I give them all the information they need to make a decision. To me, God always gives us a choice, chances. I think we have to look at the church's teachings, look at our own lives, and come to an informed decision."

—VANESSA COOKE

"I am absolutely, unremittingly pro-life. I don't think pro-life and pro-choice people should be in the same church. You can be a pro-choice person and be a lot of things, but one of them is not Catholic. As for birth control, yes, we have used it. That is a matter of conscience, not a matter of life and death."

—WILLIAM CORBIN*

"We are trying natural birth control and when we are having a hard time with it, we say the rosary together. Catholicism is a lifestyle, and there are rules. That's okay. I think sometimes we need rules. We actually feel better when we are practicing natural birth control—we are doing it for Jesus and we know that he's with us. When we cheat, yes, I feel bad. But it's never a case of saying 'I've sinned and now Jesus hates me.' He loves us all the time, and if we make sacrifices for him, I think he's with us even more. It makes us stronger as a couple."

—BETTY TORRES

# ABORTION

Non-Catholics may not realize that even the sound of this word—abortion—sends chills through Catholics. Those of us who went through Catholic schools remember that whenever it was mentioned—which was not often, for the weight of the word was so great and its impact so onerous—it was uttered in a hushed tone, as if even its use would contaminate the speaker. It is a word that drips with evil and death. Little wonder that the debate over the legality and morality of abortion is especially charged for Catholics.

Pro-life; pro-choice. The battle lines have been drawn, with each side seemingly unwilling to listen to the other. We'll work our way through this very difficult issue, but let us start with one area of agreement.

No one is *pro*-abortion.

No one—not the woman (or more often young girl) who has an abortion, not her mate, not the members of her family, and not her friends—looks upon abortion as something good. It might be considered necessary, or looked upon as the lesser of two evils; but it is never *good*. Of course, I was raised Catholic; but I seriously doubt that any girl or woman has ever walked blissfully into an abortion clinic, undergone an abortion, and walked out feeling simply wonderful. Relieved, perhaps; but there is often a profound sense of sadness, often a sadness that is never quite erased.

Abortion is a terribly serious act, and no thinking person can go through it and not be affected. In the earliest stages, tiny cells are being preempted in their ingenious scheme of combining, mutating, and growing as they seek to form a new life. As a pregnancy continues, a definable physical form is being removed from the only place that can sustain it. So it is understandable that the Catholic Church—and indeed every major religion—has historically taken a firm stand against abortion. And it is understandable that there is a continuing moral repugnance against abortion in the population at large.

For the Good Enough Catholic to make a sensible and moral judgment on this confusing and often immediate dilemma, it's necessary to trace the historical development of the church's thinking and teaching on abortion. We need to know how the understanding of the conception and development of life, and the perceived presence of a soul within that life, has evolved over the centuries.

## The Mystery of New Life

Some maintain that the church's stand on abortion has been consistent down through the centuries. That is hardly the case. For centuries, the church based its doctrine on Aristotle's *De generatione animalium*, which maintained (wrongly, it turns out) that each male seed contained a life, needing only the nutrition of the womb to thrive. A distinction was later made in the early church between a formed and unformed fetus—although such terms were being used at a time when precious little was actually known about the reproductive system. Both St. Jerome (d. 420) and St. Augustine, two of the earliest writers on this issue, taught that abortion was homicide and grievously sinful, but only when the bodily elements had come together to form a fetus. The ideas of the "unensouled fetus" and the "ensouled fetus" differentiated between what was considered only matter, and matter infused with an immortal soul. In 1713, a decree of the Holy Office actually forbade the baptism of a spontaneously aborted (that is, miscarried) fetus if there was no reasonable foundation that it was "animated by a rational soul." Thus it is apparent that the church has not always considered these early forms of life capable of having a soul.

As more was discovered about reproduction—including, in 1827, the presence of the ovum, or egg—Catholic teaching changed in response. The distinction between the ensouled and unensouled fetus was removed from Catholic canon law in 1869. Faced with a continuing stream of revolutionary scientific information, the church, perhaps in frustration, finally opted out of the abortion debate. A new understanding was proclaimed: The soul was infused at the very moment of conception, the church pronounced (although we now know conception is not accomplished in a moment at all); doing anything to frustrate that process of conception, or the attendant growth of a fetus, was akin to murder.

While no one was able to prove or disprove the precise moment at which the soul was actually infused, the church invoked a traditional posture of Catholic moral theology—that one may never act in the presence of doubt. Of course, doubt is present in many of life's decisions; but here the church stood firm upon its authority, claiming that human life was too precious to be tampered with in the face of uncertainty. Vatican II's *Gaudium et Spes* condemned abortion as an "abominable crime." Indeed, the church has stood firm on all reproductive matters, not only condemning artificial birth control (as we have seen), but opposing as well any pregnancy terminated—from RU-486, the so-called morning after pill, to outright abortion—regardless of the circumstances of conception.

There has, of course, been considerable debate on these points. From a purely biological point of view, Catholic thinkers and moral theologians have pointed out that, first of all, conception is not an instantaneous occurrence; it takes place over a period of days. Fertilization itself takes twenty-four hours. Furthermore, in the earliest days of a pregnancy, the zygote can still be subdivided; twins are not formed until about the fourteenth day. As a soul cannot be subdivided, how is it possible that there be a soul present at that juncture? Human cells are present, but they lack the structure of a human organism. True human life is only recognizable at about three weeks, and primitive brain function does not begin until about the eighth week.

Regardless of these biological facts, the Catholic Church has not only stood firm—forbidding Catholics, under pain of mortal sin, from advocating or having an abortion—but has mounted an unprecedented public campaign to ban abortions in America and the rest of the world. In consequence, abortion has been a sadly divisive issue in the church, pitting good people against good people. Certain Catholic theologians and politicians have been banned from speaking at Catholic institutions, threatened with excommunication, and reviled for their willingness to even discuss the issue openly. The staunchest pro-life and pro-choice advocates demand 100 percent acceptance of their point of view, leaving no room for debate or compromise. For the most committed, the only legitimate objective is converting the other side—and, indeed, the whole public debate—to their way of thinking.

This bold effort by the Catholic Church to influence both public opinion and the law has not only been divisive, it has been counterproductive. The church's unyielding call to make abortions illegal has actually increased public support for a woman's right to choose whether or not she will have an abortion. It appears that the church can no longer use its moral authority as a bully pulpit when addressing an increasingly independently minded laity.

It is not that the Good Enough Catholic can't easily see both sides of the abortion debate. Wanton murder of fetuses is a sickening prospect. But dissent against "ossification of doctrines" and "temptations of ideologies"[12]—words of the eminent theologian Bernard Haring—must also be heard. For the Good Enough Catholic, there is an enormous personal, physical, and moral range between the termination of a pregnancy that risks killing the mother, or bringing forth a severely malformed baby, and a pregnancy that will yield a child of a gender other than what the parents had hoped for. It might be helpful to discuss some of the different situations that present themselves.

First, consider tubal pregnancy or a pregnancy at the onset of serious disease—say, a cancer of the uterus, which, if not removed, may be fatal to the pregnant woman. More and more Catholic theologians—as well as Catholics at large—no longer hold the unyielding view that a woman should face devastating physical harm or possible death rather than have her pregnancy terminated. They see this as clearly a case of choosing the lesser of two evils—in this instance, sacrificing the fetus in order to save the woman's life.

Then come a second tier of problem pregnancies, those resulting from rape or incest. These are not conceptions resulting from mutual love, or anything resembling mutual passion. There was no intent of procreation; there was neither consent nor any semblance of intimacy. These are pregnancies that constitute perhaps the starkest invasion of a woman's body. For not only is such a pregnancy an unspeakable burden for a woman or young girl to carry, but how can she be expected to love and nurture a child that is the product of such a heinous act? Is this not too much to ask of that woman, and too great a burden to inflict upon that child?

In both of these situations, it's important not to scurry to our ideological corners simply to proclaim what we know what is the "right" course of action. Rather, the position of the Good Enough Catholic is to look at all the circumstances. Even in cases where a woman appears likely to die if her pregnancy continues, or has become pregnant after a brutal rape, it is never possible to categorically say this pregnancy must end or that one must continue. This is a time for prayer, for seeking God's guidance; it is a time to ask for the gift of discernment (as discussed in chapter 4) to make a good decision.

As Good Enough Catholics—conflicted and imperfect as we are—we struggle for the faith that God will provide an answer if we are both bold enough and humble enough to ask him. For God's grace is more encompassing than human or scientific knowledge, more wise than volumes of moral theology, more profound than our deepest thoughts. God is a loving father who wishes us to be happy; he gives us the wisdom to find our way through the worst times in our lives. He cares deeply about us, regardless of the decisions we make. We are never outside the love or grace of God; and we can make even the most agonizing decisions in our lives certain of his acceptance.

## The Education of One Catholic

A more difficult decision, one that presents itself far more frequently, is that of an unintended pregnancy—one where no force has been used, and the woman's life is not in danger. Most often, a young (statistically, the average age is 18.6), unmarried woman is involved. Viewed in the abstract—given our individual pro-life or pro-choice orientation—such decisions might seem easy to make. But for many of us, myself included, it is a much different situation when actually faced with a real person and a real pregnancy.

I grew up at a time when abortions were virtually unheard of (not that they weren't happening), and I could never imagine being part of such a heinous act. But then, like many people in the 1970s, I began to examine my once-categorical opposition to abortion as I saw how unwanted pregnancies visited heartache and grinding poverty upon poor families, both in developing nations and here in the United States. Even so, mine were all theoretical judgments—until one afternoon in Brooklyn, when a teary-eyed girl walked through the front door of the makeshift social service center and soup kitchen where I was volunteering at the time.

Alycia,* a fifteen-year-old Puerto Rican girl, sobbed as she told me she was pregnant. I knew Alycia well; she was a bright, deter-mined girl who had hoped to go on to college and break the cycle of poverty into which she had been born. I knew that if she had this child her life would instead more likely follow the well-worn path already trod by her mother and so many of her young friends. All of them were single mothers, poor, and living on the margins of society.

Alycia was despondent. What should she do? What could she do?

I was amazed with the quickness of my advice, which I offered to her the next day. By the end of the next week, I was driving her and her young boyfriend to an abortion clinic. I felt I was doing her a great service. I had rescued her; I had been the supportive parent she needed, and lacked, at a crucial juncture in her life.

I thought about that categorical decision many years later in a dark sonogram room, as a technician passed an electronic wand over my wife's slightly swollen stomach. On the screen were the shad-owy outlines of our first child—then only a months-old fetus, but an unmistakable human being nonetheless, with legs and fingers and eye sockets. My mind went back to Alycia. And suddenly I wasn't so sure I had helped her.

Did I present Alycia with other possibilities—like adoption—and offer to help her through the months of her pregnancy? Exactly how pregnant was she? What did that fetus look like? Was it as developed as the child I was seeing on the screen? What became of Alycia? Did that abortion change her life—and, if so, for better or worse? Did she go on to college—or on to a string of unwanted pregnancies by men she would never marry? Where was she today?

My position on abortion had slowly moved from the traditional Catholic stance inculcated by seventeen years of Catholic education to one I had considered both compassionate and realistic, and cer-tainly enlightened. But in that sonogram room, it was suddenly wrenched back to a point somewhere in between. No, I could never go back to the unbending stance of my church; but neither would I ever again be able to so blithely assist another person in ter-minating a pregnancy.

I'm sure my experience is hardly unique. Many Catholics are struggling to find an approach to the abortion issue that is both moral and sensible. Knowing the sheer biology of reproduction, I would venture a guess that a good many Good Enough Catholics would not have grave difficulty accepting the use of a "morning after" contraceptive like RU–486, which stops the development of what is then a small gathering of cells. Others will see as reasonable the termination of a pregnancy that threatens the mother's life, or would result in a profoundly deformed infant whose life was not sustainable. And still others would advocate ending a pregnancy that resulted from rape or incest.

Beyond these, however, there remains the rest of the problem of unwanted pregnancies, the vast majority—and these require considerably more contemplation and divine guidance.

The Good Enough Catholic can be bold enough to ask, along with today's moral theologians, ethicists, and pregnant women who wrestle with these difficult issues: Does God seek every life, regardless of the circumstances and the human cost? A person can, with the highest of moral standards, see this as a life-and-death, black-and-white, question; or, with equally high moral standards, see a continuum colored by vastly varying circumstances.

In addition to birth, we must also consider the life thereafter. There are some 1.5 million abortions each year in the United States. For whatever reasons—the highest or the most base—they are unwanted children. Would we be condemning these infants to a world of unremitting financial or emotional poverty, or to living in homes surrounded by outright pathology? Can we keep alive, by the brilliance of modern medical science, fetuses and infants who will never think or live as anything resembling a human being? For ethicist Father Robert Springer, it comes down to this question: "How great a value must be present to countervail the sacrifice of life?"[13] Or as Father Brian Jordan, who has counseled many poor and indigent women in his Maryland parish, has concluded: "I'm pro-life. But I'm also pro-person. You have to listen to every story."

The church has also instituted a program to reach out to women who have had abortions. Called Project Rachel, it now exists in over a hundred dioceses across America. Project Rachel helps women who feel guilty, depressed, and even outside the church

after their abortion, making it clear that there is no sin that can separate us from the love of God.

## Other Roads, as Yet Untraveled

There are certainly options other than having an abortion or bringing a child into an unstable, unsupported life. There are thousands
upon thousands of childless couples who seek desperately to adopt
a baby and cannot find one. Can't we somehow make it easier
for a woman to carry her baby to term, so that the child could
be welcomed into a home that yearns for it? It does not do enough
to picket abortion clinics. The violence, hatefulness, and self-
righteousness of some protesters have indelibly stained a movement
whose professed concern is respect for life.

If we are serious about these possible lives, even more must be
done to help these usually young and unwed girls and women
through their pregnancies. Then we must help them to both celebrate the birth and grieve the loss of an infant—perhaps, most important, by helping them feel sure that they are sending their child
on to a more promising life.

If the Good Enough Catholic comes to a point that abortion is a
possibility, then where and how will the line be drawn? Use of the
morning-after pill? Is a first trimester abortion acceptable, but a second trimester abortion out of the question? Does the risk of a
deformed child justify an abortion? How deformed?

Each pregnancy is a unique encounter with both the divine presence and the existential realities of life. Abortion must never be
looked upon as a convenience procedure; the potential life must be
respected and protected. But so must a woman's right over her body
be acknowledged. The point for the Good Enough Catholic is that
neither respect for the unborn nor respect for a woman's right to an
abortion can be viewed as categorical or unequivocal. We do not
allow men and women to abuse their children; neither must they be
sanctioned to arbitrarily abuse their reproductive systems.

Although the Catholic Church has sought to suppress debate on
the abortion issue and to punish those who do not agree with its

stand, the Good Enough Catholic has a unique contribution to make in this often polarized debate. We can be first to put away the language of absolutes. We can seek common ground, not conquest. We can be the people in the middle—the uncomfortable middle— looking to the highest ideals, but always ready to see and hear the human beings involved. Our mandate is love and justice, not law and necessity.

All those who have gone through an abortion or contemplate one will not find us simply turning away. We are loved by God in the decisions we make in our lives—and so are they. To accept and love them as instruments of God's love is the least we can do. They have suffered enough already.

"No young woman who has come to me talking about an abortion has done it without great pain and reflection. My important job is just to listen to them. They must make the decision. None of them come out of the abortion clinic the same person. But they know their lives are going to be ruined by having a child. Do I mask the fact that I'm Catholic when I help girls who go to an abortion clinic? No, I don't. I'm a Catholic in that abortion clinic and I'm a Catholic when I'm in church on Sunday."

—JOAN SULLIVAN

"Perhaps with the abortion issue, we are fighting Prohibition all over again. Or, we'll find the pro-life people were right and this is profoundly wrong. I, personally, am pro-life, but I think the Catholic Church is advocating the writing of laws that are unenforceable. By definition, preventing abortion is not enforceable, so why are we doing it? Besides, if we outlaw abortion, do we go back to the coat hangers and back alley abortions?"

—JOHN FIALKA

"I was pregnant, my marriage wasn't going to last, I had no job, no health insurance. I called the abortion clinic. But I couldn't take this baby's life just because of those things. Somehow, I was led to a new life of faith; I really understood what faith was. And I passed the bar exam, a job came through. It all worked out. I have this beautiful child because I made faith a real part of my life."

—MAGALIE SALAS

"I can't preach to people about anything, certainly not abortion, when I'm not in their shoes."

—MARIELSA BERNARD

"I worked with a retarded woman with cystic fibrosis who had two spina bifida kids. She became pregnant by another retarded man. They even talked of marrying. Of course, this would have never worked out. Yes, this fetus mattered, but what about the other kids and the woman herself? How was she going to cope with this? I think it's selfish to keep a child when you can't take care of it. As I think it would be selfish to abort a child you really could care for. Selfishness is the key when you look at the whole abortion issue. I did take her to the hospital to have the abortion. That was a moral decision on my part."

—MARY ANNE BARRY

# THE GOOD ENOUGH CATHOLIC CHALLENGE: ONE ACT OF LOVE

We have spent much time discussing sex, its manifestations, and its ramifications. So, let's put sex aside for now, and talk of love.

For love is not only the ubiquitous "answer," it is both the essence of Christ's message and the foundation of a fulfilling sexual relationship.

Let's focus on practicing love in the most real sense. Let us put love in its proper place—first. Let us transform what might be simply ordinary into something extraordinary. Again, the Good Enough Catholic does not promise a total transformation, but simply starts with a single act.

If you are married, make your next sexual act an act first of love. Let there be no sexual encounter that is not preceded by a display of love. You and your partner know how to do this, each in your own unique way. It can be simple; it can be grand. It might be flowers or a foot massage, or simply turning down the sheets at night and lighting a candle in your bedroom. Hiring the babysitter and taking a night for a romantic movie. Singing a favorite song from your courting days. Looking tenderly into your spouse's face and saying, "I love you."

Then let human love take you where it will. Follow the dictates, both the gentle urges and the absolute demands of love. And let divine love flow through you. This is wonderful, sensual, and holy. Here is an opportunity, through this powerful force, for a recommitment to that person to whom you pledged your love, whether many years ago, or just recently.

You are waiting to be loved. Here, for this one time, you can present love as a gift to your spouse, love as an invitation.

For unmarried Good Enough Catholics, your challenge is a little different. Experience the presence of love before its expression. You know the difference between transient lust and the feeling of transcendent love. Wait for that moment. Wait for someone you want to love.

# SELECTED READINGS

John F. Dedak, *Contemporary Medical Ethics*. New York: Sheed and Ward, 1975.

Bernard Haring, *Free and Faithful in Christ*, vol. 1 (*General Moral Theology*). New York: Seabury, 1978.

Pat King, ed., *Catholic Women and Abortion: Stories of Healing*. Kansas City, Mo.: Sheed and Ward, 1994,.

John Korte, *Simple Gifts: The Lives of Pat and Patty Crowley*. Kansas City, Mo.: Andrews and McMeel, 1979.

*New Catholic Encyclopedia*, vol. 17 ("Supplement: Change in the Church"). Washington, D.C.: Publisher's Guild, 1988.

# ❧ PART III ❧

# LIFE WITH OTHERS

*We walk in many worlds. Each has a profound effect on us; but so often we feel we can do so little to affect them. But of course, that isn't true. Each of those worlds is made up of individuals, just like us. Each person is an integral part.*

*We need a parish, a home for the Spirit (chapter 9), to nurture, enlighten, and encourage—but also to confront us with ourselves. We are individuals—no more, no less—but we are also social beings. Our most intimate community, the family (chapter 10) is our most precious gift—and greatest challenge. Here is our "domestic church," God's first dwelling place among his people. And then as we approach community life (chapter 11), we can see that our daily actions profoundly shape the many other groups of which we are part.*

# CHAPTER NINE

# PARISH
## A Home for the Spirit

It is extraordinarily difficult to sustain any commitment alone. Experience has proved this to all of us; modern sociology and psychology, echoing the tenets of ancient wisdom, proclaim it over and over again. The encouragement and companionship found in a group like Alcoholics Anonymous, teamwork on our jobs, or the support of a spouse or good friends when times are tough—each point to our need to know that we do not stand alone as we strive to accomplish something in our lives.

As Good Enough Catholics, we, too, need to know that we are not alone or aberrant in trying to live a religious, moral life in the midst of a world that often differs, condoning—even rewarding—lesser alternatives. We need to see other faces and sense other souls attuned not only to the competitive roar of the marketplace, but also to the gentle murmurings of our souls. We need a place we can return to as our moral base of operations, a place where we might be spiritually fed.

For Catholics, this has traditionally been the geographical parish. It was simple: our street address dictated the location of our spiritual home.

Some Catholics look back fondly to the geographical parish of their youth as the place where their early religious life was nurtured. For them, the parish was the active center of both religious and social events, a bustling place staffed by priests and nuns who educated and inspired them. Still other Catholics remember punitive nuns and unforgiving, small-minded priests, who littered their young lives with a veritable minefield of moral offenses and constantly harangued their parents to put more money in the collection basket.

In today's Catholic Church, the range among geographical parishes is equally wide—some are open, inviting communities with Vatican II dynamism; some are uninspired places of strict orthodoxy that see eternal damnation in every birth control device, and a pilgrim unworthy of spiritual food if the spouse next to them in the pew isn't their first. These parish experiences—good or bad, past or present—can keep us from seeing what has emerged in the Catholic Church as a new understanding of where we might find our place of spiritual mooring.

The day is past when Catholics were expected to proceed obediently to their geographical parish, where they were expected to tolerate bad liturgy or bad theology. Allowing such soul-killing would be an outrage for any person interested in nurturing a spiritual self, let alone a Good Enough Catholic. If you are concerned about seeing clearly, you do not put up with a barely tolerable pair of glasses. If you embark on a journey by foot, you don't begin by putting stones in your shoes. Why should the Good Enough Catholic be forced to seek nourishment for a spiritual life within a parish that actually impedes or stifles spiritual awareness and growth?

The Good Enough Catholic requires a Good Enough Spiritual Home. And today there are many, many ways that Catholics can come together for worship, reflection, and mutual support. Catholicism has both innovated with fresh, new approaches, and reclaimed a rich tradition from the earliest gatherings of those who sought to follow the way of Jesus Christ.

# COMMUNITY TO PARISH. . . .

In the days of the apostles and during the first centuries of the early church, small groups of believers, mostly in more densely populated areas, gathered together to share memories of Christ, to listen to others who knew him, and to share the Eucharistic meal as he had bid them do. An integral part of these primitive services was the confession of sins and settling of differences among the community members. It was considered crucial that reconciliation take place, that peace be a part of their time together—so that they, in turn, might bring that same spirit into their daily lives.

Some of these first Christians took enormous leaps of faith, answering the gospel invitation to live and share everything in common, and to boldly spread the word. A far greater number of early Christians lived normal family lives; while quietly going about their daily work, regularly and clandestinely gathered together in each other's homes on the Lord's day to worship and be educated as a community of believers. Their new religious pursuit was demanding and potentially dangerous, set as it was within a prevailing pagan and secular culture. While they could not live as lilies of the field, they knew that without mutual support and contact with like-minded people, they would not be able to carry on in their belief. When their faith was weak, the faith of others was strong enough to shore them up. When they had physical needs, the other believers came to their assistance. It was a grace-filled, religiously based support system and it worked remarkably well.

The early bishops, elected from among them, were their first pastors; and, as believers spread from centers of population to more rural areas, lay leaders (called presbyters) were appointed to preside at the breaking of the bread in these fledgling communities. Their daily or weekly rounds completed, these presbyters returned to the bishop's house, where they—and the bishop—lived with their families. Gradually, under the supervision of the early bishops, and led by the bishop of Rome (who would eventually be called the pope), boundaries delineating dioceses were drawn along the only lines that they knew—the map of the Roman Empire—so that communities within and those appointed to serve them could function in a more organized way.

When, after the conversion of the emperor Constantine (d. 337), the church was granted certain lands and properties to continue its work, Christian communities and, in effect, the first parishes, gained a new prominence. No longer did they have to operate clandestinely; now worship could safely take place in the open, and many parishes enjoyed substantial holdings. Wealthy families in feudal times, and well into the Middle Ages, considered parishes established on their land a valuable and important asset. After all, important religious rituals took place in the churches they had built and would graciously attend. They felt they were providing a valuable service: entree to eternal life. They considered the handsome income generated from church-related lands and labor to be theirs. The priest was looked upon as no more and no less than one of their servants; they chose him, gave him a pittance, and, as they did with the rest of their serfs, kept the rest of his harvest for themselves.

Temporal rulers and the princes of the church fought back and forth over who would control both the parishes and the priests within them. Monasteries also eventually came to control huge areas of land. While the structure of the parish as we know it today was still not in place, and there were many abuses of the simple faith of common folk, these were centuries of soaring holiness. Christ's message resonated throughout a world in which few had much, and most barely survived. The Christian way transcended the inequities and hazards of daily life. The mass was a powerful symbol of Christ's presence among the people; the Eucharist, a sustaining spiritual food. The message of love and peace that had resonated so deeply within the souls of the early Christians continued to spread throughout the known world. No longer characterized by tightly knit faith communities, Christianity had become the faith of the masses. But it was a faith still searching for a structure within which ordinary people—not only monks in their monasteries, or the formally ordained religious— could live out in the world.

With the historic Council of Trent, the parish system was established. The bishop would be the primary pastor of a diocese; the diocese, in turn, would be divided into geographical parishes, each to be served by one or more priests who would attend to the spiritual (and, as best they could, temporal) needs of the people within.

In contrast with past centuries, when clergy could live apart from the faithful, the bishop had to reside in his diocese, the priest within his parish.

The church, after centuries of struggle, had finally re-created on a much larger scale what was considered a perfect society, one that hoped to replicate the communities of believers that had sprung up after the death of Christ.

By the time European settlement came to America, the geographical parish was the established norm. It was an effective way to serve the faithful, and provided as well an efficient repository in which to keep records of their religious life, from baptism to burial. There were huge, dense parishes of the cities, and there were sprawling parishes of the settlers, where a priest might cover scores of miles on horseback in a week. But the American church soon realized that geography was not enough. Hundreds of parishes were created that had another overlay to them: they ministered to a certain ethnic group *within* a geographical area. Immigrants—French, Germans, Slavs, for instance—could receive instruction in the faith, and hear announcements and sermons, in their native language. Meanwhile, these and others, like the English-speaking Irish, could fraternize with people of similar culture, tradition, and temperament. The parish became a comfortable refuge within the dominantly Protestant American society of those days, a society that was hardly welcoming to these strange people speaking unintelligible languages, or English with a strange accent—and who were Catholic to boot!

Beginning around the turn of the century, American Catholic parishes blossomed. The largest religiously based educational system the world had ever seen was emerging; thousands of schools were built that educated millions of immigrant children for little or no cost in order to perform the dual mission of making them good and productive citizens while preserving in them the "one, true faith." Parishes, while fulfilling their primary function of dispensing the sacraments, often helped parents when economic hardship struck, and helped enormously to assure these new Americans a firm toehold in their new homeland.

While the parish was the center of many Catholics' social and religious lives, it's important to note that the religious practice of the day was largely composed of attendance at events at which the faithful were little more than a passive audience. Whether it was mass (at which the worshiper sat mutely), or at a novena, the stations of the cross, or other devotions (where rote responses were recited), the person in the pew had been taught that mere attendance and the desire for communion with God were sufficient to bring the graces that would assure them a place in heaven. Participation was an unthinkable word, one few would have been so bold to even consider.

That they should "feel" anything, that they should in any way regard the priest as a human being and anything other than Christ's proxy, was to approach apostasy. Organized and efficient, yes; but certainly distant in spirit from those first faith communities.

## . . . . PARISH TO COMMUNITY

The winds of change that resulted in the social and political firestorm of the 1960s and 1970s began to be felt even within the bastions of Catholic belief and practice that were the geographical parishes. A better-educated and widely traveled Catholic laity—many of whom attended college after World War II—began to grow restive in a church that still conducted its primary community worship in a language few of them knew. It was a church that many began to perceive treated them as perennial, incorrigible children in need of guidance, children who were expected to be seen (at mass and parish functions) but not heard (on any decisions affecting parish life, or in any matters encountered in their own spiritual journeys).

Wholesale defections from Catholic parishes had not yet begun when Vatican II concluded in 1965. In fact, informed Catholics who actually read the Vatican II documents—and the much greater number who found out about the proclamations through the media, or heard about them in church (while many priests welcomed Vatican II, a substantial number were uncomfortable with sharing their once-unquestioned power)—were encouraged. A new church was being born, one that upheld a new awareness of God as a loving father, not a punitive bookkeeper. A new parish was also being forged, one where lay people could be co-workers with the priest, where their talents and input were essential, where their opinions would be heard. As the council's "Dogmatic Constitution on the Church" proclaimed:

> Upon all the laity rests the noble duty of working to extend the divine plan ever increasingly . . . let every opportunity be given them that, according to their abilities and the needs of the times, they may zealously participate in the saving work of the church.[1]

The excitement surrounding the movement to build a new church within the old parish structure, utilizing the abilities of the laity as well as being open to "the needs of the times," was energizing—but, to many minds, quickly truncated. A new pope elected in 1978, John Paul II, sensed that the church had gone too far in its attempt to understand those needs; it had become too lenient, accepting, open. Only by returning to a Vatican-regulated orthodoxy could this fragile bark, tossing about on a sea of relativity and emotion, be brought to calmer waters. The new shoots of faith life—base communities and other small groups who gathered for support and worship, members of the hierarchy who saw collegiality and not only papal dictates as the imitation of Christ—had to be carefully watched and controlled.

Even before John Paul II was elected pope, Catholics in parishes all across America had begun to witness the departure of some of the best priests and nuns they had known. Catholics listened week after week to those who remained, some of whom knew little more theology than they did—and many of whom were sadly out of tune with the new complexities of lay peoples' lives. It wasn't that there were not excellent men and women who still remained in religious life; there were. But to many Catholics, there seemed to be precious few of them—and, in any event, Catholics grumbled, not in *my* parish. The largest, voluntary exodus from the church swept millions of

Catholics out of parishes entirely, or sent them to the periphery of
church life. Their children grew up largely unchurched; the active,
involved, productive Catholic life their parents once knew grew
dimmer each year in their memory.

# THE PLACE FOR YOU

It is certainly not rare to hear a Catholic, burned by bad church experiences or already burdened by too many organizational commitments, recite a litany along the following lines: "Yes, of course, I
want a spiritual life—but I don't need a parish or any other structure
to achieve it. I can do this on my own and be a better Christian
without having to deal with still another Catholic institution, filled
with small-minded people. I need to be fed; I can't give anymore.
I've got to take care of myself. I'm stretched to the breaking point
as it is."

This modern-day religious rugged individualist may be right. But
usually, he or she is not.

Many things have changed in church life and Catholic spirituality
over the centuries, but one thing has not: Catholicism, for the vast
majority of us, is not a solitary pursuit. By its very nature, Catholicism is communally based—the community at once being worshiping body, educator, and support group. Like a marriage, a Catholic
community provides both a sheltered place for our beliefs to grow,
and a testing ground where the imperfections of our human lives,
and of the day in which we live, might be addressed in an openly religious and spiritually hopeful context.

Quite simply, we Good Enough Catholics need the company of
those who share our basic beliefs—even while the expression of
those beliefs might be wildly and painfully diverse—to know that
we are not alone in our pursuit. We need reminders that other
people are struggling. We need to worship together, to share the
Eucharistic meal, to allow that special grace to flow where "two or

three are gathered in my name." We need regular times set aside to tend to the needs of our souls—and to be called out beyond the walls of church, home, and self. Most religious loners eventually can't sustain what may begin with the best of intentions.

In the past, to find a place for Catholic mass and access to the sacraments (mutual support and a testing ground were not usually included in the criteria), a Catholic dutifully went to the nearest parish church. This is not a bad way for the Good Enough Catholic to begin the search for a community of faith, even today.

Both the earliest Christian communities and traditional, geographic Catholic parishes came into being on practical grounds: people living near each other could regularly gather in a designated place of worship. People bounded within a small town or a geographical area of a city have common interests; they see each other on a daily basis. What better reasons than these to then come together to share the Eucharist and have a spiritual base close to home?

Catholic parishes throughout America have come to fill still another role in our extremely mobile society. For Catholics who covet a sense of place and belonging—whether they remain in one place or move often—there may be no better place than the parish. A geographically defined parish makes a spiritual statement that God has a place within every community, and that the church stands for what is best in all people. Hundreds of parishes have also found themselves taking on other crucial roles—that of stabilizing or invigorating city neighborhoods. Two Chicago parishes dramatically point this up.

St. Gertrude's is on Chicago's changing and multiethnic North Side. Dorothea Tobin, a mother of eight whose husband is a psychologist, is one of those Good Enough Catholics whose commitment to living in urban Chicago is rooted in her family's involvement with St. Gertrude's parish. "Yes, we could move to the suburbs like a lot of couples with kids," Dorothea said, "but Edgewater is an exciting and fertile neighborhood. Without St. Gertrude's, it would be taken over by violence and poverty; with St. Gertrude's, it works. It's not easy. The church is the lightning rod, a place for the warring tribes—conservatives and liberals, old-line ethnics and people of color—to meet and find what they have in common and not what divides them."

Some seventy blocks to the south of St. Gertrude's, with Chicago's soaring skyscrapers peering down upon its venerable walls, Old St. Patrick's was the epitome of a moribund downtown parish. Today, it is a beehive of religious and social activity. Lawyers and financiers from prestigious Loop firms tutor poor inner-city children; as many as a half a dozen weddings take place every Saturday. Masses are jammed, as are programs on everything from the meaning of Christmas to living as a Jewish-Catholic couple. Why?

"Because people are looking for a heart and a home for their spiritual belief," said Father Jack Wall, the pastor. "We are a mission-driven church. We don't try to get people on the books as parishioners. We try to call people to service. And they *want* to be called."

At St. Joseph the Worker in New Orleans, parishioners run a food pantry and a hot line for people who request prayers by phone. Most Holy Trinity parish in San Jose, California, established a parish nurse program, appointing these health professionals and volunteers "ministers of health." St. Theresa's parish in Harrisburg, Pennsylvania, boldly takes out an ad in the local newspaper each year and issues a blanket invitation for those "who feel separated from the church by divorce, birth control, lifestyle, invalid marriage, or any reason" to "come home for Christmas." The Church of St. Francis Xavier in New York City offers courses in "bio-spiritual focusing," and hosts a lesbian women's group in addition to the expected volleyball games and bridge tournaments. The parish also is used to having guests for dinner; it serves an astounding 1,000 free meals on Sunday afternoon.

"Too many people see the parish as something on an ecclesiastical organization chart. We don't see the pope every day; we see each other. It's here in the parish that my faith is fostered, here, from insights and experiences of ordinary people and an ordinary priest—not from the hierarchy or theologians. The way I feel about our kind of parish life is that we are guerrillas living up in the hills, living a countercultural existence. Yes, a dictatorship would be easier; then we'd know all the answers and exactly how to act. This way it's exciting, dangerous, and wonderful."

—PAT REARDON

"Praying in my parish is like praying with my family."

—MINNIE DIANA

"I had drifted away from the church and as I was moving all the time, and on top of that plenty angry with a lot of the church's stands, I never latched on to a parish. When I started taking in foster kids, I realized I couldn't do this alone. I wanted a community life for this strange family: fortyish women and goofy teenagers. But there we were in the pews, like everybody else, struggling to be better people, each in our own way."

—JOAN SULLIVAN

"I am continually tempted to switch parishes; I vehemently disagree with my pastor's progressive ways. But these are my people, my family has a webbing through this parish. After twenty-three years, I'm just going to leave?"

—MARTY GERAGHTY

But how many other Catholics have walked through the doors of their local parish and, after trying honestly to make it their spiritual home, simply could not? Perhaps they've tried other parishes as well, and did not discover a St. Gertrude's, a St. Joseph the Worker, or a Most Holy Trinity. Individual parishes may have struck them as unappealingly traditional or painfully trendy. More often, perhaps, they came across as spirit-killing, uninspiring places.

The traditional parish may not be the place for you. But in searching for a spiritual home, the Good Enough Catholic needs to be willing to search within as the search goes on without. I am certainly not advising a return to the old Catholic approach—toughing it out at a parish Sunday after Sunday from a sense of duty or guilt, or tolerating an inadequate parish because you are desperate to have your children receive their First Communion or confirmation *someplace.* You should go to church because you want to go, because it enriches your life, because you derive benefits from being there. Parish affiliation must be a relationship; you go out of desire, not out of obligation.

But perhaps something else is at work; a brief examination of conscience might be in order. In your confusion about what it really means to be a Catholic today, are you reluctant to make a commitment to a certain place? Is there a concern that when you stand up ready to be counted, you might find yourself standing in the wrong place? Or in the deepest recesses of your mind, is there the downright fear that bringing God into your life is going to upend it? What if you are called upon to participate in parish life? The perfectly valid rationalizations you have lived with all these years may have provided you with perfectly good excuses to stay away from the church.

Don't try to sublimate all of your reservations and fears; they are real, and you are not perfect. Equally, don't let those reservations and fears stand in the way of making this important first step. Don't worry—the perfect parish doesn't exist, so don't spend a lot of time looking for it.

Let me offer my own story as an illustration of some recent parish-shopping and parish-hopping.

Before I married and had children, I had not been affiliated with a Catholic parish for about seven years. Although I usually attended Sunday mass, what corporate spiritual life I had centered around a Trappist monastery, St. Joseph's, in Massachusetts. It was, for me, a refreshing change from an ordinary parish, a place where, blessed by silence, the call for greatness and sacrifice was clear. Oddly, the monastery stood against everything that I was invested in, devoted (as I was then) to a self-centered life as a single, divorced man. The liturgy was beautiful and transcendent at St. Joseph's, and some of the monks I came to know were models of what it meant to be both human and holy. It was blissfully quiet, a still point in an otherwise chaotic life.

When I married, I still attended mass at St. Joseph's, but I soon realized that the monastery could not be a spiritual home for my family of four. Somewhat reluctantly, and expecting very little, I began to attend my local parish church.

The young priest there, a brilliant, well-read and well-traveled man, was—to my mind—traditional beyond belief. He faithfully mouthed Vatican pronunciations, allowed no room for dissent, and seemed to regard parishioners as sinners first, human beings second. His sermons were indictments. He served up dogma I didn't accept, and which I could not, in conscience, follow. I couldn't take it, and I didn't want to leave the church; so I decided instead to leave this parish.

In a neighboring parish I found a quite different kind of priest. He appeared a good if simple man, who never had an original thought, seemed to put little time into his sermon preparation, and was great with the kids—even if he had absolutely no ability to converse with an adult on an adult topic. Yet, as he meandered through his Sunday sermon, I could let my mind wander where it might, strolling through the fields of the Lord. My wife and I tried to make the best of the situation, and soon found ourselves key members of a basically leaderless parish. We served as lectors and helped organize some parish events; my wife taught a CCD class.

That this particular priest was eventually found to be a minor-league pedophile (he had been taking revealing pictures of young boys on various church-sponsored outings for all his twenty years of priesthood, and was finally discovered) was certainly dispiriting; but again, I was not about to leave the church over one such person. His replacement presided at mass with a pronounced lack of reverence and decorum, and preached sermons that were torturous in their repetitiousness, lacking in insight, and often contained glaring grammatical, theological, and historical mistakes. I knew I couldn't stay. So it was back to the original parish and the young, traditionalist priest.

He had not outwardly changed in my four or five years at the other church, and neither had I: but this time the fit worked better. Maybe it was just a case of each of us maturing in the faith, acknowledging that the Catholic community is bigger than our individual approaches to God. More likely, and more basically, I think we simply had agreed to disagree, that we had found in each other a worthy opponent, a sounding board for our individual approaches to Catholicism. We both knew that it's hard enough to find anybody with whom you can have a good discussion about religious belief these days.

I found myself starting to go more and more often to weekday mass at that tiny church in the middle of a faded New England mill town. There, with a handful of worshipers, all older than me, I found I could quietly worship; hear of local concerns, needs, sicknesses, and deaths; and hear a short daily sermon. On Sunday, the priest was hellfire and brimstone; during the week, he offered lovely, spontaneous lessons springing from the Scripture, lives of the saints, or church history. He never failed to educate me or present a slant I'd never considered. And he provided inspiration. I rarely got up from my pew the same man I was when I sat down. And then, as I left mass, I found myself lingering on the front steps to argue over the latest papal proclamation, the foibles of our local bishop, or some recent article or book. In a strange way, I came to feel we needed each other—I needed the priest to give me some stiff, unequivocal marching orders, and he needed me to temper his views with those of a concerned layman, husband, and father.

As I look back, this parish "shopping and hopping" worked for me at those points in my spiritual journey. Had I given up in exasperation, or just stubbornly stayed at one place, without listening to the yearnings of my heart and considering my own and my family's needs, I would have done so out of some mistaken sense of duty, not the desire to be closer to God. I now live in North Carolina. After being attracted initially to a suburban, almost exclusively white parish, populated by young couples with young children, my wife and I chose the downtown parish, with an older, integrated congregation. Somehow, this is a better fit for us. It is far from the perfect parish, but for this struggling Good Enough Catholic, it's certainly a Good Enough Parish.

You can do the same—and not just because of the 1983 change in canon law that gives Catholics the right to attend any parish they choose. There is nothing wrong with visiting a good number of parishes in your search for the right one. Ask Catholic friends whose opinions you trust and whose lives you admire. When you go to a new parish, give it a chance; don't make a quick judgment because you don't like a particular statue, the color of the sanctuary, or the content or delivery of that morning's sermon. Talk to the priest, ask him what his view of the parish is. Oddly enough, he's not asked that question very often. If he's the kind of person you want as a partner in your spiritual pursuit, he'll have a response. If you find him defensive and deflective, that might be your answer.

A final note on parishes. None are perfect; most good ones resemble a happy if somewhat fractious family, where different points of view compete. It's good to have our ideas tested; it's good to kneel and sit beside people who don't really see the world as we do, yet who are linked to us by a common religious tradition, the desire to someway, somehow, be closer to our shared God. But if the parish turns out to be a truly dysfunctional family—where conflict and doctrinal arrogance prevail, and charity and laughter have no place—find another religious base of operations, for your own spiritual and psychological salvation.

## OTHER VOICES, OTHER PLACES

If, after visiting several geographical parishes, you still haven't found a spiritual home, there are still many other options. After all, a parish is basically a community of believers gathering together periodically for worship and mutual support, attending to each other's needs and the needs of the world around them. It's heartening to reflect back to Christ's followers and the first Christian communities. They didn't sit in neat rows of pews, put their weekly donation in an envelope and have a choir and organ music. They were pretty much making it up as they went along.

I'll guarantee that within walking, driving, or public transportation distance of where you are sitting right now, there is at least one—and probably more—communities of Catholic believers whose different approaches will surprise you. These small faith groups are quietly revolutionizing the Catholic Church.

In Hartford, Connecticut, there are no fewer than *five hundred* small faith groups that meet regularly for prayer, liturgy, and discussion. The Woodstock–St. Paul Community, with about sixty regular members, has been worshiping together for twenty-five years on New York's Upper West Side.

People in small faith groups "get used to making a difference," Father Art Baranowski said in an interview with *U.S. Catholic* magazine.[2] "And not because they're 'involved' or they're 'good Catholics' or they 'know Scripture.' They might not even like going to church." They care because they have found God among others and within their own hearts. "People are dying of loneliness . . . so there's a crying need for belonging—for people we can be safe with, who know us and something of our struggles. Small communities . . . offer a way of belonging to the church measured not by what people do but by who they are. That's what Jesus taught. . . . Small communities are not just a nice idea for personal growth; they're a more effective way of structuring the church."[3]

These faith groups range from those who make a strong commitment to common worship, daily spiritual reading (such as the Divine Office), and a specific mission (for instance, among immigrants, the homeless, or the dying), to those who simply gather for periodic prayer and open discussion of their inner lives. Some groups are charismatic and pray in tongues, others attend Tridentine Masses in Latin. Members of these faith groups speak Vietnamese, French, Spanish, and other languages, including English. Basically, the group responds to the needs and desires of the people forming it.

One of the most fertile religious periods in my life some twenty years ago was spent within such a small community in Brooklyn. Not finding ourselves entirely satisfied with formal parish life, a dozen of us banded together. It was a rather ragtag group, with various levels of commitment and belief, but for years we prayed together, hosted a home mass (creating our own liturgy when a priest was not available), and eventually started a soup kitchen and shelter for the homeless that still exists to this day. There are a number of good books about such small communities.[4]

At your local college or university, the Newman Center provides an excellent community of believers. Here is a nontraditional parish, usually headed by a thoughtful priest, that can provide intellectual stimulation and spiritual enhancement.

Small groups of nuns who no longer live in convents are often the center for communities of lay people who pray with them and often assist them in their work. Monasteries and convents can provide a spiritual oasis and, while certain cloistered orders discourage interaction between their members and the public, you can still worship with them and even find, if you choose, a way to help in their work. For instance, I know of a woman who founded and operates an inviting residence called Mary House near St. Joseph's, the Trappist monastery in Massachusetts, which offers a place of solitude, rest, and prayer for couples or women who are not able to stay at the monastery retreat house.

In virtually every major city and in many smaller towns, there are Catholic Worker houses of hospitality; at last count, there were almost two hundred throughout the country. Catholic Workers, lay people who live a life of voluntary poverty and work primarily with the poor, while also being activists for peace and social justice, are interesting, committed people—and they are believers in the need for communal prayer and worship. You might want to visit the Catholic Worker house near you.

There is no listing in your Yellow Pages for "Spiritual Homes: Traditional and Nontraditional," but once you begin asking your Catholic friends, Catholic college students, priests, and others in religious life you might meet in passing, you'll be surprised at the variety of Catholic religious experiences close by. There is a network, a Catholic subculture out there. Within it you can seek—and find— your spiritual home.

# THE GOOD ENOUGH CATHOLIC CHALLENGE: FINDING YOUR SPIRITUAL HOME (AND THEN?)

We need a spiritual oasis, a place where we can gather with other Good Enough Catholics to pray and talk and celebrate, a place where we can render nourishment to others on life's journey and obtain that nourishment for ourselves.

The challenge for this chapter is to set out to find a home for your soul, always open to the various possibilities that will present themselves. You may start with your local parish or a Zen-Christian group, at a monastery or in the back room of a soup kitchen. Listen to your needs, and to the sounds of your soul. Perhaps for now you just need to sit in the back row of a massive church; or you may want to find a place that immediately calls you to service in some outreach or social ministry. God does not judge by what you do or produce. He invites—and treasures—your presence. Other seekers need you as you need them.

Once you have found a spiritual home, that may be enough, or at least enough for you at this point in your spiritual life. It is already a great achievement to have found such a place. Making the commitment to regularly attend mass, a prayer service, or a small-group discussion will allow God and the gentle tides of your own soul to tell you when it is time to do more.

At some point the Good Enough Catholic will usually find that they are ready to do something more. It is a desire that rises up out of gratitude and happiness, not with a sense of begrudging obligation. Rarely would the Good Enough Catholic use the words "working to extend the divine plan," but that's exactly what you'll be doing.

Many Catholics in parishes bemoan the shortage of priests today. I happen not to be one of them. Looking at the number of men who will soon reach retirement age and the scant numbers of seminarians, the shortage will become even more pronounced in the years ahead. To me this shortage affords lay people the opportunity to do things unimaginable just years go. Vatican II reconfirmed the priesthood of the believers. I believe in that. It makes Catholicism more egalitarian, exciting, and powerful when all of us see ourselves as the anointed.

One of the most needed, and most rewarding, works in all parishes is that of the Eucharist minister. Taking the consecrated host to a shut-in or a sick person can be a deeply spiritual experience. You are bringing the most precious gift that person will receive that day. And you are bringing yourself. You will find yourself intimately and immediately involved in the life of another pilgrim. And you don't have to be a saint to bring the Eucharist to another; this sinner can testify to that.

If your parish seems to be lacking in interesting programs, you might want to organize some. There are other Good Enough Catholics just waiting to be asked about how faith and religious belief work in their lives. You can help counsel young couples about to marry; you can participate in a new program where lay people act as advocates for those seeking a marriage annulment. With the shortage of priests, the parish today is a blank slate, ready to be written upon. Just look around: What do people seem to need? What would you enjoy doing?

You might find yourself starting a new kind of men's or women's club—one that meets on a designated morning for mass and has breakfast together. Such a group of businesspeople meets in downtown Hartford once a month for a 7:00 A.M. mass, following which one of the members gives a short talk about how he or she links Catholic spirituality with daily work. In Massachusetts, I belonged to an ecumenical group of men that met on the first Friday of every month. We had no organization or speakers; after mass at the Trappist monastery, we went out to breakfast and talked about whatever we wanted. But inevitably the conversation turned to subjects that men usually don't talk about together, like child rearing, poverty, and the state of our souls. We began to sponsor an annual dinner that honored one of our townspeople for service to the community, and informally raised money for local causes, from the rescue squad to a hospice program.

Choose what you want to do, when—and if—you feel the call. Being a lector is exactly right for some people, and exactly wrong for others. If you like to cook, you might get a kick out of cooking a meal for a couple hundred hungry souls at a soup kitchen. The opportunities are limitless. And remember: this is not all pain and sacrifice. That is not the Good Enough Catholic way. If there is no satisfaction or sense of joy, something is wrong.

## SELECTED READINGS

Arthur Baranowski, *Creating Small Faith Communities*. Cincinnati, Ohio: St. Anthony Messenger Press, 1989.

———. *Praying Alone and Together: An Eleven-Session Prayer Module for Small Faith Communities*. Cincinnati, Ohio: St. Anthony Messenger Press, 1988.

William V. D'Antonio, James Davidson, Dean Hoge, and Ruth Wallace, *Laity: American and Catholic*. Kansas City, Mo.: Sheed and Ward, 1995.

Thomas A. Kleissler, Margo A. Lebert, and Mary C. McGuinness, *Small Christian Communities: A Vision of Hope*. New York: Paulist Press, 1991.

# FAMILY
## The Gentle Crucible

No institution has been more shaken by the upheavals of the past few decades than society's most basic and revered unit—the family. The tremendous social, political, and economic convulsions, the sea-change in women's roles, our mobility, and our quest for self-fulfillment, all have conspired to test the strength of this venerable cornerstone.

Not too long ago our idealized world was right out of Ozzie and Harriet, with dad working, mom at home, and kids having the time, and the carefree, safe environment, to just be kids. Of course, it was not that way for many families who didn't live in neat suburban communities, but in the commonly held perception across America, this was what family life was all about. Moral, decent—a bit goofy at times—but intact and holding the promise of a happy ending.

How things have changed.

Now, with fewer and fewer children living in a family with both natural mother and father present, with more and more children being raised by either a single parent, a grandparent, or a foster parent, with singles and the widowed living alone, the intact, biologically correct, one-income family seems now but a quaint slice of Americana. Have we given up on the family as out of date, or somehow unnecessary?

Hardly. Disoriented by a fast-paced world, our values buffeted by the harsh and ever-changing winds of public whim and popular culture, we yearn for a strong family life even more. "If only we can do *this* right," many a young mother and father have said, looking down at their newborn and realizing that a vastly different life lies ahead. "If only I *had* done that right," others have bemoaned; after the years insidiously crept by, comes the realization that things somehow went wrong.

With all its limitations, and even in its modern, fragmented state, it is the family—"the first and vital cell of society"[1]—that offers the elemental hope of providing a place where we can take the first steps toward living in harmony as human beings, and transforming the various worlds in which we live.

For this reason, it is in the family that we most need to feel the presence of God, the sense that Christ is with us. For it is here that we learn daily and exquisitely about trust and forgiveness, suffering and loss, accomplishment and rapture, disappointment and despair. It is here that we are provided the tools with which to fashion our lives and undertake tasks not easily accomplished by our own willpower alone. It is here that we learn to sacrifice for others.

There is perhaps no greater or more formidable challenge before us. Never before has it been so crucial, both to our own sense of personal well-being and for the greater good of our world, that we live well with those with whom we live most intimately. They profoundly affect us; we, in turn, profoundly affect them. Within this complex, changing tidepool of human and divine love resides the very origins of our humanity.

# WHAT FAMILY?

Two-parent families, single-parent families, blended families, "empty nest" families. Families headed by foster parents or adoptive parents; by grandparents or other relatives. Same-sex couples, couples without children, couples who live together by need or desire. Extended families, nuclear families. Intact families, broken families. Church marriages, civil marriages, common-law marriages. The separated, di-

vorced, widowed, and single. This list of family possibilities is dizzying—and probably incomplete.

Each type of family promises its own rewards, and, in turn,
makes its own unique set of demands. Yet all are similar, in that—
regardless of circumstance, choice, good fortune or misfortune, good
choices or bad—each is a group of people with whom we will live
and interact intimately. These are the "cells" that will grow and
prosper with nurturing, or die from neglect. Each cell contributes to
a better society, or contributes to its demise.

For Catholics, not that long ago the idealized family was a variation on the Ozzie and Harriet theme—and, in a certain sense, a
bigger-than-life variation. The archetypical large Catholic family,
with its four, five, or more children, lived in a friendly neighborhood; attended a parish church that was the spiritual, social, and educational center of their lives; and had a network of relatives living
close by (or even upstairs). Their lives might have seen financial
struggles, and their souls may have doubted their worth under the
church's watchful eyes, but they did possess the "one, true faith." As
for this world, they experienced the comfort (as we see it in retrospect) of coexisting with people of a basically similar temperament
and lifestyle.

In fact, while the Protestant and Jewish children that Catholics
grew up alongside had differing religious dogma and practices, all
had been steeped in—or at least exposed to—the same broad moral
code: the Judeo-Christian ethic. Virtually all went to church or synagogue; those that didn't were quiet about their unbelief. The Ten
Commandments cast a long shadow over tenement buildings, down
suburban streets, and across farm fields all over this land.

Today, Catholics have been absorbed into the mainstream in
more than merely economic and professional ways. Catholics divorce and remarry; they have no less than a proportional share of
dysfunctional families; unwed Catholic women have babies. Catholics
intermarry and marry outside the church. A smaller and smaller percentage of Catholic families are comprised of two parents living
with their biological children. And Catholic families with a biological dad working and biological mom at home—the "Ozzie and

Harriet" family model—comprise the same declining slice of the population as in the rest of America.

In other words, the majority of Catholics and other Americans do not even live in the same sort of families in which they grew up. And a religious tradition—once a given—is no longer the integral part of a child's upbringing it once was.

> " 'You guys don't fit into the gay scene and you don't fit into the straight scene,' a priest told us when my partner and I talked about adopting children. He said it was going to be tough, but he felt we could do it. 'People may not accept it, because you're on the cutting edge, establishing a new lifestyle—a gay couple with children living in a very settled way. You are forming a new kind of family,' he said. Well, we went ahead and adopted a South American baby, and one from the rural American South—both of mixed race, considered the least adoptable. They complete our life. It is simply wonderful to be a family together."
>
> —TOM EAKINS*

# THE DOMESTIC CHURCH

Intoxicated by the burgeoning of scientific discovery, thinkers of the seventeenth century (Newton, Bacon, Hobbes, Locke, Descartes, and Spinoza), whose discoveries laid the foundation for thinkers of the eighteenth century (Diderot, Rousseau, Hume, and Kant) found themselves questioning the need for God. These authors of the Enlightment, who developed a school of philosophy called rationalism, were dissatisfied with the divine explanation of the human condition and human destiny, and sought instead to offer one that was secular and blessedly logical. This, of course, led to assaults on church authority—and to its claims on personal and public morality —as unnecessary, restrictive, and intellectually unsustainable.

In response, what would be a series of encyclicals were promulgated under the seals of successive popes, articulating a new understanding of the centrality of family life in church teaching.

The social encyclicals of the past century—which we will discuss in more detail in the next two chapters—dealt with macro issues: political, economic, and civic life. Paralleling these documents were another group of encyclicals, addressing still another set of perceived threats to far smaller units of society. There was then, as there is now, a crisis of faith about marriage and family life.

In their book examining these documents, William Urbine and William Seifert wrote, "They are meant to guide and direct the people of God in their pilgrimage of faith. The church is concerned that the values of marriage and family life, seen within a sacramental context, be understood and accepted as achievable goals for individuals, couples, and families to live within their lives."[2]

There were generous servings of church doctrine in these texts—oftentimes in starchy, theological prose—but, equally, there was an ever-increasing compassion. Like the social encyclicals, they were hardly known and rarely read by the average lay Catholic, but the marriage and family encyclicals unknowingly laid the foundation for the dramatic revelations of Vatican II—and for the even more compassionate letters that would be issued both by the Vatican and local bishops in the years after Vatican II.

Not surprisingly, the documents stressed the absolute inviolability of the sacrament of matrimony and stubbornly condemned all forms of artificial birth control—even as growing numbers of Catholics were divorcing and using contraception. But to accentuate only those two themes in the documents is to lose sight of the timeless, enduring values about family life that were advanced. Perhaps the most revolutionary concept on family life that Vatican II produced, in its document *Gaudium et Spes* (the Pastoral Constitution on the Church in the Modern World), was in fact a resurrection—that of the family as the "domestic church."

Judaism had always maintained that the home was the first place of worship and ritual, where ordinary events—such as simply sharing a meal—were moments of holiness, brimming with grace. The most important Jewish rituals, both at the weekly *shabbas* observance and during the high holy days, take place in the home, not the synagogue. Jewish sanctity was accessible through the ordinary. The believer did not have to sit in a magnificent edifice to acknowledge the presence of God.

It was natural for the first Christians to continue in this Jewish tradition (after all, that's what most of them were and still considered themselves), gathering in each other's homes for worship and fellowship. Even when worship became more complicated and the formally ordained presided over the liturgy, the home was still revered as a holy place of gathering. It was St. John Chrysostom (d. 407), a revered doctor of the church, who went so far as to call the family a "domestic church."

Christ's words, "Where two or three are gathered in my name, I am there among them," were taken literally. It was there, in the home, that an invisible God's love was revealed in the lives of visible family members, and in how they treated each other. If God was not sought within the sanctuary of the home, the church fathers understood, he would not be found in the sanctuary of a church.

While a goodly portion of the early papal encyclicals on family life were devoted to admonishments, it is refreshing to see how church teaching has matured over the years. It is not that the idealism called for is any less; rather, the teachings are more connected to how people live today, frankly acknowledging the many different starting points for our various journeys to holiness.

For instance, the U.S. Bishops' 1994 pastoral letter on the family, "Follow the Way of Love," addresses those who

> . . . consider their family too "broken" to be used for the Lord's purposes . . . remember, a family is holy not because it is perfect but because God's grace is at work in it, helping it to set out anew everyday on the way of love. . . . Wherever a family exists and love still moves through its members, grace is present. Nothing—not even divorce or death—can place limits on God's gracious love.[3]

Regardless of a family's conventionality or unconventionality, the bishops were saying, God wants to be present in each home. And as Mitch Finley notes in his book *Your Family in Focus*, "It is in our life together as a family that we discover both God and ourselves."[4]

Where else, really?

## LIFE IN YOUR "DOMESTIC CHURCH"

When Vatican II upheld the family as the "domestic church," it marked the unearthing of a basic Christian reality that had for too long been covered by layers of ecclesiastical silt. After all, most Catholics had been taught that the parish was religion's true home. But, of course, that could not be so; we spend but a fragment (if any) of our week in our parish, but we spend countless hours, waking and sleeping, with our family. Our family is our first community, ". . . the most basic way in which the Lord gathers us, forms us, and acts in the world."[5] The family is where Christianity first took root; it is where our faith is tested and lived out in real terms, with real people. The family is our own religious community—no different in certain basic ways from a group of monks living in a monastery.

I compare the family to a community of monks for good reason. For in both of these places a group of people, committed to each other and a common purpose, seek to give and receive support for their life's journey. Each has the health of their "cell" at heart— embracing not only concern for personal well-being, but for the entire entity.

I have been privileged to know in some depth members of various monastic communities throughout America, from those committed to urban parish work to contemplatives in secluded places. Their "family" is anything but the peaceful, prayerful oasis that many Catholics imagine it to be. Of course, it is a place of support and love; but it is also a place of conflict, where differing ideas and personalities alternately mesh and clash. In a monastery, some people talk too loud and too often, while others are selfish with their time and emotions. The quirks of some become intensely annoying to others; moments of unsolicited affection cause tension and embarrassment. Salvation is not attained by the moments of serenity and like-mindedness, but through the crucible of daily experiences when difficulties present themselves.

Most of us have been taught to avoid conflict; but conflict, when it happens, actually can draw us together, into a deeper relationship. Conflict necessitates honesty; it requires us to reach within ourselves to face what is best and worst, honest and dishonest, weak and strong within us. And so, while conflict should never be deified for its own sake, it can be a potent force for family intimacy.

In one of the *National Catholic Reporter*'s series, "Teaching the Faith," the Foley family of La Jolla, California, sat down with reporter Arthur Jones to talk about their faith lives. The rich mix of an evening's conversation showed many conflicts: various levels of observance; vast differences in opinion about birth control, treatment of gays, the priesthood, and prayer life. There was old-school Catholicism and Generation X Catholicism. But religion and religious values were unmistakably an important part of this family's life and discussion. Jones found ". . . an openness, but one qualified . . . by the Catholic Christian message learned at home, in the parish groups and at school."[6] This is the vital combination for today's Catholic family.

In our own "domestic church," there are boundless opportunities for holiness. Going on vacation, sorting out how to spend money or allot time, deciding what movies and clothes are appropriate, the tone and content of conversation around the table at mealtimes, caring for a sick child or an elderly relative, recovering from death or disappointment—all can make the family more cohesive, and its members better able to live as happy, healthy individuals who can make a positive difference in the various communities they are part of. But addressed the wrong way, such issues can be bitter and corrosive, thus crippling both human and spiritual growth.

# WHERE VIRTUE IS BORN

Most Good Enough Catholics would agree that much of the moral climate of today's society is not conducive to good family values or to raising children with moral fiber. Overwhelmed by our busy schedules, with the demands of earning a living, participating in children's activities, and the sheer logistics of life in late-twentieth-century America, too many of us feel powerless to do anything about it. After all, who can stand up to the power of television, of advertising, of song lyrics? What can counter the continuing stream of unsavory revelations about some of our most honored public figures?

Chastened by what they have heard or read about the art of negotiation, the necessity of listening to their children's point of view, and the difficulty of deciphering the inner storms of youth, many parents find themselves insecure about making definitive statements about right and wrong in our relativistic world. They even become reluctant about trying to instill basic values within their own family—that crucial unit of society over which they have the most control.

As we look about us in everyday life, seeking that one person who will stand up against the moral turpitude, hungering to discover signs of decency and righteousness in the world, our children are doing the same thing. Hidden behind youthful indignation at being told "No, you can't do that" is a sigh of thankfulness that a line has been drawn. Behind a sullen face is one beaming with relief that a firm decision has been rendered.

The parent who tolerates nearly any kind of behavior in an effort to create "an independent thinker" is a parent who has morally abandoned the child. Children want guidelines; they want a moral beacon by which to steer their fragile bark across the stormy seas of infancy, latency, puberty, adolescence, and young adulthood. They appreciate clear messages. They are enraged at those whom they find guilty of the grievous sins of abdication or indifference.

All of which goes right to the heart of what being a Good Enough Catholic parent is all about. What so many parents fail to realize is that your best, most thoughtful, prayerful, parental instincts *are* good enough. And if your children do not hear from you what is right and wrong—as best you can determine—the only voice they hear will be the siren call of the popular culture.

This does not mean that you need to be a moral bully. You must listen to your children. Whenever I bring up examples from my growing-up days, my children have a ready response: "That was then and this is now." They are right. But, while five-cent ice cream cones will never come back, the values of respect for others, honesty, standing up for the outcast, and hard work are never out of style.

The family has been, and will always be, the first school of social virtue. The child who learns at home that violence is not the answer to resolving differences will take that same attitude to school and out to play. If honesty and generosity and compassion are family practices, so, too, will they infuse a child's actions outside the home. Giving generously within the home predisposes a child to act likewise. Law enforcement and social service agencies must step in only when the family has not imbued true moral behavior in its members.

This does not mean that you must constantly preach "Catholic values." It does mean you must do your best to *live* them. When you go to church with your family, you proclaim that worship and community are important. When you give of yourself beyond your four walls—at that food pantry, soup kitchen, or home for the aged—you are making it clear that service to others is important.

My own upbringing taught me, by my father's example, that simple, daily acts have profound repercussions. My father never uttered a single word that I can remember about morality or Catholic values. But his actions spoke eloquently for him. Once, when I was old enough to work with him, he was confronted with a particularly difficult piece of molding that had to be installed behind a radiator. It was late; we were both tired. I wanted to just slap it in and be done. No one would ever see this thin, three-foot-long piece of wood; no one would ever know.

But my father said no. He would know about it; he would always see it in his mind's eye. While he didn't say it, I began to realize that he was faced with tiny decisions every day about taking shortcuts in his work as a carpenter, about doing things no one would ever see.

What he showed me in this was that so many of our actions, seen or unseen, carried either merit or shame. Yes, those are pretty absolute terms. Of course, he knew he would fail, and that his children would fail. But he also knew—and we learned by his example—what was the objective of a considered, Catholic life. The target may have been distant and small, but it was well defined. You had to do your absolute best, regardless of the situation. In that once-in-a-lifetime, unexpected moment when we are called upon for a truly heroic act, we will do no more or less than we have been doing all our lives before.

I thank my father for that lesson. I only *hope* I can stand for as much in the eyes of my own sons.

"My family was active in the Catholic Family Movement; they didn't talk about it much, but they lived it out. For instance, we would take food to the migrant workers who came through our part of Michigan. It was a powerful message."

—TOM LENZ

"We agree on many things, but on certain things we don't, and I won't budge. They're not going to watch awful TV shows like *90210*, because my commentary on those people's lack of values will drive them so nuts they'll turn it off."

—MARTY GERAGHTY

"There was a standard, and then there was a Geraghty standard. My parents were so strict when I was growing up—they wouldn't let us do what 'other kids' were doing—and it was totally embarrassing at times. When I told other kids I went to college with, they didn't think it was weird at all. And some were from very permissive homes. They really admired me for having parents that stood up for things so strongly."

—DAUGHTER, MAUREEN GERAGHTY

"As a service project we try to do something as a family, so one year we manned a Salvation Army kettle out in front of a grocery store for one entire holiday season. It blew the minds of our parish people to see us doing Salvation Army work, but nobody could walk by without at least stopping to think of what was going on here."

—CAPPY KUSTUSCH

# QUALITIES OF A GOOD ENOUGH CATHOLIC FAMILY

The components of good family life are simple. Love, acceptance, and sharing might immediately come to mind; but I'd like to consider two other components, time and attention—and to make it a good Catholic family life, let's add another: ritual.

"Quality time" is a popular concept these days, the idea that we can somehow concentrate the little time we spend with our children, filling each moment together with a certain intensity. Contrary to what harried, upwardly mobile working parents say, as they hire out so much of their children's care, when it comes to kids there is no such thing as quality time; there is only time. Here, we should distinguish between parents who need to work as much as they do simply to assure their family's survival, and those who have options—and opt for career over kids. We might be able to focus our attention in order to solve a management problem by a deadline; we might be able to condense a half-hour workout on a treadmill into fifteen minutes by running at double speed. But when it comes to family life, such intensity is not only self-defeating and selfish, it is downright manipulative and antagonizing.

We do not live in some idealized, bucolic world cast in sepia tones, blessed with background music by Vivaldi and conversation by Emily Post. Often we are rushed; there are not enough hours in the day to accomplish everything. By the end of the day, if not before, our energy is sapped. Yet it is not good enough to simply say to our children (or our spouse), "As soon as I can find the time, I will"; that makes me as angry as it does you. It is like seeing someone bleeding to death and piously saying, "I'll say a prayer for you." It just doesn't meet the clear and present need.

It takes *quantity* time to build a loving relationship, as we well know from courting our spouse or significant other. A family needs similar time—time to listen to what happened at school, what's happening on the block, about the agony at the first outcropping of acne, a friend made or lost. One of the best (and easiest) times for this is at meals.

Now, I can hear the cry of protest go up from families who haven't eaten together for days, even weeks. If I might be dogmatic, didactic, preachy, pushy, fervent, and even the bully I warned you against, let me say this: try to hold mealtimes as precious as you do church times, maybe even more so. For the dinner table is the altar of the domestic church.

Gathering together for food and talk at your table is the domestic church's counterpart to parish liturgy, where that larger community comes together. Both are occasions to take nourishment, food for body and soul; both anticipate God will be among those gathered.

Mealtimes are the only times during the day when the entire family actually faces one another for an extended period of time. Mealtimes are moments when all are equal, when everyone's opinion matters, when the clan gathers on its journey for sustenance and a review of where that day has taken them, and to lay plans for the days ahead. Think of yourselves as the Israelites wandering in the desert, or the early Christian communities; you are gathering together as they did.

What is more important than this time together? Which of your activities or your children's activities? A moment of reflection will help each of us sort out what we want our family to be about, the moments we will want to remember. Will it be that extra meeting, another soccer practice, the quick haircut—or will it be a family meal that you held sacred and insisted upon?

As we discuss ritual in the next section, a key consideration revolves around what Good Enough Catholic families might do on their Sundays. Preserving Sundays is a way of giving honor to God, but it is essentially an issue of time—and whom you give it to. God ordained the Sabbath as a day of rest to offer an opportunity for the human community to lay work aside and get to know each other again. It is not a day to wallow in or even consider our sins and shortcomings; it is a day to have a good time together.

It was a rainy, muggy Sunday here in North Carolina, and as we had been to mass the evening before, the day yawned wide before us: father, mother, and boys eleven and nine. No place to run, no ready-made outdoor possibilities. The boys came up with an idea— a poker game! I groaned. A poker tournament! I groaned again. A *marathon* poker tournament! I groaned even louder. But, trying to take my own advice, I listened.

So, when we picked up the Sunday paper at the drugstore, we got four tiny candy prizes at the discount counter and some poker chips. After allotting blues, reds, and whites equally, we embarked on a daylong adventure of five-card, seven-card, nothing wild, deuces and treys wild, day baseball, night baseball. A morning session, lunch, rest. An afternoon session. Supper. An early evening session.

Finally, near bedtime, the chips were tallied, and the prizes awarded. As we put the boys to bed, I had to admit to myself that we had just spent one of the best Sundays of the year—one that we would remember and fondly recall.

I'm sure we could have used this time much better for the sake of the Kingdom, scouring our closets for clothes to give to the needy, reading Bible stories, or doing some religiously based art project. But our little tribe rested on our journey, listened to the rain, and had some fun together; simple, innocent, time-consuming fun.

Some would wag fingers at the idea of playing cards on the Sabbath; the Wilkes family stands accused. Your own flights away from the world and into your individual time warp may be different, much different—a videotape film festival of the best of classics, from *Little Women* to *Twenty Thousand Leagues Under the Sea*. Camping out in the backyard and not entering the house all day. A hike, a drive, a marathon game of Dictionary, Monopoly, or Scrabble. The options are multiple, the intent is singular: taking, making time with your family.

# THINGS CATHOLIC IN A CATHOLIC HOME

Many of us can look back to the Catholic homes in which we were raised and, mentally walking through that front door and into those rooms, see that it was distinctively, decidedly, unapologetically Catholic. The thick-stemmed crucifix that slid apart to reveal tiny vials of oil, holy water, and candles for the administration of extreme unction. Pictures of the Sacred Heart, the Blessed Virgin, and St. Peter; statues of St. Francis, St. Therese, or St. Jude. A church calendar in the kitchen with religious art, saints days—and the name of the local Catholic funeral director. Reciting the rosary together as a family; kneeling before a parent for night prayers.

Opening our eyes to survey our own homes, we might have a tasteful Miró print on our walls and a Sierra Club calendar in the kitchen. And the family gathers—nightly and faithfully—in front of the television set.

It is not that Impressionist art, ecology, or entertainment are not good; but if we want our children to know they are God's own—and the Catholic version of God's own—the time has come to replace some of the symbols, and restore some of the reminders, of that belief in our homes. We Good Enough Catholics must reclaim ritual from its trivialization by the time-consuming, mind- and soul-numbing noise of modern life. Watching a favorite TV show or the evening news is fine, but it does not take the place of family religious ritual.

"Catholics do a disservice to themselves and their children by keeping their Catholic identity under wraps," Patrice Tuohy has argued in *U.S. Catholic*.[7] "Dispensing with religious rituals, such as nightly prayer and grace before meals, and not displaying religious art in the home is as un-Christian as failing to vote and refusing to display a flag is un-American. They're not absolutely essential expressions of allegiance, but they should come with the territory."

Today's Catholics may feel tentative—or unsure—about reintroducing religious ritual into our family life. We may feel that we are merely Good Enough Catholics, not Superb Catholics, so what authority do we have to call for such observances? Few of us feel sufficiently holy to be instituting religious practices. But this is our "domestic church"; here, we are both hierarchy and congregants. It is here in the home that parent or parents are the most important teaching authority in the church. We need meaningful ritual in our family life. And our children want and crave ritual. As the exemplary Quaker, Hannah Whittal Smith, wrote, "Act as if you believed and you will come to believe."[8]

Religious ritual must flow naturally out of your family's rhythms, temperament, and desires. What might seem perfectly transcendent in a church setting could feel forced and unnatural in the "domestic church." There are natural times of pause or transition in a family's daily life, and these are usually the best times to begin simple rituals.

The evening meal is a good place to start. Initially, you might just go around the table and allow everyone to tell what was the best and worst thing that happened that day. In a few days, you can introduce a simple prayer. You can use the standard "Bless us O Lord and these thy gifts . . ." or, you can offer more specific prayers of thanks for the food, for strength, for patience, for good weather—whatever you and your children want to tell God about.

It is amazing how a prayer changes the tenor of a meal. Prayer unifies. It is spoken in a different tone, one that indicates people can feel free to talk about the truly important issues that might be on their minds. It calls us out of our ordinariness. It makes us stop the drone of a day. Prayer sanctifies and refreshes the "domestic church."

My wife and I started to say a short, spontaneous prayer before supper when we married, and continued it—as best we could—even when our boys were infants. We voiced our thanksgiving for the food before us and each other, and always tried to reach out beyond our table and house to "those who have nothing to eat, no one to share it with, or no place to rest this night." Our boys expected a prayer, and as they grew they were invited to offer their own prayers. On more than one occasion it has brought a lump to my throat—even after a giant family fight—to hear them thanking God for what we have, and then immediately remembering those less fortunate than we are.

We also pray when we have guests, and those who know our practice look forward to this moment of thanks and reflection. We always try to offer specific prayers about our guests—thanks that they are new friends or old, or have traveled a distance to be with us, whatever might be going on in their lives. Often a member of our family is asked to offer a prayer before a meal when we are visiting in other homes. I've been amazed to find that children—once they see that normal concerns are exactly the things that can and should be prayed about—enjoy leading the prayer.

Family religious ritual is as simple as sending a child off to school or play with a "God bless you" as well as a hug. At night, kneeling or sitting on the edge of the bed is a perfect time to review the day ending and anticipate the day ahead with a short prayer. Lighting a candle sets a mood and says that this is a part of the day different from all the other hours.

We now understand how profoundly important the first three years of life are in shaping the psychology of every child. The same is true spiritually during those tender years. When my boys were infants, I wanted some sort of night prayers for them. I dutifully went out and bought some prayer books; but when I read them, I found them too saccharine for my taste, too dogmatic, or too punitive. One night, as I exhaled with exasperation at the latest book of prayers, my oldest son Noah simply began, "Dear God, I know you love me so much"—and we began from there. Every evening, beginning with this simple prayer, we prayed about playmates and visits from relatives, the sun, dirt, days of happiness, days when nothing turned out right—whatever that day's experience had been. I felt nervous and uncertain when I began to compose those first prayers, but soon they seemed to take on a life of their own. New things to pray about just kept cropping up.

The religious seasons of the year, like Lent and Advent, are also good times to begin family rituals. The Advent wreath or Lenten offerings for the poor are good reminders that important religious days are approaching. At Christmas in my Slovak parish in Cleveland, my family always shared the blessed unleavened bread called *oplatky*. Today, whether through a local parish or a member of my family, we always obtain *oplatky*. My boys love to break the bread, pour out the honey it will be dipped into, and then distribute it to the family. At Easter time in Cleveland, we prepared a basket and had it blessed. You'd be amazed to find that many parishes continue this tradition today.

The old rituals can be reinstituted today, or you can begin your own. However you perform them, you are saying your family stands for faithfulness and steadfastness, a continuum, a presence always there for them; in a word, security. While the world may change and your children will grow up, certain things will remain with them. As you may recall religious rituals of your youth, so will your children remember those you do as a family. Don't be timid; you will find your children are more than willing to be a part of something that is at once natural and holy. They will thank you for giving them a religious tradition that is an integral part of their heritage and character.

Rituals can be so simple and ordinary. In my youth, we always made the sign of the cross when we passed a funeral procession on the street. I still do it; now my family does. We do the same if we have a close call in traffic. It is not that we are pious or holy. Rather, we want to send that soul off to heaven—and we want to stay here on earth for as long as possible. We are simply communicating that to God by signing ourselves in his, his son's, and the Holy Spirit's name.

Just the introduction of a piece of religious art can be a way to begin to set a tone in your home. With many interreligious marriages today, the piece of art can honor one of many traditions. Miró and the Sierra Club need not be sent to the attic; they have their place, too. But a simple cross or religiously inspired print can both beautify a home and inspire its inhabitants, making a statement about and *to* those who reside there.

> "My foster kids had no routine, no ritual in their lives. When I took them to church and I'd come back from communion, I'd touch it to their foreheads. I didn't exactly know how to do this, but it was my way of sharing Jesus with them. I had this one kid who was very, very hostile and angry; one Sunday I just stayed away from him. He looked up at me and said, 'Aren't you going to touch me?' It meant something to him. Was I just *acting* as if this was a family? Maybe. But it worked. We seemed like a family, in church at least."
>
> —JOAN SULLIVAN

# THEIR RELIGIOUS TRAINING—AND YOURS

There have been a number of studies done on the effectiveness of the religious training that many Catholic children receive today—that is, an hour of religious instruction a week. The sad but predictable conclusion is that, in and of itself, such training means almost nothing, and has little or no effect on what place religious belief and values will have in their lives.

This is surely not to say that you shouldn't expose your children to some religious training—if that is all you can muster. But if your home is one where gospel values are not discussed or practiced, where a Catholic way of approaching life is not a value, or where church attendance is negligible, dropping children off for an hour's forced feeding of Catholicism once a week is simply not going to do much. You may raise wonderful children, but they will not be Catholic children. They may even learn the language of faith, but they will not receive the faith.

Many parents say that they are not imparting a specific religious belief because they want to allow the child to decide what religion he or she will follow. Or, hearkening back to some painful experience of their own Catholic upbringing, they say they do not want to subject their children to the same shame or guilt or narrow-mindedness they found.

The fact is that children will decide for themselves anyhow when they reach adulthood, and may embark a number of times on different religious and spiritual quests. But to withhold from them a sound religious tradition is akin to not schooling them in impulse control, manners, or good study habits. People don't just automatically develop good habits when they turn twenty-one.

One way to impart the Catholic faith is through the classic means: Catholic schools. Every study ever done shows that Catholic schools provide not only quality education, but moral training besides. Sometimes Catholic education requires a significant sacrifice, both in terms of tuition and the logistics of simply getting the children to and from a Catholic school. But it can yield enormous benefits.

In most cities and towns, we no longer have the cohesive neighborhoods that once provided the moral petri dish in which children could grow. A Catholic school can provide this, a framework for a unique way of living. As the editors of *America* magazine put it: "Catholic schools have always aimed to walk a narrow path between aloofness from the secular culture in which they find themselves and an uncritical acceptance of every aspect of that culture."[9]

Speaking of education, we might make mention of our own. Adult Catholics—even those of us who were educated in Catholic schools—are in constant need of refresher training in our religion, and new insights and inspiration to keep our faith alive. Parishes, religious communities, campus ministries, even dioceses offer dozens of courses in everything from understanding Scripture to coping with single parenthood. Retreat houses, houses of prayer, and monasteries provide the opportunity for a quiet retreat—for one day, several days, a week. They come in all of the many variations of Catholic practice—from ultra-orthodox to creation-centered and New Age. They are there for the seeker—all you need do is seek.

A good Catholic bookstore (or your library) will have hundreds of books that can speak to your soul. Catholic newspapers and magazines make accessible an amazing diversity of religious experiences, sometimes in the most unexpected or out-of-the-way places. Don't necessarily look to the best-seller list to find God. What masquerades as spirituality today often is no more than adoration of self. God—a lasting, true God—is our goal.

"All our kids went to Catholic schools. It simply works. They not only learn their studies, but they learn a way of living a life."
—DOROTHEA TOBIN

"My kids are CCD Catholics, twenty-four and twenty-six now. They're good kids, but they don't attend church. I wouldn't do it that way again; I would definitely send them to Catholic schools. They need as much Catholic education as they can possibly get. What a Catholic environment offers—and I had it when I was growing up—is a haven where you can try your wings before you have to fly."
—JOHN FIALKA

"We have a Catholic-Jewish Sunday school so that the children of these mixed marriages can be exposed to the rich tradition of both faiths. Families are unified in that class."
—FATHER JACK WALL

# THE GOOD ENOUGH CATHOLIC CHALLENGE:
# AN EVENT IN YOUR DOMESTIC CHURCH

We are members of large families, or we live alone. But all of us are joined to natural families, adopted families, pickup families. Whatever the configuration, whoever the participants, these are the members of our tribe, fellow pilgrims on the road of life.

Our family, our "domestic church," provides daily opportunities to sense God's presence in the world. It is our shelter from the storms of life, our first community, our first school of virtue. We want it to work. We realize we cannot transform it overnight; indeed, it may never be that perfect place of love and compassion and cooperation we dream of. But we can take one small step.

And so, the Good Enough Catholic challenge is to begin one ritual in our own family. It can be a prayer before supper for a week; reading or reciting evening prayers with our children; "God bless you" as a parting blessing.

Or, make this Sunday a family day. No malls, no television, no work. Listen to what all members of the family would like to do— and then do it, to the best of your abilities. Or do nothing at all. Just know that this is a day unlike any other day. God ordained it not for himself, but for us. All we need to do is graciously receive the gift.

# SELECTED READINGS

Walter M. Abbott, ed., *The Documents of Vatican II* (esp. "Decree on the Apostolate of the Laity). New York: Herder and Herder, Association Press, 1966.

Mitch Finley, *Your Family in Focus: Appreciating What You Have, Making It Even Better.* Notre Dame, Ind.: Ave Maria, 1993.

Bridget Mary Meehan, *Prayers, Activities, Celebrations (and More) for Catholic Families*. Mystic, Conn.: Twenty-Third Publications, 1995.

National Conference of Catholic Bishops, *Catholic Household Blessings and Prayers*. Washington, D.C.: United States Catholic Conference, 1989.

National Conference of Catholic Bishops, "Follow the Way of Love" (pastoral letter). Washington, D.C., 17 November 1993.

Gertrud Mueller Nelson, *To Dance with God: Family Ritual and Community Celebration*. New York: Paulist Press, 1986.

William Seifert and William Urbine, *On Life and Love: A Guide to Catholic Teaching on Marriage and Family*. Mystic, Conn.: Twenty-Third Publications, 1993.

James Vollbract. *Small Acts of Kindness*. New York and Mahwah, N.J.: Paulist Press, 1995.

Paul Wilkes, *My Book of Bedtime Prayers*. Minneapolis: Augsburg Fortress, 1992.

# COMMUNITY
## A Way to Live Together

- Individualism is our American birthright, fundamental to the functioning and vitality of a democratic system.
- Individualism is an essential element in our character, needed so that we might stand up for who we are and defend what we believe in.
- Individualism is a quality we seek to instill in our children, so that they might be independent thinkers capable of making up their own minds, and not be swayed by the crowd.
- ". . . Individualism may have grown cancerous . . . threatening the survival of freedom itself."[1]

Most of us, I assume, would readily agree with the first three statements—and shudder at the last. Taken from *Habits of the Heart*, an academic book about the American character that surprisingly became a best-seller, these haunting words waft across the collective conscience of a nation that seems to be morally adrift. How could this be?

After all, this is a nation that, while holding up individualism as a precious right, and believing firmly in the liberation and vindication inherent in free speech, always prided itself on its ability to pull together. Yet the ascent of the "Me Generation" signaled a new kind of Americanism; we have become a nation in which the social and political fabric seems nearly torn asunder by the impassioned demands of so many competing groups, each with an ideology they maintain is *the right one*. We have become a nation where public debate has turned into shrill accusation, and where ridicule, intimidation, and fear-mongering in the service of anything calling itself a cause are acceptable—and successful.

It seems we are citizens of a nation where a New Selfishness ("I want mine; I worked for it") has replaced the Old Concern ("There's enough to go around if we all sacrifice a little"). In our quest for self-fulfillment and unfettered individualism, words like altruism, self-sacrifice, and deferred gratification seem like relics of another day, another people.

How could this powerful trait—individualism—have taken such a turn? After all, it was political individualism that set this country free from colonial overloads, rugged individualism that settled this vast land, entrepreneurial individualism that forged the most impressive economic machine the world has ever witnessed.

How? Because, frankly, individualism only reaches as far as our next interaction with another human being. In today's world, we have contact—personally and electronically—with so many people. Somehow, we have lost our ability to see beyond our own needs, to seek the greater good. For in each of these interactions we encounter someone else who also can lay claim to their own individualism. They, too, have rights, hopes and dreams, which may correspond—or directly clash—with our own. Whether it suits our purposes or not, our personal needs must be looked at, and possibly altered, each time they meet up with the needs of another.

Some say they are not about to do that. Sensing that the moral fabric of our society is wearing thin, we are tempted to retreat even farther into our safe areas, to pull up our physical and psychic drawbridges so that none might trespass. Down deep in our souls we know something is missing in such an approach, something basic to our lives as citizens, parents, friends—and Good Enough Catholics. But so often we feel alone, powerless to do something about it. Our proud individualism has, in some ways, imprisoned us.

It is a paradox. We are an economically affluent country. Many of us have accomplished and obtained things our parents and grandparents never even dreamed of. And yet, we have grown less—not more—willing to share ourselves and our possessions. As a recent study indicated, Americans are giving less and less time and money to charity—and Catholics are leading the retreat. In fact, Catholics give even less to charities than people who profess no religious belief.[2]

The answer to our moral crisis is simple, as are most answers to profound and complex questions. And, while sometimes uncomfortable to face and difficult to live out, it is an answer that ultimately works. It stands ready as the antidote for the epidemic of righteous individualism and narrow self-interest that has swept across our nation and up our front steps. "It" is called *community*. Not some geographical area, this community is a state of mind.

If we reflect for a moment, we realize that we are part of a variety of communities throughout each day, each woven into society's fabric. Our family is one community, our neighborhood another; but so are the people in the supermarket and those around us in the workplace. Those we worship with, socialize with, study with, even those with whom we sit in a traffic jam—these are all our community. As we read a newspaper or watch the news on television, we form community, if even for a fleeting moment, with those who go hungry while we eat, those who suffer in war while we live in peace. Each has an impact on us—and, in ways perceptible and imperceptible, we have an impact upon each of them.

At first the thought of so much community can be overwhelming, an understandable and seemingly legitimate reason to circumscribe our lives, cutting off anyone other than those who agree to live their lives as we live ours. The demands, the needs of all these communities, give ample reason to retreat to the safety of our small group and the comfort of our stock responses.

But once again, Catholicism offers both the road signs and the reliable compass to guide our interactions and dealings with others. Catholicism looks upon individualism and pronounces it good—in fact a crucial element in the moral ecosystem of character. But individualism is not and has never been the Catholic ideal, and this certainly is true for the Good Enough Catholic as well. Interdependence is the ideal. God created us to live in community, as we all inhabit the same earth. Jesus Christ constantly reminded his followers to look out for the needs of others. Divine wisdom was trying to tell us that if everyone held a concern for others, the world would indeed be a wonderful place.

## COMMUNITY AMONG AMERICANS

In the 1830s, a French social philosopher sailed to America on a reporting assignment. Fascinated by what he had heard about the people of this vast new country, Alexis de Tocqueville wanted to view firsthand this experiment in self-rule. Ours was a unique, revolutionary system of government, and after a half-century of experience it seemed to be succeeding. The power unleashed by these rugged-individualist Americans, who had proclaimed (and then fought for) their independence from the powerful British Empire, had not imploded in anarchy—as many on the Continent had predicted would happen.

Tocqueville found that there were three main strands, woven together, that formed the American character: a strong sense of family, adherence to religious traditions (then dominantly a puritanical Protestantism), and the ability to participate, through local politics, in the very system to which these newly minted citizens had ceded a certain degree of control over their lives. But there was something else as well. Tocqueville concluded that the essential social ligaments connecting individuals to the wider political community were set in place by a network of voluntary associations. This, Tocqueville argued, was unique to America.

From book clubs to charities, choral groups to fraternal societies, New Americans sought out every conceivable way to band together. These, the flotsam and jetsam of other countries, religious idealists and political miscreants, had been tempered in the New World by a strange, internal force—a spirit of cooperation. In essence, they had

constructed a new kind of society—at once emblematic of the American character, so fiercely possessive of its hard-won freedoms, yet
willing to associate with virtually anyone in pursuit of common needs.
Strangers all, in a strange land, Americans sought common ground
where they could pursue goals beyond their individual capacities.
Through their natively concocted associations, self-seeking individu-
alists found themselves growing into another role: public-spirited
citizens and communitarians.

Constantly in need of fine tuning, experiencing a continuing series
of deaths and births, a community-oriented civil society worked amazingly well. Many, many worlds, intricately interrelated, orbited
within a democratic universe. Trust, sacrificing for the good of the
whole, proved to be the true genius of America. "Habits of the heart,"
as Tocqueville would write in *Democracy in America*, had transformed
and saved the American people from themselves.

When, beginning in the nineteenth century, Catholics came to
America in significant numbers, this was the social and civic ambi-
ence they found—but from which they were largely excluded. In
theory, America stood for the welcoming words emblazoned on the
Statue of Liberty: "Give me your tired, your poor, your huddled
masses yearning to breathe free. . . ." In practice, it was quite the
opposite for Catholics. Because of their particular type of Christianity, their beliefs and practices were at best suspect—and often de-
meaned—by the Protestant power structure.

A network of Catholic parishes became their anchor, their ethnic
and fraternal organizations, a way of serving both their emotional and physical needs. In doing this, of course, American
Catholics were merely replicating the voluntary associations they
saw all around them.

Not that Catholic immigrants landed on America's shores as perfect, loving, sharing Christians. But community had always been a
part of Catholic upbringing in the villages of Central Europe, Ire-
land, Italy, and eastern Europe whence, in successive waves, the vast
majority of them came. Concern for the other; a welcome for the
stranger, who was to be regarded as Christ himself. How badly they
wanted to feel this kind of welcome in America; *they* were now the

other, the stranger. They knew how important it was for a community to stand together through good times and bad. When they did not find that kind of community in America, they created it.

Catholic neighborhoods, Catholic parishes, Catholic organizations and institutions—comprising a vast network of hospitals, orphanages, and social service agencies—in turn exerted an enormous impact on the ethos of American life. A people with scant material resources shared what they had. Catholicism, at its best, stood for caring not only for one's own, but for the faceless stranger, the indigent, the poor, the ill. Catholic social services were eclipsed in scope and dollars only by the federal government itself. No religious group had ever done as much for themselves and for others.

There was another overlay of moral teachings for Catholics, though few really knew it existed. These were the social encyclicals and pastoral letters, written by popes and the American bishops over the period of a century. The encyclicals boldly proclaimed that the Catholic way could not always be in tune with what were often the dominant economic, governmental, and social voices in America. In fact, these Catholic social documents often opposed prevailing sentiments that Americans held dear.

Material goods, for instance, were not for the Catholic to jealously guard, but to keep in trust ("As for riches and other things that men call good and desirable . . . it matters little; the important thing is to use them aright").[3] Labor could be organized and bargain collectively, so that a just and living wage could be secured. Neither a socialism that vested all power in the state, nor laissez-faire capitalism—the bedrock of America's economic faith—were to be idealized and slavishly followed. Catholic social thought always looked to the good of society as a whole, condemned blind faith in impersonal market forces, and looked to judicious government intervention to bring about a moral social order. Perhaps most important, in a sweeping concept that extended each Catholic's sphere of concern to the ends of the earth, there had to be a "preferential option for the poor." ("God himself seems to incline to those who suffer misfortune; for Jesus Christ calls the poor 'blessed'. . . . He displays the most tender charity toward the lowly and oppressed.")[4]

Though few had ever read them or were familiar with them, these documents of religiously inspired social thought profoundly influenced American Catholicism. In their parishes and schools, Catholics were continually summoned to look back to the words and inspiration of Christ, and then out onto the world in which they lived. Theirs was to be another America—other-directed, community-conscious. Even though Catholics populated the lower echelons of America's economic and civic strata, many believed and practiced a commendable, religiously inspired selflessness.

As we reflect back over the past hundred years, it is an amazing transition that American Catholics have experienced. Catholics at first found themselves marginalized, but soon became a crucial sector of a nation unified by World War I. They were humbled by the Depression, only to be uplifted by the New Deal. They believed in community, both their own and that facilitated by a benevolent government. After they and the rest of the nation pulled together for World War II, Catholics were well represented among the millions of Americans accorded access to education and an upward mobility unknown in human history. But the silent, satisfied generation of the 1950s would be the last to know the comfort of intact parishes, neighborhoods, ethnic communities, and families. The cultural and political upheaval of the 1960s and 1970s presaged a turning inward for Catholics in the 1980s. And now, in the 1990s, there is an unprecedented suspicion—sometimes hate—of government and even society, a shunning of community obligations, and a reluctance to accept the responsibilities that rights presume. The distributive justice at the core of Catholic social teaching has gone out of favor.

"I moved into this neighborhood in the early 1960s; it was a wonderful place, safe, filled with kids. Well, it's not that way exactly anymore, but I've made a moral choice to stay here—to stay here and raise hell. If everyone with resources leaves neighborhoods like this, it becomes a self-fulfilling prophecy and the neighborhood will go down. I think the message of Jesus was to cast our lot with the poor. So this is my mission. Just to live here, to be part of this community."

—MARY ANNE BARRY

And the result? A review of *The Lost City*, a book that zeroes in on Chicago communities just like Mary Anne Barry's, appraises our current outlook:

". . . a world of restless dissatisfaction, in which nothing we choose seems good enough to be permanent . . . in work, marriage, in front of the television set." So, too, the "suspicion of authority has meant the erosion of standards of conduct and civility," while the transformation of sinners into passive victims who have been dealt "bad cards in life" places us "a step away from deciding that there is no such thing as right and wrong."[5]

Many of today's Catholics, the children of those who were immigrants just a generation or two ago, hold up—not out—their hands to today's immigrants. Some, who benefited enormously from government programs, want today's programs curtailed. Some, whose families were once among the least of American brethren, look upon today's poor with dismay—and sometimes disgust.[6]

What has happened to the community spirit of so many American Catholics? Do the gospel mandates no longer apply? Are the poor no longer our concern? Is our neighbor no longer to be treated as ourselves?

"Hal Gordon had just completed one of these New Age, personal empowerment experiences that leaves a person feeling gitchy-gitchy good, with a great sense of fulfillment—but he had no place to take it. The institutional church has all the vehicles; I told Hal to take what he found and apply it through what the Catholic Church was all about."

—FATHER RAYMOND KEMP

"As a black man, I was never in love with the Catholic Church, with all the uncaring people; but Kemp got to me somehow. All his talk about unabridged caring, service, service, and service. 'Well, okay, Kemp,' I said to myself. I took what I had learned about spirituality through that secular experience, wrestled with it in a Bible study with a dozen other people, and decided I had to do something. So here I am, in the middle of a crime-infested neighborhood, in a community-action center I started, with a motto, 'God Up Front in the War on Drugs.'

"A little community action, a little help from the Catholic Church. We use the structure when it works; we bend the rules when we have to."

—HAL GORDON

# DESIRES IN OUR HEARTS

Perhaps life is not a race whose only goal is being foremost. . . . Perhaps the truth lies in . . . [the idea] that there are practices of life, good in themselves, that are inherently fulfilling. . . . Perhaps enduring commitment to those we love and civic friendship toward our fellow citizens are preferable to restless competition and anxious self-defense.

—*Habits of the Heart*[7]

We are a social movement aiming at shoring up the moral, social, and political environment. Part change of heart, part renewal of social bonds, part reform of public life. Change of heart is the most basic. Without stronger moral voices, public authorities are overburdened and markets don't work. Without moral commitments, people act without any consideration for one another.

—*The Spirit of Community*[8]

God did not create human beings for life in isolation, but for the formation of social unity . . . "into a single people."

—*Gaudium et Spes*[9]

The insistent summons of these two recent, well-received books offering a way out of our amoral miasma echo what Catholic social thought has consistently maintained. A moral code must be honored; we must look beyond our needs. But the current sentiment, as documented in many a public opinion poll, seems to point in the opposite direction, confirming that our hearts are hard and immune to change. This, I think, paints an impoverished picture of our national soul. Yes, there is a public outrage. But there is also private aspiration.

When the researchers of *Habits of the Heart* talked to a broad range of Americans in the quietness of their homes, they found them ". . . eager to discuss the right way to live, what to teach our children, and what our public and private responsibilities should be. . . ."[10] They wanted to live a morally coherent life. The problem is that Americans—American Catholics among them—would say they do not know how. Where to begin?

Good Enough Catholics, struggling to live moral lives, may feel paralyzed by a society that seems to sanction lawlessness, reward greed, and encourage dependency. While we may have a private desire to be good and decent, too many of us have allowed public moral calluses to grow. We have grown reluctant to say something specific is wrong or immoral in a time when it is easy to point to a hundred things that are wrong and immoral. The tiny pinpricks of conscience that once stirred us are faint. But the instincts will not go away.

Can the Good Enough Catholic tend to and enhance the various communities, people, and groups that call out to us, and still maintain our individuality—and our sanity?

# LOVE IS NOT THE ANSWER

As John Donne reminded us, none of us are islands; no one stands alone. We are parts of dozens, hundreds of other communities, some forming, some enduring, some dissipating each day. In each of them, we are constantly negotiating—consciously or unconsciously—how much and what part of ourselves, our individuality, our talents, energy, attention, and means, to invest in them.

Our family, as we saw in chapter 10, is our first community. It is a community of those we know well, and to whom we are inextricably bound for life. Catholicism—and even the primal instincts of survival—charts out its demands. Regardless of where we go, or what other communities we are a part of, this one will never be dissolved.

Most of our other communities are composed of strangers. Some have common bonds: religion or sex or age, specific interests, geographical area, voting district. But many others occur far more randomly. Every day we confront people who are at once strangers, yet to whom we are linked. They are God's creatures just as we are, fellow pilgrims on life's journey. As Good Enough Catholics, how are we to be guided in our interactions with them?

Love, right? Love is the answer, the Perfect Catholic might offer. To which Reinhold Niebuhr (d. 1971) would respond with a resounding "no."

Niebuhr, an eminent Protestant social ethicist, stunned the religious and theological worlds in the midst of the Great Depression—when social programs were literally keeping people alive—by declaring that disinterested love for our fellow human beings was, in fact, *not* the answer. There was no such thing as pure love, Niebuhr maintained, sending angels' wings fluttering skyward from this sinful human lot; so why masquerade that it was otherwise?

What Niebuhr was advising in his seminal work *Moral Man and Immoral Society* (a title that itself resonates with our current conundrum) was that simple Christian moralism would do little to alleviate social inequity. A certain hard-headed pragmatism, tempered by Christian values, would go much farther. Man and woman were a mixture of the noble and the debased, as was the society around them. While animal instincts might stir people to preserve what they have, protect those closest to them, and reject all others, humans were not animals. They were separated from animals by their ability to control their impulses, to measure whether or not their impulses were correct, and *then* to act.

The objective of the moral person was not to live a life of absolute love and social self-abnegation, frantically straining to create an atmosphere of disinterested love. Rather, Niebuhr maintained, the objective was to practice a realism in which various interests were considered and, ideally, balanced. It was a matter of Christian justice, a kind of justice where claims were recognized, though not necessarily granted. Only in this way could people be saved from their own selfishness. Mediation was the answer, not adversarial confrontation to see who could prevail.

It takes no stretch of the imagination to realize that inevitable conflicts make life within communities difficult. Religious fundamentalists may want to create a Christian state, or an Islamic state. Taxpayers may not want to bear the burden of caring for those terminally ill with AIDS. Parishioners may want to return to a Latin mass with organ accompaniments, while others want liturgical dance and synthesizer music.

The reality we face is that we cannot escape these conflicts. By isolating ourselves, we allow those few with the loudest voices, the most impassioned beliefs, or the basest intentions to prevail. By refusing to be part of the solution, we *are* part of the problem. In the fragile moral ecosystem that is our democratic society, each person's input and attitude and concern really do matter.

Most important of all, by turning our backs, we do not follow the example of Christ, who confronted the inequities and needs of his day. He took on the moneychangers who were commercializing worship. How different is that from our saying no to the blatant commercialization of Christmas? He challenged a judgmental crowd by demanding that the person without sin be the first to cast a stone at the woman caught in adultery. How different is that from our standing up to the morally righteous of our day, whose narrow scope of concern sees only as far as is convenient, or beneficial, to them?

# ME? NOW?

Good Enough Catholics see and sense moral indifference all around us. But often, we pronounce it ubiquitously "out there" someplace. It is not, of course, in our family, our friends, or ourselves. It is "they" who are to blame, whoever they are. We are hardly alone in this attitude. As the sociologist M. P. Baumgartner found in studying an American suburb, most people didn't feel it was their place to express their own convictions when they encountered somebody doing something wrong.[11]

Unfortunately, Good Enough Catholics can't have it both ways. Good Enough Catholics cannot have a moral society unless we ourselves, within the various communities that we inhabit, are moral. We must lay moral claims on ourselves—and, without preaching or being holier than thou, on others. There is no other way if we want a moral society. Each action knits or rends the moral fabric.

I seriously doubt that my good friend Father Greer ever read Niebuhr. But he understood Niebuhr's line of thinking perfectly— and practiced it.

As Father Greer and I sat talking one day I asked him about his role in the crisis that engulfed Boston in the early 1970s, when forced busing was ordered to integrate the schools. Father Greer was hardly a social progressive, and certainly no bleeding-heart liberal; yet when the call went out, he volunteered to ride the buses with black children. They were stoned, spat upon, and jeered—and so was he.

"Look," he said, "I don't love blacks as much as I love my own Irish people. But God made us all, and he didn't make any garbage. . . . Was I enthusiastic about . . . it? No. Did I jump into my clerical collar every morning and say, 'Greer lands a punch for equality'? No. I was ordained to help people, and right then, the blacks needed help."

At the time, his most intimate community was the diocesan priests of the Archdiocese of Boston. Many of them, like Joe Greer, were Irish, and had less than tender feelings about blacks. Racist jokes were sometimes part of their humor. He could fall prey, as many of us do, to condescending comments about racial minorities. Father Greer had never volunteered to serve predominately black Boston parishes; very few of his contemporaries had.

But here was a moment when he was called upon to make a decision. Would he, by his presence, wearing a Roman collar, help prevent violence as the schools were integrated—a move he personally opposed—or would he merely stand aside, as virtually all his priest-friends were doing? Father Greer could hardly have been faulted if he had done nothing. He might have privately consoled himself by offering a mass for the intention of the schoolchildren.

What he did was make a more public stand. Busing was certainly questionable; but violence toward these children was unquestionably wrong. He would not allow this to happen if he could help it.

I've often reflected on that moment in Father Greer's life. I'm sure his friends didn't agree with him. He might have been the butt of jokes himself. This was not an easy or clear-cut decision. But Father Greer, not really seeking to make any sort of statement, sent a clear message to his community of priests, to his parish, even to his own family, about what the Catholic faith meant for him at that particular time. It was not an act of love—he said so himself. It was an act of *fairness* to a group of people whose need he knew—and which, he knew, he could do something about.

Fairness is enough. God asks for no more of the Good Enough Catholic.

"The topic of '. . . whatever happened to those nuns who taught us grade school . . .' came up in a conversation, and I was shocked to find out that many of the orders didn't have enough money in their retirement funds to take care of the sisters when they got old. I looked into it and found nuns living on food stamps, in a crummy motel, in real poverty. I can't be a social worker in my job, but this was a great story. After the story I wrote appeared in the *Wall Street Journal*, a group started up that raised $2 million to take care of them. Now there are yearly collections that have raised over $20 million. Look, if we can't take care of our own, who gave and gave and asked nothing in return, forget about the Third World and poverty. I found poverty right in our own church."

—JOHN FIALKA

Few of us are blessed with the selfless love that Christ embodied and the saints practiced; few of us are satanically evil. We are composites of good and evil, generosity and selfishness. We wrestle with our best and our worst instincts all the time. That is the human condition. But, in the encouraging words of good St. Rose of Lima, ". . . the gifts of grace increase as the struggles increase."[12] The Good Enough Catholic will receive the courage to face difficult moral choices, as needed.

# MAKING—AND LIVING—THE MORAL CHOICE

"Truly I say unto you, just as you did it to one of the least of these my brethren, you did it to me": these familiar words of Scripture present a sweeping recognition of the importance of our interactions with others. The words mean exactly what they say; a hand extended to an elderly person crossing a street is a hand extended to God, a check for a good charitable cause is a divine offering. Father Greer on that bus was protecting Christ from his oppressors.

Jesus' message, set within the moral economy of life, makes all our actions potentially holy. We have many guidelines for our behavior—the Ten Commandments, the social encyclicals; but I want to suggest another set, beautifully practical and clear.

In Catholicism there are two groups of invitations, acts toward humans, that are—according to Christ's promise—acts toward God. They are called the works of mercy. Rooted in the example of Jesus Christ, they are directed toward the needs of people we will encounter in life, both those known to us and those who are strangers. They are needs we also will experience. These works are based on the simple wisdom, "Do unto others as you would have them do unto you." They ingeniously form a basis for living the Good Enough Catholic life.

While the works of mercy constituted an answer (now dimly remembered) to a Baltimore Catechism quiz for Catholics of a certain age, many younger Catholics hardly know of their existence. It might be beneficial to list them and see how they apply in our day, in our attempt to structure a morally coherent life in our interactions with others. They are broken down into two categories: corporal works of mercy, tending to bodily needs, and spiritual works of mercy, tending to needs of the soul.

## Corporal Works of Mercy

- Feed the hungry.
- Give drink to the thirsty.
- Clothe the naked.
- Shelter the homeless.
- Visit the sick.
- Ransom the captive.
- Bury the dead.

## Spiritual Works of Mercy

- Instruct the ignorant.
- Counsel the doubtful.
- Admonish the sinner.
- Bear wrongs patiently.
- Forgive offenses.
- Comfort the afflicted.
- Pray for the living and the dead.

The works of mercy lay out for us a set of varied opportunities to live as Good Enough Catholics. As your eye passes back over these two lists, they can be considered in many different ways: actually and metaphorically, individually and collectively, acts of heroism and acts of daily decency. You may be surprised to realize you have probably performed—or had a chance to perform—many of the works of mercy within the past week.

*Actually and metaphorically:*   "Counsel the doubtful" can mean that midnight ride you took with a friend who was having marriage problems. "Ransom the captive" can mean that time you came to the aid of the new kid on the block who was being shunned, or the clumsy new clerk at the supermarket who couldn't quite get the hang of it. You buried the dead when you looked into that woman's eyes and told her that her late husband was a wonderful man. You sheltered the homeless when that acquaintance you really didn't like needed a place to stay overnight, and you willingly provided it.

*Individually and collectively:*   There are many works of mercy, like those suggested above, that a person performs as an individual. But some works of mercy are collective efforts. You choose (or refuse) to be a part of them by the way you vote, the way you speak, the kind of social programs you help support. Collectively, you "instruct the ignorant" when you make sure that all children receive a good education in your area. You "give drink to the thirsty" when, after reading of an impoverished Third World community in the paper, you contribute to help them sink a well. And, if you think about it, you "bear wrongs patiently," "forgive offenses," and both "feed the hungry" and "clothe the naked" by paying taxes that— even though you certainly don't appreciate being parted from your hard-earned dollars—go to caring for those in need. Imagine— paying taxes can be considered virtuous! Holy!

*Heroic and daily decency:*   Father Greer's bus rides might be looked upon as heroic, and perhaps there have been times when you did something similar. But the works of mercy are more often performed as little acts that are part of our daily lives. Theologically, they are means to our redemption and true humanization. Practically, they are the balm that soothes our interaction with others, the oil that lubricates society's gears.

As Good Enough Catholics, looking out upon the many communities of which we are a part, it is not difficult to recognize that we can have an impact—positive or negative, profound or fleeting—on many, if not all, of them. In the workplace, what do we stand for? A quality product or service, respect for those we work with? Do we help someone who's having a hard time, or make their life even more difficult? Do we pitch in when a team effort is required, or reserve ourselves only for those occasions that will prove to be of benefit to us personally? At the convenience store, where a new employee is being broken in as the line grows longer, do we join in the huffing and complaining? Or do we try to ease the tension with a smile or a lighthearted comment so as to ransom that captive of a bar code reader or a balky cash register?

Our lives are full of opportunities to be Good Enough Catholics. Tiny opportunities in which we make this a better world for everyone—or we do not. Tiny, grace-filled moments.

"We had a restaurant for twenty-five years, the neighborhood place where senior citizens hung out. Whether people had money or not, they ate. The neighborhood started going downhill and the drug dealers took over. I reported them to the police. They told me I'd better get out or I'd be dead. I wasn't leaving. So they burned the restaurant down one night. They stood there and laughed. Well, I wasn't getting out of there. That was my neighborhood, my community. So I started working with the gang members; I even took them into my home. I forget how many foster kids I eventually had. Three are now in college. I gave them all a cross to wear. They love it. They love jewelry. They may hate God because they think God did them in. But when they touch that cross maybe they think God does care for them after all."     —DOROTHY PAPACHRISTOS

# THE GOOD ENOUGH CATHOLIC CHALLENGE: ONE, UNASKED-FOR ACT

Our actions have an impact every day, in so many places and many ways, perceptible and imperceptible. Yet most of us Good Enough Catholics would personally find it extraordinarily difficult—impossible, in fact—to wake up in the morning determined to impact, in a positive, Good-Enough-Catholic way, every person and group we came in contact with that day. It is a worthy ideal, but one we know we would fail.

My father—one of those people who never preached a word, but taught by his actions—said his idea of being a decent person was to do one good, unasked-for deed a day. He was the kind of man who *did* help the new kid on the job as a carpenter—the kind who, working in the coal mines as a younger man, shared a sandwich with the new immigrant on his first day at work. He met immediate needs as he encountered them. I'm sure he wouldn't have passed by anyone lying on the side of the road—and he would have thought nothing of it.

And so let the Good Enough Catholic challenge be just that: one good deed, based on one of the works of mercy. You may want to try this for a single day; you may want to do it for a week. The idea is not to take the works of mercy and say you're going to practice a specific one. You may want to glance at the list again. But don't worry, an opportunity will present itself—in the place where you work, the store where you shop, the voting booth you enter, or in the very place in which you now sit reading.

Your attitude will make a difference; that one small act will send ripples. An attitude of human decency, of human concern, is extremely contagious. If Good Enough Catholics cannot return to the good old days, we can be the start of the good new days, creating an atmosphere in which it is easy and natural to be good. And we are not alone. Other Good Enough Catholics are making the same attempt.

# SELECTED READINGS

Robert N. Bellah, et al., *Habits of the Heart: Individualism and Commitment in American Life*. Berkeley: University of California Press, 1985.

Amitai Etzioni, *The Spirit of Community: Rights, Responsibilities, and the Communitarian Agenda*. New York: Crown, 1994.

Leo XIII, *Rerum Novarum*, in Michael Walsh and Brian Davies, eds., *Proclaiming Justice and Peace: Papal Documents from Rerum Novarum Through Centesimus Annus*. Mystic, Conn.: Twenty-Third Publications, 1991.

Allan Luks, *The Healing Power of Doing Good*. New York: Fawcett Columbine, 1991.

# ✥PART IV✥

# THE CHURCH
# AND YOU

*The Catholic Church forms the basis of our approach to God, our spirituality. It is through the church that we first understood who God is and how he works in the world.*

*Church teaching (chapter 12) presents a vast array of knowledge that we must not be intimidated by, but can learn from. There is an art to understanding what the church teaches, and how to incorporate those teachings in the circumstances of our individual lives. The authority vested in the pope and the hierarchy (chapter 13) serves a noble purpose, providing teachers to interpret ancient truths in the modern day—but again, we must be thinking partners with them. The priesthood (chapter 14) is not limited to the ordained. We are all members of a royal priesthood, the priesthood of believers.*

# CHURCH TEACHING
## The Art and Practice of Belief

The most prestigious graduate school of theology and religious education in Rome—and the largest in the world—is the Pontifical Gregorian University. Founded in 1552 by St. Ignatius Loyola, the Gregorian has been a staunch defender of the Catholic faith down through the centuries, and the training ground for thousands upon thousands of priests, 850 bishops, sixteen popes, and no fewer than twenty saints. It is here that a significant portion of what we know as modern church teaching finds its theological origins.

One afternoon I sat in a rather simple office within the Gregorian's ornate and imposing neoclassical building, talking to the man personally chosen by the pope to lead this distinguished institution. Father Giuseppe Pittau, the Gregorian's rector, leaned back pensively in his chair at my question.

Many Catholics had bristled before at the strong, unequivocal words of Pope John Paul II. And now the latest papal proclamation, declaring that the issues of priestly ordination—of mandatory celibacy and a male-only clergy—were categorically closed and no longer to be discussed, had sent still more Catholics into paroxysms of disbelief. What was the thinking Catholic, the Good Enough Catholic, the theologian searching for truth to do?

Father Pittau smiled as he began his answer, a wan look, at once of theological detachment and of trust in the wisdom of the ages. "Even the pope's point of view must be studied," he replied. "But we must always be open to solid research, not just points of view. And, while we have a love for tradition, we must enrich it, or it dies. Too many in the church are timid today, therefore they go the safe way. That is not always the good way."

I marveled then, and I marvel now, at the simplicity, depth, and wisdom in those words. Father Pittau was saying that Catholicism's teachings could be transmitted neither by dictatorship nor spoon-feeding. Catholicism's teachings required thought—of his students, of all Catholics. The church was not a democracy, where the votes of the faithful steer the course of doctrine and dogma; no, that could not be so. Church teaching needed different wisdoms: the authoritative voice of the bishop of bishops, teacher of teachers—the pope—as well as the insights and findings of theologians, and the experiences of the actual people who were attempting to live out Christ's mandates.

The truth will ultimately win out, our faith has taught us, painful or tedious as the process may be. Equally, while no pope can dictate what we must believe, the pope's words—spoken from the chair of St. Peter, the rock upon which Catholicism is built—must be honored with attention, respect, and our own careful discernment. This is essential to the nature of Catholicism and Catholic belief.

It is not enough to either blindly accept or stubbornly refuse official church teaching; neither response represents the kind of Catholicism that Father Pittau wanted his students to take into the influential teaching and leadership positions they would occupy in the world. Equally, neither is good enough for the Good Enough Catholic.

# A THEOLOGY IS FORMED

From the very beginnings of the church down to this day, there have been misunderstandings, disagreements, conflicts, and downright battles about how to exercise moral leadership in the church, about how to guide people in the way that Christ intended for them. The small group of believers that Jesus left behind—which only gradually discovered that its beliefs were destined to be significantly different from the Judaism of its founder—were aflame with the Spirit, but lacking in practical experience. They had to find ways to pronounce specific actions worthy and unworthy of the followers of Christ, efficacious or detrimental to their spiritual lives—and to guide their new adherents through all the infinite possibilities between these extremes. But where to turn for this guidance?

Of course, the word "theology" was not mentioned; neither was "church teaching," "doctrine," or "dogma." What was sought by the earliest Christians were a set of practical guidelines for that time and that place, to be employed in real people's lives.

At first, there was a simple litmus test: Is this what Christ would have wanted, what he himself might have done in similar circumstances? To find that, the early Christians looked back to the life of Christ and searched the stories about him that had been passed down orally. There was no religious authority to readily turn to, so these communities gathered together and prayed for guidance in facing the moral and practical issues of their day. It was confusing, coming, as they eventually would, from varied religious and cultural traditions. As best they could, they had to sort out what was truth and what was heresy, what was acceptable behavior and what was not. And they looked to their elders—elected to positions of leadership because they were perceived as actually *living* the way Christ had proclaimed.

Eventually, the stories and portrayals of Jesus' life were assembled. Letters from the earliest disciples to their fledgling communities throughout the Mediterranean world were gathered together and, combined with the four gospels, formed what we now know as the New Testament. This would be the repository of truths that formed the basis for church teachings.

The number of Christians grew, and communities were founded in ever-increasing numbers far from Palestine; the issues they faced grew increasingly complex. Not only were the "spiritual sources"—

the words of the New Testament—called upon to form Christian codes of faith and morals; the most substantial and tested secular sources were also consulted. Key within this secular body of knowledge was what was known about the natural law—or the very nature of things—especially as distilled in the writings of the preeminent pre-Christian Greek philosopher Aristotle (d. 322 B.C.).

Of course, formulating a body of authoritative church teachings was an enormously complicated procedure that required reading of both holy and secular texts—an ability possessed by precious few of the early Christians. While the church always maintained that authority rested in the community of believers as a whole, more and more the discerning of moral law became the work of clergy, members of the hierarchy, and scholars who specialized in philosophy—and a field that would be known as theology, an area of inquiry later characterized by St. Anselm (d. 1109) as "faith seeking understanding."[1]

Schools of study and religious instruction grew up in centers such as Rome, Antioch, and Alexandria. Early fathers of the church, such as Origen (d. 254) and Augustine (d. 430), synthesized and explained the Christian approach. Various teachings emerged from both the pope's own communications and the various churches and communities. There were teachings that proved to be true to the life of Christ and Scripture, and resonant with an evolving tradition. And there were incorrect interpretations—some of which were deemed so potentially harmful to the faithful that they were denounced as heresies.

Almost from the start, there were voices within the church that, seeing the wild fluctuations in interpretation, warned of the dangers; they wanted absolute surety to be preached and taught, and absolute obedience demanded. And there were others who were more willing to take Christ at his word, confident that the Holy Spirit would stay with the church to guide it. As St. Vincent of Lerins (d. before 450) said, even as he was battling the myriad heresies of the day:

> Is there to be no development of religion in the church of Christ? Certainly, there is to be development on the largest

scale. Who can be so grudging to men, so full of hate for God, as to try to prevent it? . . . The religion of souls should follow the law of development of bodies. Though bodies develop and unfold their component parts with the passing of the years, they always remain what they are.[2]

Gradually, the concept of a more definable and authoritative body came into being. It was called the magisterium—which initially meant "teaching." It was composed of the leaders of the various Christian communities, bishops, and Peter's successor, the reigning pope. Theologians informed their deliberations and judgments, and the faithful were constantly consulted as the potential recipients of such teachings. The authority of the magisterium was understood to be in keeping with Christ's example. The magisterium would attempt to discern the truth, then convince the faithful through the inherent truth and goodness of the teaching it proposed—not through coercion or threat.

In the Middle Ages, another outpouring of theological works—anchored by the writings of the seminal thinker Thomas Aquinas—further advanced the body of church teachings. Both the early and medieval periods had been characterized by a certain openness and continual questioning, but the rise of Protestantism stopped that in the later Middle Ages. The church responded defensively, claiming that it alone had the right to speak authoritatively on moral issues, or on what Christ would have for his people on earth. Strict, inflexible doctrine and moral coercion took the place of what had been a more pastoral approach to religious instruction.

Starting with the First Council of Nicaea in 325, on through the five Lateran councils (1123–1517), to the momentous Council of Trent (ending in 1563), and on to the Second Vatican Council in 1962–1965, the church has periodically found it necessary to stop in its teaching role and gather leaders from throughout the universal church in order to address pressing religious issues. It is interesting to note that except for Vatican II, *all* the previous twenty councils were called to address specific heresies or threats to church unity—from Arianism (Nicaea), which denied the divinity of Christ; to the

Protestant Reformation (Trent), which questioned everything from the church's teaching authority to the sacraments; to the question of papal infallibility (Vatican I, 1870).

Thus, Vatican II stands apart in the history of church teaching. There were no major threats to Catholicism in the late 1950s and early 1960s; in fact, the church had never seen more uniform practice and belief, and such great numbers. But Pope John XXIII sensed a world about to change. He believed the church needed "updating"—or, in an oft-repeated metaphor, the church needed its windows opened to allow in fresh air and light. Pope John felt the church needed to change its attitude of defending the "one, true faith" from the onslaught of the world. Instead, it needed to confront how the world had changed, and what that world might have to say to a body of dogma, doctrine, and practice assembled over the previous nineteen centuries.

"I wanted to join the church, so I went to our pastor and asked him, point blank, 'What do I have to believe to be Catholic?' He said, 'The Apostles Creed and the Nicene Creed.' We kept talking, and either he or I said that a lot of people don't think of the Blessed Virgin Mary from this year to the next and whether she was a virgin or bodily went to heaven. What he was telling me was to get into the basic stuff and not worry about the rest; it would take care of itself."

—CAROLYN SWEERS

"We really don't know where the church is in the whole growing process. Maybe the church is just in its infancy stage and not adult at all."

—VANESSA COOKE

# MAJESTY AND MISTAKE

When those who question or criticize the teaching authority of the Catholic Church look for examples on which to base their case, they have an ample array of egregious mistakes and missteps to choose from. At times, the church has been plainly wrong, a moral bully, and woefully shortsighted.

It was the Catholic Church—and Pope Urban I (d. 1099)—that urged on the Crusades, making the slaying of "infidels" an act worthy of heavenly reward, not a breach of the Sixth Commandment.

It was the Catholic Church that condemned Galileo for having the audacity to assert that the earth revolved around the sun, contradicting church tradition that held the earth was the center of the universe. Galileo was not only forbidden by the Inquisition to teach or seek to prove his finding, but was forced to recant and lived the last eight years of his life under house arrest.

It was the Catholic Church that pronounced slavery acceptable; decreed charging interest on loaned money a grievous sin; condemned pagans and Jews to hell unless they converted; and, in our own century, declared that a morsel of meat eaten on a Friday guaranteed an eternity in damnation. Worshiping in a non-Catholic church? What is now a sign of Catholic openness was for centuries decried as a mortal sin.

And yet, with all its monumental blunders and errors of judgment over the centuries, the Catholic Church has produced the most comprehensive set of moral teachings in history. There is nothing like it in any religious tradition. While at times terribly narrow-minded and belligerently incorrect, church teaching for the most part has stood the test of time, proving after all to be a true and good path for humankind. Catholics have a right to be proud—and a need to beg forgiveness—for their church's strong stands.

Indeed, the church has not only proclaimed religious doctrine. With the increasing realization that the work of God is *in* the world and *among* people—and not only a heavenly quest—a rich body of encyclicals has addressed a wide spectrum of contemporary issues as well. We briefly discussed the encyclicals dealing with family life in chapter 10, and the social encyclicals in chapter 11. In addition to documents issued under the pope's seal, individual bishops and bishops' conferences throughout the world have spoken out on an even wider range of issues, from treatment of the poor to the dangers of nuclear arms, human threats to the ecology, and a Catholic view of the economy.

> "I don't get too worried about what comes down from the Vatican and the pope, because they are people. They have their views and they're trying to interpret what's in the Bible, the same way I am. It doesn't mean you don't believe that church teaching has some place in your life. But you realize these are man-made rules, not God's rules. The 'church' shouldn't keep you from coming to church."
>
> —NATASHA WITSCHY

> "Church teaching deviates so much from the teachings of Christ, and yet there is so much good in it: social justice, concern for the immigrant, the worker, the poor. But there's so much about us that drives me nuts. I'd like to have an unquestioned faith, but, unfortunately, I don't. I'm not a child anymore, and I have to think things out for myself."
>
> —MARIELSA BERNARD

## "TRUTH" AND HOPELESS RELATIVISM

We live in a time when even the mention of the word "truth," once so venerable a concept, raises our intellectual hackles. With Pilate, we ask: What is truth? And whose truth is being offered to us?

No matter how we try to run from it, or how instinctively we throw up our shields of rationality, we yearn for a bedrock of truth upon which to build our moral lives. We know the basic realities of life don't change every day; yet those who have promised unquestionable truth have so often disappointed us. As a result, many of us find ourselves foundering somewhere between the safe but unlikely promise of unchanging truth, and the miasma of hopeless relativism. We want truth, but we will not blindly give up our God-given ability to think for ourselves.

As we look at church teaching, then, it is important to understand it for what it is—and to understand ourselves for who we are. For church teaching, at any given moment, is the product of men and women—humans who, given their individual abilities, virtues, and faults, praying for God's inspiration and guidance, and looking to the church's rich body of tradition, attempt to show us a way to live in keeping with Christ's words and example. Church teaching exists within a specific historical framework, embracing—or denying— the body of knowledge available at that time. Church teaching may claim elements of divine inspiration, but it is not divinely written.

And we, in turn, are the products of a time and place, limited by our own particular social, economic, political, and historical framework. We may choose extremes: we can choose to put all that aside and obediently follow the church's teachings to the letter, claiming the church knows more about life's mysteries than we do; or we can live and view life exclusively through the prism of our own experiences, emotions, and thoughts. This latter course comes with all the limitations of a thoroughly existential approach. As Richard McBrien writes in *Catholicism*: "The more history we know, the less likely we are to distort the reality of Catholicism by shaping it to our own predispositions or by identifying it with one razor-thin slice of its long and richly diverse history."[3]

Most people acknowledge the need for the guidance of an authentic religious tradition in seeking a true spiritual and moral life. It is not something we can merely concoct out of thin air or a mélange of modern philosophies or self-help techniques. "Without tradition, learning is arduous at best, impossible at worst," writes Robert L. Wilken. "The ideal of the autonomous individual is glaringly inappropriate, for we recognize that here the true mark of rationality is to apprentice oneself to another rather than strike out on one's own." He goes on to say there is time enough "for originality when the apprenticeship is done."[4]

Church teaching provides that apprenticeship. Our own natures will dictate how we express our individuality in dealing with this great body of doctrine and dogma.

Vatican II documents delineated quite clearly two important aspects about church teaching—that it is at once immutable and mutable. "The church also affirms that underlying all changes there are many things that do not change; they have their ultimate foundation in Christ, who is the same yesterday, today, and forever."[5] But: ". . . if the influence of events or of the times has led to deficiencies in conduct, in church discipline or even in the formulation of doctrine (which must be carefully distinguished from the deposit of faith itself) these should be rectified at the proper moment."[6]

These two seemingly opposed statements shed light on the premise of what it means to be a Good Enough Catholic. There is an eternal, unchanging message and lifestyle in Catholicism. Sometimes our church not only proclaims the message, but lives it; sometimes it does neither. We Good Enough Catholics are members of a Good Enough Catholic church—a church that has certainly made its mistakes, but one that preserves a magnificent tradition and body of truth. It deserves our allegiance. After all, as Peter said when the Jewish leaders turned away and Jesus asked if he, too, would be moving on: "Where can we go, Lord? You have the words of eternal life."

Catholic teaching embraces creed, sacraments, encyclicals, canon law, dogmatic formulations of the ecumenical councils, liturgy, theological writings of both the early church fathers and the theologians of our day, the Sermon on the Mount, the practice and example of the church down through the ages. And while we might say that it can be reduced to an ethic of "love God and love your neighbor as yourself"—which, indeed, it can be—Catholic teaching is vast, complex, and, for all practical purposes, unknowable for any individual. Each of us is given only a partial understanding of the mystery of life, of God, of our church.

Yet it makes neither good sense nor good theology to think that we must start afresh in each generation to reinvent Catholic belief. We cannot adopt the easy and misleading idea that one Christian's ideas of religious belief and practice are every bit as good as another's, or that we have the right to take or to leave what our church has taught and does teach. Rather, it is our task to take this vast body of knowledge and tradition and adapt it, making it alive and meaningful in our day.

In some ways, the kind of teaching authority the Good Enough Catholic looks for in the church today is no different from the kind of authority that the Good Enough Parent would hope to exercise. It is not the kind of authority that commands this, or restricts that, simply because of its inherent power. For, as St. Augustine said in *On True Religion*, "Authority invites trust and prepares human beings for reason." Interestingly enough, Augustine's word "invites" also has been translated by the more doctrinaire as "demands." But how can anyone *demand* trust? Augustine, in his wisdom, was speaking not of coercion but rather of truths that engender our confidence, simply because of the source that we have learned we can trust. It is not that we *have* to believe; because of the authenticity of the source, we *want* to believe.

"The American culture wants things changed instantly, but these are things of lesser value and they don't endure. I have a problem with 'cafeteria Catholics.' The beauty of the Catholic faith and the magisterium are very, very crucial to me because their job is to discover the truth, then present the truth. The individual then has to go through the internal dialogue to figure out how they play those truths out in their own lives."

—JOHN BUTLER

"I admire the church for its steadfastness. It's the only thing in my life that doesn't move with the trends. It should stand aside from the world and have its own drumbeat, but when it's so impossibly out of step with people, that's where Catholics like me can't go along with it."

—JOHN FIALKA

"I cannot be publicly pro-contraception. But privately, I can be. That's the difference for me. If I am putting it in the face of the church, I am defying that authority, and that is wrong."

—MARTY GERAGHTY

# THE ISSUE OF INFALLIBILITY

When the phrase "church teaching" is even mentioned, too many Catholics feel that there is a certain body of truths—a check-off list of doctrines, perhaps all the material contained in the new Catholic Catechism—that must be accepted unquestioningly and completely. The alternative, they believe, is that they cannot consider themselves Catholic, cannot receive the sacraments, and, in effect, are excommunicated from the church. Many also think that virtually all of the pope's pronouncements—instructions, encyclicals, letters, even practical rules (like not eating meat on Fridays, or not keeping holy days of obligation)—carry with them the stamp of infallibility.

Nothing could be further from the truth. In fact, infallibility has been invoked only once in the 125 years since it was defined—for the declaration of Mary's bodily assumption into heaven, by Pope Pius XII in 1950.[7] In fact, many theologians seriously doubt that any pope—as a matter of practicality—can speak infallibly, *ex cathedra*, from the chair of St. Peter. What many theologians propose is that only those pronouncements that are *certainly true* can demand our unquestioning acceptance. It makes little sense to try to name them, but their number would indeed be few. What we can say with certainty is that infallibility has *never* been invoked on a matter of Catholic morals or practice.

Clifford Longley, writing in *The Tablet*, confronted this issue, noting that sometimes

> . . . the church leaps out of this world of evidence and rationality, in order to close the gap from probability to certainty by invoking its supernatural authority. This appeal to faith does not always lead to humble obedience, but sometimes to a dishonest separation of faith from reality. It is a demand that the human mind should split in two, in order to believe with one half what it doubts with the other. We cannot separate our religious selves from our civic or everyday selves in this way.[8]

## THE PROCESS OF DISCOVERY

The theologian Yves Congar (d. 1995), whom we will discuss more in the next section, explained the necessity of an evolving Catholic tradition and teaching by citing one of the great influences in his life, Paul Claudel, who compared tradition to a man walking. "In order to move forward he must push off from the ground; if he kept both feet on the ground, or lifted both in the air, he would be unable to advance. If tradition is a continuity that goes beyond conservativism, it is also a movement and a progress that goes beyond mere continuity."[9]

Once arriving at doctrinal points, the church has historically shown a marked reluctance to alter any of its positions, sure its teaching authority would be undermined if it said it had in any way been wrong. This is understandable. Think of the impact church teaching has on the lives of hundreds of millions of Catholics. Think of who it is that the church looks to as the authority for its authority—God who became man in Jesus Christ. If we, in our individual kayaks, can readily alter our course, the institutional Catholic Church involves all the power, momentum, and difficulty of navigating a supertanker. It cannot, and actually should not, make many sudden moves.

Throughout its history, the church has spent much time, effort, and even blood defending its positions. Most were substantial and right (for example, that Jesus was fully human and fully divine), some were insignificant, and others proved misguided or plain wrong (for example, that the sun revolved around the earth). Some scholars and theologians even extend the status of infallibility over the entirety of church teachings. Others have attempted to show that church teaching is not a series of definite end points, but rather a process of discovery, given new insights in history or science or human development. In other words, church teaching could be seen as a continuing revelation only gradually unfolded in the church's life and among her people—never complete, forever seeking to accurately mirror the spiritual truth revealed by Jesus Christ.

One of the key proponents of this later approach was John Henry Newman (d. 1890), a convert from Anglicanism, who eventually became a cardinal. "His mind, teeming with images, offered a variety of ways of understanding how the church's doctrine of today was not literally the same as the church's doctrine of yesterday, but yet the church was faithful to her Founder," wrote John T. Noonan, Jr. (a federal court judge, not a theologian), in an excellent article in *Theological Studies*.[10] ". . . development became one of the 'principles' of Catholic christianity. . . . Newman confessed that changes had occurred in the doctrine of the church but maintained that the changes had been rooted in the original revelation and were a perfection, not a distortion, of it."

"I don't want to have to try to convince anyone about religious belief. When I find people critical of the Catholic Church and they say, 'I don't want to be part of such a place,' I just tell them, 'That's not my experience.' And then I pause. If a person wants

to go further, I'm happy to talk about it, but I'm not about to convince someone to go to church or 'come back to the faith.' People
know I'm Catholic and I hope who I am, rather than my ability to
'defend the faith,' is a testimony to what being Catholic today
means."

—TOM LENZ

"Perfection" not "distortion." Newman's words are a cooling
breeze to counter the hot winds of absolutism that blow over the
church from time to time when the hierarchy feels impelled to try
to rein in its errant flock not through the trust engendered by legitimate authority but by the raw exercise of power. How well Newman knew from personal experience how religious thought could
and did develop. He had once argued that the *via media* of Anglicanism represented true "catholicity"; but when authorities in the
Church of England asked him finally to cease his writing and
preaching, he withdrew into a long period of prayer and meditation—only to find in Catholicism his true spiritual and intellectual
home. Newman's ideas about the development of Catholicism as a
series of imperfect steps toward the revelation of God's perfection
would take a century to have its real impact—in the theologians
whose work laid the foundation for Vatican II. (And, in his memory, Newman Centers for Catholic students have been aptly named
on secular college campuses throughout America.)

There are those Catholics, still angry with a church that once
would condemn a person to hell for a Friday hamburger, who want
to continue to vent their rage, and thus hold themselves apart from
such a seemingly arrogant and myopic institution. We can sympa-
thize with them.

The church can be faulted for (though it may choose other terms)
a certain immaturity of thought, of which institutions, just like the
people who populate them, can be guilty. But to unequivocally
condemn actions of the church really produces no gain, regardless of
how justified a specific indictment may be, or how personal were

the injuries inflicted by insensitive church teachings. It is the same as freezing in time any person's actions, calling them to task for those actions performed then with limited knowledge or experience, and judging them against the standard of the knowledge and experience they possess today. We forgive children for their many foolish acts. As they grow, we expect higher and higher levels of wisdom. We must do the same with the church.

Changed historical conditions bring about changes in church teaching. What was right in one century can be wrong in the next—and vice versa. Change, even in something so seemingly etched in stone as church teaching, need not be feared. As Cardinal Newman said, "Here below to live is to change. And to be perfect is to have changed often."[11]

"Someone gave me a subscription to one of these ultra-right-wing, conservative Catholic publications, so I'm on this ultra-right-wing, conservative mailing list. It's amazing the literature that comes out, scaring Catholics: that Catholicism isn't being taught right, either in Catholic schools or CCD. It's such a campaign of fear. I teach in a Catholic school, and I know how good we are; it shocks me that these people think that unless we teach the strictest view of Catholicism, it's not Catholicism at all."

—GAIL SMITH

"I know all the rules. But that's not what it's about, not the way life works. The rules are not the same as you go along in years. A child is told not to use matches; as an adult, you know how to use them."

—PETER HEBEIN*

# EXILE AND VINDICATION

Recent history presents us with some stunning examples of how eternal truths are resurrected and modern insights eventually embraced in the Catholic Church. Reflecting on these examples might provide us with a little more patience with our church, and that sense of detachment that Father Pittau exhibited in our conversation at the Gregorian in Rome.

Many of the greatest Catholic theologians of our century— John Courtney Murray (d. 1967), Henri de Lubac (d. 1991), Congar, Bernard Haring, Karl Rahner (d. 1984), and Pierre Teilhard de Chardin (d. 1955)—were at one time unmercifully pilloried for their ideas, fired from teaching positions, forbidden to publish, and effectively banished. In the period following World War II, they saw the doctrinal uniformity and presumed certitude of church teaching not as uplifting, but instead deadening to the Catholic spirit. They saw a need to break out of the shackles imposed by the neoscholastic approach to Catholic thinking that prevailed throughout the church; and they were brave enough to say and write this openly.

It is important to understand this neoscholasticism, because it formed many of our priests—and, in turn, a large percentage of Catholic lay people. As Brendan Hill has reminded us, "The classic resources for such theology were 'manuals,' which stated a teaching of the church in the form of a thesis, explained the thesis in a series of notes, and then demonstrated how the teaching was supported in the statements of church councils, passages of Scripture, and in the teachings of the fathers and Aquinas."[12] The accent was on *defending* the faith; church teaching was regarded not only as correct and complete, but in no need of periodic review. To question implied a lack of faith—or perhaps a suffusion of arrogance, holding one's self above the teaching magisterium.

But Murray, de Lubac, Congar, Haring, Rahner, and Teilhard

saw the faith in another light. They wanted to break through the rigid and lifeless categories of the time and return to the rich sources of the Bible, the early church fathers, and the profound thinkers whose work had been whittled down to fit neat, legalistic theorems. Their theology took classical church teaching and exposed it to the critical light of historical biblical research, the thoughtful examination of Scripture in both the social, political, cultural contexts of the time when it was composed and those of today. These writers felt that a reassessment of church teaching was called for by the dramatic forces unleashed by the changes in world economies; the new anthropological and archaeological research, which yielded a much clearer picture of Christ and the early church; the advances in science, psychology, medicine; and the changing social roles of women and men. An understanding of linguistics, symbolism, metaphor, and myth provided new paths for interpretation.

Congar saw the laity in an entirely new light, not as sheep to be led, but as partners with the clergy. De Lubac worked toward an integration of natural and supernatural, refusing to grant each a discrete world. Rahner and Haring conceptualized an entirely new vision of the church, no longer seeing it simply as the setting for quaint and obligatory ritual, but rather as a dynamic, organic community, constantly adapting itself to the ever-changing world. Murray believed that everyone—Catholics included—had the religious freedom to choose their own path to God. Teilhard drew out a link between paleontology and theology, of human and spiritual evolution.

Banished to the perimeters of the church before Vatican II, these writers would usher in the most profound and most rapid renewal in Catholic history. Why? Because what they were proposing made rational and spiritual sense for twentieth-century people. What is also quite remarkable is that these seminal Catholic thinkers did not lapse into bitterness or despair when they were being rejected by the official church. They had faith and confidence that the truth for this age would emerge. Eventually, some of them were even elevated to the status of cardinal—although none had ever been a bishop!

And of course, like the doctrines they critiqued, neither should their hard-fought ideas be enshrined. In fact, de Lubac, while acknowledging the enormous benefits of Vatican II, bemoaned a Catholic "collective loss of balance" after the council, declaring that the newfound "openness to the world" left Catholics "as poor creatures without an identity, trailing along in a tow."[13] Not a few of Vatican II's innovations are now under attack as being counter to what a hierarchical church should promote. Still other theologians advance even more radical solutions—from those seeking a return to strict, neoscholastic orthodoxy, to those advocating (for example) women's ordination or a dismantling of the Vatican bureaucracy.

Yes, church teaching is confusing. No wonder Good Enough Catholics ask: To whom can we listen? How can we, untrained in theology, find the truth for ourselves? How can we stay in a church that silences or intimidates our best theologians?

# THE ART OF AN ENLIGHTENED FAITH

To add to the confusion even further, consider these two statements:

> Even when the magisterium does not intend to act definitely . . . a religious submission of will and intellect is called for. . . . [T]he teaching of the magisterium, by virtue of divine assistance, has a validity beyond the argumentation it employs.[14]

> Yes, American Catholics want to be faithful to their spouses, their families, their communities, and even their church, which is considered the Bride of Christ. But, as a bride and groom are called to be faithful to each other, they are expected to challenge any dysfunctional behavior. Likewise, American Catholics want to be faithful to their bride, but will refuse to be co-dependents to her dysfunctional decisions.[15]

The first statement comes from "Instruction on the Ecclesial Vocation of the Theologian," a 1990 Vatican document that attempts to ban public dissent from church teaching. The second is from

Father Brian Jordan's letter a few years later to his congregants at St. Camillus Parish in Silver Spring, Maryland, after the Vatican banned divorced and remarried Catholics from receiving the Eucharist, refused to accept a New Revised Standard Version Bible with inclusive language, and a nearby bishop decreed that female altar servers would no longer be allowed in his diocese.

Such diametrically opposed views of church teaching are common today. It is not important or necessary that the Good Enough Catholic subscribe completely to one or the other. What is important is that the Good Enough Catholic take seriously both what the church is saying today and what it has said down through the ages—in addition to taking equally seriously what their own life circumstances, experience, study, prayerful reflection, and common sense reveal.

What we seek is an "enlightened faith." We seek to live not by the *letter* of church law, but by the *spirit* behind those laws, which should have their foundation in the life and witness of Jesus Christ. To simply ignore the church's teachings and traditions is to turn our backs on a rich treasure. To use only our own mental abilities is to impoverish and limit what the mighty church founded by Jesus Christ can mean in our lives. That would find us gazing intently and hopefully into a mirror—but all we would ever see is ourselves.

The gospel mandate that the church used for many years to condemn usury—the lending of money for profit—is a perfect example of how an enlightened faith transcends the literal or dogmatic, looking to the spirit, not the letter, of the law. Scripture reads, "Lend freely, hoping nothing thereby." As we now understand, this is a call to generosity, not a prohibition against lending money for profit. Indeed, lending money for profit is good and necessary to healthy economic systems and, in turn, gainful employment and bountiful production. Likewise, "What God has joined together, let no one put asunder" can be interpreted as setting the goal of a life commitment for all marriages, rather than an absolute prohibition of divorce. Only by a realistic and compassionate application of those words is Christ's message realized in practical terms.

Seeking an enlightened faith. Living by the spirit of God's law.

We need not fear to be at once bold enough, and humble enough, to make those our goals.

> "My job is to help change the church from within. All the doctrines are not true, but I don't let those doctrines get in my way. There is a lot of room for respectful disagreement. In the gospels Jesus is constantly saying not to get lost in the details. That's the trouble with the church today. We ought to keep to the major principles and set aside the little things that divide us."
>
> —ALLEN STRYCZEK
>
> "It's very important to note that the teaching church can only teach what the believing church believes. In the past fifteen years, the whole spirit and concept of the *sensum fidelium* has been dashed. This is sad. We need to rein in the magisterium. We need to practice more discernment and not so much doctrine. Because, for instance, sometimes God is saying that ending a life is a holy thing. We can't preserve it at all costs. We know that now."
>
> —DICK WESTLY

## THE GOOD ENOUGH CATHOLIC CHALLENGE: OPEN TO INSPIRATION

We are fully aware that our Catholic Church has much to teach us, yet we have seen its horrible abuses of ecclesiastical power—by means of church teaching. At the same time, however, we realize that if we arbitrarily pick and choose what parts of our faith to follow, we will be cast upon a sea of relativism, with no beacon to guide us.

We may believe that truth eventually triumphs in Catholicism, but the reality is difficult to accept, especially when we find ourselves on the other side of a church teaching—condemned, perhaps, for whom we have married or divorced, for how we approach birth control, or for our view of the priesthood and hierarchy.

Yet, as imperfect as this human institution of the church is, it is founded on the life of our leader, Jesus Christ, and—realistically—where else, where better, to seek guidance? And so, we need to give church teaching the credence it deserves.

When the next document is issued by the Vatican or our own bishop, let us challenge ourselves to read it. We will afford these teachers the opportunity to instruct us, inspire us, change us. We will not come to this reading as pliant, naive Catholics. We cannot change or repress our nature so easily. But we will come as *open* Catholics. We are ready to hear messages other than those we already agree with and not just the words that convey our sentiments at that moment. We will look at this document and see what it says to our own lives. Even if we violently disagree, we will read it, this one time, as we might read Scripture. We will let it churn around in our brains. And then . . .

We trust in God for what follows.

# SELECTED READINGS

John P. Boyle, *Church Teaching Authority: Historical and Theological Studies.* Notre Dame, Ind.: University of Notre Dame Press, 1995.

Brendan R. Hill, *Exploring Catholic Theology.* Mystic, Conn.: Twenty-Third Publications, 1995.

Bernard Lauret, ed., *Fifty Years of Catholic Theology: Conversations with Yves Congar.* Philadelphia: Fortress Press, 1988.

Pierre Teilhard de Chardin (Bernard Weil, trans.), *The Phenomenon of Man.* New York: Harper and Row, 1965.

# CHAPTER THIRTEEN

# CHURCH AUTHORITY
## Thoughtful Obedience

The primacy of the pope, along with a hierarchal network of bishops overseeing the spiritual lives of the faithful around the world, can comprise either the *best* reason for being a Catholic or the *worst*. Whichever it is for you, make no mistake—it is precisely this comprehensive ecclesiastical and hierarchical structure of the church that separates Catholicism from all other religions.

In the pope, Catholicism claims a direct descendant of Peter—the rock upon which the church is built, a representative of Christ on earth, its single, identifiable religious voice. The papacy is one of the few remaining institutions that has survived since ancient times. At the lower levels of its hierarchy, Catholicism has local shepherds to tend to the unique needs of the faithful flocks, be they in New York City or New Zealand, Byelorussia or Bangalore.

Yet many Catholics and non-Catholics alike counter: Is the pope no more than an autonomous religious monarch? Is this a man answerable to no one, whose episcopal vassals enforce his bidding over subjects who may only have access to God through a labyrinth constructed by human decree, and not by divine command? What of free will? What of conscience?

In the previous chapter, we discussed church teaching; in this chapter and the next we will concentrate on how, through the work of human beings, Christ's message has been (and is being) made known to the world. In the next chapter, the priesthood—what we might call the individual ministry of the church—will be examined. In this chapter we will concentrate on the quite visible, yet often misunderstood, structural ministry of pope and hierarchy. The intent is simply to help Good Enough Catholics better understand their history—and, more important, the place of the hierarchy in our spiritual and moral lives.

To understand that the Catholic Church is a church of religious structure, providing a fabric for our moral lives, assuring, as the *Encyclopedia of Catholicism* says, ". . . an authentic unity of faith, charity, mission, ministry, and sacraments."[1]

First, a look back.

## HOW THEY CAME TO BE
### The Shoes of the Fisherman

It is quite a stretch to connect an instantly recognizable pope—who flies in jets and is seen on television by millions upon millions of people around the world—to an obscure fisherman by the Sea of Galilee whose prosaic life was profoundly transformed by a chance meeting with an itinerant preacher some two thousand years ago.

Until quite recently, it was taken for granted by most contemporary Catholics that Christ specifically named Peter the first pope and that, in some way, divine providence continued to place the papal mantle on other equally worthy and holy shoulders down through history. This is hardly the case. For, while the essence of Christ's message hasn't changed, the papacy—indeed, the whole concept of an ecclesiastical hierarchy—has changed dramatically, at times fitfully, evolving as church and human history unfolded. As with any human venture, it has been blessed with an abundance, and a range, of human characteristics.

At the dawning of the Christian era there was, of course, the seminal figure of Peter, called by Christ. Peter, along with Paul, surely held a dominant position both in spreading the good news that Christ preached, and in serving as a pastor to the rapidly growing early church. Actually, we do not even know if Peter actually served in Rome as bishop. But because of the tradition that both he and Paul were martyred in Rome—and surely because Rome was the center, not only of the Roman Empire, but of the known world—the leader of the Christians in Rome was considered the de facto leader of the entire religious movement called Christianity.

It was to the leader of the church in Rome that Christians looked continually for guidance and for rulings on matters of faith and practice. Gradually, the bishop of Rome—a title that first appeared only in the second century—was, more or less in retrospect, seen as the successor to Peter, whom Christ had called "the rock upon which I will build my church."

The power and the prestige of the papacy continued to grow because of the jurisdiction ceded to Rome, to the extent that eventually the bishop of Rome was seen not only as a spiritual, but as a temporal leader as well. As the only model of the day was that of monarchy, it was natural that a leader who commanded the allegiance of so many would also be considered something of a monarch. When Christianity was eventually declared the official religion of the empire after the conversion of Constantine in the fourth century, lands, properties, and businesses were restored (or given) to the church. A new era with a new kind of power—vast, temporal, and appropriate to the pope's new worldly status—was at hand.

This was no longer a group of Christians loosely joined together in secretive, persecuted communities, with their eyes fixed on an eternal domain. This was a large, visible, and earthly kingdom, that had to be defended and managed.

Popes over the centuries have had to struggle not only with the natural temptations that come to those wielding temporal power, but with theologians and canonists trying to discern the limits of papal authority—to say nothing of their brother bishops who worked strenuously to maintain their own autonomy and authority. Yet even as they juggled this enormously complicated mix of worldly and otherworldly domains, most popes lived lives of exemplary holiness, spreading the word to the corners of the earth, holding off barbarians and heretics, brokering peace agreements—while protecting and accumulating one of the world's largest troves of music, art, and books.

Some of the giants were the most humble, and saw their role clearly. St. Gregory the Great (d. 604), when he was addressed as "universal bishop" by another member of the hierarchy, responded, "Away with those words which inflate vanity and wound charity! I know what I am and what you are."[2]

Others among the 264 popes did not acquit themselves as well. Some led armies into battle; fathered illegitimate children, and named the children of favored patrons as archbishops, assassinated their rivals, and excommunicated some rulers for defying them—while obsequiously toadying up to others. John XII (d. 964), elected pope at the age of 18, led such an immoral life that he was deposed—but then, because a pope is pope until death, was reinstated!

The process for electing popes—and for determining who actually *was* pope—has an equally uneven past. Temporal rulers imprisoned cardinals to make certain their choice for pope was named. Some popes demanded the right to name their successors. Coups, intrigues, deals, and even murder are all part of papal election history. At one chaotic time, there were no fewer than three men who claimed simultaneously to be pope. In fact, from Hippolytus in 217—who was later declared a saint—to Felix V in 1439, there were no fewer than 39 antipopes.

While Gregory the Great brushed aside adulation, one of his successors—Gregory the VII (d. 1085)—saw his position rather differently: "The pope is the only one whose feet are to be kissed by all princes."[3] Pope Boniface VIII (d. 1303) went even farther, clutching tightly the keys of the kingdom he contended resided exclusively in his office: "We declare, state, and define that it is absolutely necessary for the salvation of all that they submit to the Roman pontiff."[4]

When the pope was finally forced in 1861 to divest the church of the Papal States, which comprised a sizable chunk of Italy, a long era of worldly control came to an end. But the debate over that far more powerful jurisdiction—the souls of men and women—continued unabated, and in fact intensified. The issue was authority:

how much the pope would have, and with whom, if anyone, he would share it. Still unsettled was the central question: Could this authority extend to the ultimate reach of teaching? Could the pope in fact speak without error—infallibly—on church matters?

The First Vatican Council proclaimed that he could, and that all ecclesiastical power ultimately rested in his holy office, in his person. The Second Vatican Council drew back from such absolutism, saying that the voices of the pope's fellow bishops also had to be heard in determining the will of God.

The papacy we experience today is vastly different from what it was for virtually all of church history. Although the pope's temporal domain is no more than the 107.8 acres of the Vatican city-state, he wields enormous moral power. With modern communications, a pope has the ability, both personally and through the vast infrastructure that is the institutional church—the Vatican bureaucracy, bishops, parishes, centers of learning—to proclaim his vision of Catholicism. In the papacies of Pius XII (d. 1958), John XXIII (d. 1963), Paul VI (1978), and certainly that of John Paul II, the pope has been a visible, recognized international leader, whose words on a broad range of social and moral issues are directed not only to Catholics, but to the world at large.

Yes, the office of pope has had a decidedly speckled career; but somehow, despite episodes of degradation and triumphalism, it has retained its unifying power. As Cardinal Newman wrote in his "Essay on the Development of Christian Doctrine," it is the Holy See that historically kept the fragile shoot of Christian belief alive and growing. Something was at work here far beyond human comprehension.

> "If you look back over two thousand years of popes, we've had saints, fools, thieves, lechers, poseurs, and everything in between. There must be something beyond the ability—or lack of ability—of ordinary men that keeps this church going."
>
> —JOHN FIALKA

# Elder/Episkopos

Of course, the office of pope was not specifically mandated in the New Testament (nor were the sacraments or the Christian Church itself, for that matter); rather, leaders of the various early Christian communities gradually emerged as organic, necessary components of church life. No group can function for long without leadership.

In Scripture, the word *presbyteros*, or elder, and *episkopos*, bishop, were used interchangeably, not so much as titles of honor but of function, signifying the pastoral leader of a certain area. They were chosen from among the members of Christian communities to be leaders by virtue of the witness of their own lives, as well as for their ability to instill the Christian way in others. They were to have both spiritual and practical capabilities, as St. Paul outlined in his first letter to Timothy:

> A bishop must be irreproachable, married only once, of even temper, self-controlled, modest, and hospitable. He should be a good teacher. He must not be addicted to drink. He ought not to be contentious but, rather, gentle, a man of peace. Nor can he be someone who loves money. He must be a good manager of his own household, keeping his children under control without sacrificing his dignity; for if a man does not know how to manage his own house, how can he take care of the church of God?[5]

In addition to teaching the tenets of the faith to the catechumens, preaching the gospel to the unconverted, and generally serving as spiritual guides, these early bishops presided at the Sunday celebration of the Eucharist and performed other sacramental functions. But as Christianity spread, a bishop could no longer be present for each community's Sunday worship, and so presbyters—who would eventually be called priests—officiated at the breaking of the bread. The church was organized along the grid of localities and provinces of the Roman Empire, and eventually these geographical areas would be called (as they were by the Romans) dioceses. But in early Christianity, these were only geographical boundaries of a religious nature, carrying little worldly power. Almost as an afterthought—the promise of such a lineage was hardly contained in Scripture—the local leaders began to be spoken of as "successors of the apostles."

The conversion of the emperor Constantine marked the beginning of a dramatic ascendancy for the office of bishop. Within their geographical boundaries, bishops were given previously confiscated lands and the ability to generate revenues; Christianity now functioned as the state religion. Once known as "fathers of the poor," bishops controlled lucrative businesses and took on regal trappings: fur-trimmed garments, jewelry, a court and residence worthy of royalty. By the Middle Ages they were known, appropriately, as "princes of the church." Bishops had alternately to fight off and compromise with secular monarchs in order to retain their lands. They also had to deal with a pope in Rome who, depending on his own vision of the needs of the universal church, sought their complete allegiance or a substantial portion of their wealth (or both). The needs of individual believers and the importance of priests receded farther and farther into the background.

The worldliness of bishops and the high-handedness of the Vatican, which increasingly called for higher and higher levels of obedience to its decrees, gave rise to a group of protesters. They found the strict distinction between clergy and laity, the emphasis on sacraments to the exclusion of the ministry of the word, and the pretense of a divinely ordered hierarchy—among other ecclesiastical excesses— hardly in keeping with the teachings of Jesus Christ. The church responded to Martin Luther (d. 1546) and the Protestant Reformation with the Council of Trent (1545–1563), which rid the church of the most blatant abuses of power and codified church practice— but centralized power in Rome as never before. Rome fought to seize the critical power to appoint all bishops. National churches, which had been able to choose bishops from among their own priests—as well as secular rulers, whose "recommendations" to Rome were akin to selections—fought to retain their influence.

In the seesaw contest of episcopal versus papal prerogative, each had its own often differing views as to where the will of God was leading. The pope claimed the necessity to strengthen the unity of the church by appointing those who agreed with his vision. The bishops stood their ground as successors of the apostles, not delegates of the pope. Individual bishops and bishops' conferences often spoke out and, while acknowledging the pope as "bishop among bishops," attempted to represent to Rome the state and nature of their people's souls. These bishops, along with their priests, dealt with the problems of living a moral life. They worked on a practical level, not in the rarefied theoretical and theological atmosphere of Rome. Movements such as Gallicanism rose up, through which the bishops of France contended that Rome's teachings did not go into effect until ratified by the national church.

The First Vatican Council (1869–1870) countered Gallicanism head on, proclaiming forthrightly that the pope had supreme, even infallible powers. Its document "Eternal Pastor" declared forthrightly: "The primacy of jurisdiction over the whole church was immediately and directly promised to and conferred upon the blessed apostle Peter by Christ the Lord."[6] The pope was Peter's successor; thus, there was a religious chain of command that had to be observed: God-pope-bishops-priests-people.

Less than a hundred years later, the Second Vatican Council turned the equation around. The people, the faithful, were now all-important, dynamic co-formulators of an evolving body of doctrine and moral leaven for the world, not simply loyal, unthinking servants. A priesthood of all believers was proclaimed, and bishops were also restored to a place more in keeping with their early tradition. They were again leaders in their own right in their dioceses, who were to act *in concert* with the pontiff in guiding the universal church. The bishop's authority came from God, not from the favor of the pope.

Vatican II struck a decidedly pastoral note in its decree on the role of bishops:

They should present Christian teaching in a way appropriate to the needs of the times . . . in a way that meets the difficulties and problems that people today find a special burden and source of anxiety. . . . In handing on this teaching, they should manifest the church's motherly love for all, believers and unbelievers alike.[7]

Today, while we live in a church where the selection of bishops is Rome's exclusive prerogative, this was not—and very likely will not always be—the case. The election of a bishop from among the priests of a region has considerable historical precedent. Moreover, the naming of an outsider, a common practice today, has a much shorter history to support it.

This thumbnail sketch of the offices of pope and bishop, and the realization of the tension between centralized versus local control that has existed between them for centuries, might leave Good Enough Catholics even more confused about the role of the hierarchy in their individual lives. This confusion is only compounded by the flood of pronouncements from the Vatican, and the vast range of teachings that emanate from American bishops—from the arch traditionalists to the progressives. By what voice or voices should we be guided?

## FINDING THE BALANCE

When we strip away all the hierarchical trappings and set aside, at least for the moment, the many volumes of Catholic doctrine, the continuing debate on how much moral power the pope and bishops have over an individual Catholic's life all comes down to a rather simple truth: pope and bishops are all seeking to discern God's will, and how it should be made known in our day.

It might strike the Good Enough Catholic as strange that the Catholic Church—which takes as a fundamental article of faith the premise that the Holy Spirit continues to guide and enlighten it—has often been fearful of the free exchange of ideas. Popes and bishops routinely quash new ideas and attempt to curtail debate.

On the one hand, trust in the Spirit; on the other, distrust of the people.

As theologian Bernard Cooke has written, "All too often Christ's continuing presence to the church was overlooked and certain structures or agents were thought necessary to bridge the supposed gap between heaven and earth."[8] Cooke goes on to point out that Christ explicitly rejected a monarchical model for his church; yet this is what we have constructed.

It might seem as though the luckiest Catholics are those who can take on faith that their pope and their local bishop are indeed wise, inspired, and complete guides, that whatever issues forth from their mouth or office must be followed. Alternatively, perhaps the luckiest Catholics are those who will have nothing to do with the whole business of an ecclesiastical hierarchy; they pronounce and declare it irrelevant to their spiritual and moral life.

Good Enough Catholics stand in the middle. A childlike faith, while in some ways admirable, just won't do, as we've discovered time and time again. Our experiences, our instincts, our prayerful reflections, our troubled consciences—all sometimes tell us that what the official church promulgates somehow doesn't help us to better follow the word and example of Jesus Christ. This may lead us to feel guilty, that we are somehow presuming to know more than the church, the pope, the bishops—or even that we don't need pope or bishops, that *we* are the supreme authority. We don't need these "bridges"; we can travel directly to God.

Certainly, we have authority over ourselves and our actions. But we also know all too well that there is nothing supreme about us. We are totally human, and woefully imperfect. We need guidance; we need leadership. We need to learn from others' experiences and from history. We need to hear from the theologically and spiritually enlightened. We need to seek unity with fellow Catholics.

But we ask respect for our individual diversity. There must be some balance. Credence needs to be given not only to the teaching authority of the church hierarchy, but to our own intellect, to growing bodies of knowledge, research, and human experience—so that we might be helped in an effective way to make the hundreds of moral judgments we are faced with each day. Our culture, and this moment in history, have their place. After the issuance in 1968 of *Humanae Vitae*, the encyclical that reconfirmed the ban on artificial birth control, Bernard Haring, one of the eminent moral theologians of our era, proposed a way for Catholics in the middle—Good Enough Catholics—to reflect on their disputes with the church:

> Those who are doubtful whether they can accept it have to study it thoroughly, have to read it with good will, but they also have to accept other information in the Church. They cannot dissociate the pope from the whole of the Church. They have to study it, consider it, but not alone, not isolated.[9]

Not alone; not isolated. Herein lies the very essence of what can be the Good Enough Catholic's way of regarding church authority. As Philip S. Kaufman, a Benedictine monk, has observed: "To be authentically Roman Catholic it is not enough to be Roman, to listen only to the Vatican. It is also necessary to be catholic, to consider many ways, past and present, in which the Spirit has guided and continues to guide the church to truth."[10]

As the reception of *Humanae Vitae* so dramatically illustrated, a new era has opened in the relationship between pope and people. What Catholics said by not adhering to the encyclical's ban on artificial birth control—and yet continuing to acknowledge the primacy of the pope as Catholicism's leader and first moral teacher—was that they could and would go against a pope's individual ruling, without undermining the necessity or importance of his office. What Catholics said was that they did not agree with the encyclical's basic premise—that every sexual act had to hold within it the possibility of procreation; that to interrupt the flow of sperm toward egg was morally wrong. Their human experience informed them otherwise; they would not agree to live within this false construct.

Is such seeming disobedience sinful? Does this posture mean excommunication? These questions were probably agonized over more in 1968 than they are today; Catholics have gradually, but in ever-increasing numbers, come to realize that the answer is no. No action in sincere fidelity to one's own prayerful conscience, that sure pathway to God—the "kindly light," as Cardinal Newman described it—can be sinful. The American bishops, in a pastoral letter, pointed to an "enlightened conscience, even when honestly mistaken, as the immediate arbiter of moral decisions."[11]

Of course, Good Enough Catholics must be careful. Our own instincts and intelligence, the insistent demands of what we might think of as a well-formed conscience, sometimes prove to be little more than rationalizations designed to confirm what we wanted to do in the first place. Catholicism is a religion of doctrine and dogma, of structure, of hierarchy. But it is a religion that must be practiced artfully, not dogmatically. We were not given a mind, a free will, a conscience only to set them aside when approaching important decisions in our lives. We are not to be so caught up in an elaborate church structure that we forget the simplicity of Christ's message.

"In the Vietnamese culture, we don't usurp authority. When someone is put over us, we listen to them and obey them. That is our kind of Catholicism, also. We believe in the pope 100 percent. I am shocked that Catholics defy him."

—LE TRONG PHU

"I'm an educated man, but the whole business of the pope goes right over my head. It has no relevance for my life, although I am a Catholic through and through."

—TOM EAKINS*

"I raised two teenagers. Through earrings and shaved heads and major attitudes. But I gave them leeway, so they could find the way that was right for them. The pope should do the same as our spiritual father. Set high standards, but realize they are not always going to be met. We need to be reminded of the flexibility of God, because we don't see flexibility in the church. That leaves a lot up to the individual, but it's a freer and richer life when you listen to all the voices, to your own conscience—and then make a decision."

—DAVID SULEY

"A lot of people complain about the pope and all the structures. We're lucky to have a structured church. How else can you have principles? I'm glad the pope is slow to change. God's word doesn't change, does it?"

—HAL GORDON

"The pope and all the Catholic rules formed me, but they are not part of my reality now. Picasso learned to draw straight lines and faces and then went to express them in an entirely different way. In Catholicism, it's the same: you learn the basics and then express them in your own way."

—PETER HEBEIN

# OF COLLEGIALITY AND COUNCILS

Good Enough Catholics, who have seen their church go from a rigid triumphalism to the innovations and transformation of Vatican II, only to return to a more traditionalist posture, may rightly wonder: Is there a middle, sensible road for the hierarchy to travel? Where is the way that at once hews to Christ's message and yet responds to the cries of the faithful?

*Collegiality* was one answer explored during Vatican II. Collegiality is a doctrine holding that bishops throughout the world, with the pope as their uncontested leader, have pastoral authority and governance, as a body, over the universal church. In fact, Vatican II— itself a gathering of bishops in an ecumenical council—has a teaching authority as strong as (some theologians would say, *stronger* than) papal pronouncements and encyclicals.

While there have been a significant number of bishops' synods held since Vatican II, they are consultative bodies. Often, when bishops read the final document issued from a particular synod they attended, they are puzzled at what was included, excluded, and emphasized. Ultimately, of course, the final report and recommendations are issued by the Vatican. While Vatican II transformed Catholicism's view of the world, the role of its priests and lay people, and its liturgy, the central government of the Vatican's institutions, and the role of the pope himself, remained virtually untouched. There had been a call for a balancing of powers at the time of Vatican II, for a slimming-down of both curia and papacy; but this did not occur.

In the church today, there is both ferment and open dissatisfaction with the relationship between the office of the pope and that of the bishops. The bishops have little power outside their dioceses, and even within them they are closely monitored by the Vatican lest they deviate too far from an accepted norm. Certain bishops have found themselves censured for their activities; national conferences of bishops have had the Vatican intercede in their deliberations; and (perhaps most troubling to church observers) bishops often seem to be chosen more for their adherence to a certain approach to Catholicism (such as a firm stance against contraception or the ordination of married men) than for their pastoral acuity or personal abilities. The appointment of some bishops has even been perceived as punishment for a previous bishop's reluctance to bow to Rome's wishes.

As one writer put it, "John Paul has created an intellectual desert and called it peace. Bishops and theologians have been cowed into silence. . . . Heads that pop up above the parapet are lopped off."[12]

And yet—as was clearly demonstrated by the German bishops who, invoking documents of Vatican II, offered a way for divorced and remarried Catholics to receive the Eucharist—members of the hierarchy continue in their struggle to find ways to serve their people, and the universal church. They unequivocally honor the primacy of the pope, but they are unwilling to abrogate their own pastoral duties.

In 1995, forty American bishops sent a letter to Rome calling for an end to the veil of secrecy that shrouds the work of the curia—the Vatican bureaucracy—and for a greater degree of collegiality between the pope and the bishops. The letter also noted that certain areas declared closed to further consideration—from priestly celibacy and women's ordination to abortion and annulment—needed an increase, not an absence, of informed debate.

Such disagreement over issues of collegiality and the teaching authority of councils marks still another time in church history when the sentiments of a wide range of Catholics—theologians, historians, lay people, priests, hierarchy—indicate that the balance of authority is not appropriate to the day.

It is also a time when the foundations of belief and practice are being examined anew. Many within the church maintain that by honestly, charitably, and prayerfully gathering together, the twenty-first-century church can discern as wisely as the church of the first century. Humans may err, Catholic tradition allows, but the Holy Spirit will not permit the church to go fundamentally astray.

"I was in Rome for the 1987 Synod on the Laity. We had done enormous preparation and there was so much good stuff that came out of the meetings and conferences we had. But when the documents came out, there was nothing of that inspiring material. It showed me the workings of Rome. They give the appearance of listening, but Rome will portray exactly what Rome wants portrayed, regardless of what individuals have to say."

—MARY ANNE BARRY

"Love is not in the lexicon of the pope or the curia. Sad but true. Their job seems to be about power."

—MARTY HEGARTY

# WHOSE WORD TO HEED?

There are bishops who still prohibit altar girls from serving mass. Others have incorporated them for years, even before Rome's official sanction. Some bishops fight bitterly against the use of anything approaching inclusive language; others quietly use it. Eucharist on the hand, Eucharist on the tongue. The sacrament of reconciliation must come before the Eucharist; no, vice versa. Bishops who let it be known that divorced and remarried Catholics are not welcome at the Communion table; others who reach out in welcome. Bishops who stalk those speaking out against church statements on everything from birth control to sexual preference; others who accept them. Places where innovation is extolled; places where traditionalism is the answer. One pope who preaches there is but one truth, Catholic truth; another who says there are many religious paths to God. One pope calls for bishops to assist him collegially; another proclaims his is the sole voice of authority.

There is hardly uniform observance or practice in this hierarchical, structured church of ours. It is not the monolith that we once thought it was.

But this is to be neither bemoaned nor feared; it is a sign of life, vibrant, forever regenerating and replenishing life. It is a sign that under the wide canopy of a universal church spanning continents, cultures, and changing times, there are different understandings of Jesus' message of compassion, love, and service, different approaches to living as he would have us live, different paths to God.

We must be willing to live with both the ambiguity and the complexity of Catholic belief, tradition, and practice. Our own desire for sureness can stand in the way of a truly full, ever-evolving life as a modern-day, Good Enough Catholic.

Yet we cannot be careless as we attempt what we might call the art of thoughtful obedience to our church's leaders and teachings. We cannot disregard the basic tenets of our faith. The teachings of Jesus

Christ haven't changed—care for others, to be a force for peace. Love still is a necessity. We cannot shrink from the challenge it presents by explaining that modern psychology tells us sacrifice or concern for others is counterproductive to our mental health; that modern economics precludes our helping the homeless, the abandoned, the sick, or the needy; or that political realities sanction hate, rancor, and division.

The writings of the pope and the bishops address the myriad moral and public policy issues with which we are confronted and on which we must often make decisions. These writings uniquely attempt to place the template of universal Catholic teachings over what are often confusing, conflicting, and sometimes contradictory realities. Concrete proposals are often boldly forwarded, as (for example) in recent documents on world peace, the economy, and treatment of the poor. These efforts are a sign of a church that continually chooses to interact with society—with us—to bring its wisdom and authority to bear upon the world.

There are threads that run through the fabric of centuries of Catholicism that must never be forgotten as we weave each day's cloth. Religious practices will change, doctrine will evolve, history will alternately cloud and reveal, science's mysteries will tantalizingly yield to and stubbornly resist our inquiries. Bishops and popes will come and go. But we carry with us the promise of Christ that he will never leave the people of his church on earth. His divine spirit— the Holy Spirit—is ever present, at once invisible and yet palpable to those who seek its guidance.

How will we perform in our moral pursuits? Imperfectly, but hopefully, good enough.

As we discussed in an earlier chapter, Jewish tradition contains 613 *mitzvot*—rules, obligations—that govern ritual, civil, and ethical behavior. Does anyone perform all 613? Of course not. Yet all Jews have before them these goals of the righteous, godly life.

By the same token, if you find that you cannot live by the edict of a bishop in your part of America—an edict that has no standing (and, in fact, might be contradicted) in another bishop's teaching in another part of the country—have you failed as a Catholic? Of course not. How little faith we have in the Holy Spirit, how little faith in the durability of Jesus' message, when we fume at the parsimonious souls in our hierarchy who want to contain Christ's power in a tiny container of their own making.

These are not people who inspire our faith or our trust. Why allow them to divert us from the important work of finding Christ in the world, of having a rich, Catholic, spiritual life? Perhaps sometimes it is easier to say what is wrong with the church and point to the flaws in hierarchy than it is to work toward the transformation of ourselves and our world. But where does such criticism leave us? With a fine list of offenses and offenders. And then what? There are too many treasures in Catholicism to spend time and energy pointing out the dross.

It is better to find members of the Catholic hierarchy who inspire you, who speak to your heart. Perhaps it is your very own bishop, to whom most of us haven't paid much attention lately. Or, equally, a pope whose life and words hold a vision of Catholicism that is at once holy and sensible. It can be Pope John Paul II, whose powerful presence and unyielding vision is felt throughout the world; or someone like Pope John XXIII, whose humility and openness both charmed and inspired a generation of Catholics and non-Catholics alike.

Look to your pope and your bishop as you would a parent, a spiritual parent. He *does* know more than we do about the Catholic faith and tradition. Don't turn from his words when they are difficult, or when they contradict our perception of Christ's message. This is not just another voice, this is a voice that, by church teaching, should have a central place in our religious life.

But remember also that you are not a child; you are an adult, both in secular and in spiritual life. A parent's word is no longer *the* answer. It is an important *element* in our decision-making process.

" 'But the pope says . . .' I heard that all the time. In fact, I said it myself when I was younger—what the pope said was what

Catholicism is all about. Now I'm at the point where, who cares what the pope says? My job is to live the best, moral life I can."

—MARY MURPHY ZASTROW

"Catholics need to be obedient to the pope. This is what you have to do to be the best possible Catholic you can be. You need to support the institutional church. If you are a good Catholic, you take into serious consideration what the pope says."

—MARTY GERAGHTY

"I teach CCD for twelve- to fourteen-year-olds. I try to convey who the pope is: the head of the church, in Peter's place. But he is not always right. Yet sometimes he sees a need for a major change that we don't see yet. I try to teach all of this to students. Look to him for guidance. I know someday women will be ordained, even though the pope says they won't be. Maybe it's too soon now, too abrupt. But he can't be in the middle. He has to say yes or no. That's difficult, because many situations are in the middle."

—MINNIE DIANA

# THE GOOD ENOUGH CATHOLIC CHALLENGE: LISTEN TO A VOICE

Catholicism is fortunate to have so many visible pastors. We have a pope who traces his ministry back to St. Peter, who walked with Christ. We have bishops who carry on as the apostles once did, spreading the word of Christ's wonderful, liberating ways. Both pope and bishops have a rich history—and through them our faith has been transmitted, brought to this very day.

Our challenge is to find among these leaders, both past and present, voices that resonate deep within our souls.

Find the hierarchical voices that speak with holiness, wisdom, and

informed reason, those that don't demand our allegiance just because of their formal authority.

The voice may be that of John XXIII or Cardinal Newman; it
may be our current bishop or pope. Listen carefully to these voices
as they enter our lives in the days ahead. Take their words seriously.
Let them rest with you.

Take just one line or one thought that you hear from one of these
voices and put it into practice. Let it be as simple or as difficult as the
moment requires.

## SELECTED READINGS

Peter Hebblethwaite, *Paul VI: The First Modern Pope*. New York: Harper-
   Collins, 1993.

John XXIII, *The Journey of a Soul*. New York: McGraw-Hill, 1965

John Paul II, *Crossing the Threshold of Hope*. New York: Knopf, 1994.

Philip S. Kaufman, *Why You Can Disagree and Remain a Faithful Catholic*. New
   York: Crossroad, 1995.

National Conference of Catholic Bishops, "Human Life in Our Day" (pastoral letter). Washington, D.C.: 15 November 1968.

# PRIESTHOOD OF PRIESTS
## Priesthood of Believers

Central to our understanding of Catholic worship, tradition, and practice is the office of priest. The priest, we have been taught, is the holy mediator between humans and God, a person who stands in Christ's place at the altar to transform bread and wine into the Divine Presence, the Savior's body and blood. The priest is our counselor and teacher, pastor of our parish churches, the embodiment of a lifelong commitment to the highest vocation within Catholicism. Called from among people to serve people; set apart, yet one of us. The priest is our role model and the unmistakable symbol of Catholic identity and cohesion within a secular culture.

Sadly, too many of our priests have proved unworthy of the trust we once so readily placed in them. Some have left the priesthood, when we cared so deeply for them. And some have stayed—when their inadequacies were embarrassingly evident. Others have committed unspeakable sins, abusing those whom we entrusted to their care. Once, their position and regard in society was unmistakable; that has changed, but their exclusive gender and marital status remains. All are men; for all practical purposes, they are unmarried. Some Catholics cannot abide the exclusion of the married and women from this critically important and respected vocation within the church.

Compounding all the controversy surrounding the role of priests today—or, as some would question, their right to continue in such a dominant role—is the undeniable paucity of their number. In rectories once alive with three, four, or five priests, now but one man's footfall echoes. Some rectories are already long vacant. The statistics are staggering. Resignation from the priesthood—once not only unheard of but virtually impossible—is something we have almost come to expect of the best priests. It is estimated that some 100,000 priests have voluntarily resigned since Vatican II. Some seminaries have been closed, others forced to consolidate. The number of men in priestly training has dropped precipitously; the quality of those who have come to be trained is cause for concern. Our Catholic schools have fewer and fewer priests on their faculties; the very character of Catholic education is in question.

Meanwhile, growing numbers of Catholic men, and an even greater number of Catholic women, pursue religious study around the country. Far more Catholics study theology in secular institutions than in seminaries, some at the most prestigious schools of theology. Lay people, young and old alike, declare constantly their willingness and desire to serve their church, but find certain avenues open to only male, celibate, permanent clergy.

Few groups have been studied and agonized over more than our priests. Yet, for now, the future of the ministerial Catholic priesthood remains clouded with uncertainty. As for its past, it is one marked by both dramatic change and continuing evolution.

# A PRIESTHOOD, <u>THE</u> PRIESTHOOD, DEVELOPS

As the vast majority of the first Christians were Jews, the role of the priest was central to their understanding of religious life. In Judaism, all priests came from the tribe of Levi, and their function at the time of Christ was primarily to properly carry out ritual sacrifice and conduct worship. Rabbis were the teachers. A designated high priest was additionally charged with the responsibility of entering the innermost sanctuary of the temple in Jerusalem on Yom Kippur, the day of atonement, to offer a sacrifice so that God might forgive the sins of the people.

But there was another, deeper, understanding of priesthood, one that encompassed the entire Jewish people. For the Jews had entered into a unique covenant with God; he would be their God, and they would be his people. Not only temple oblations were to be offered up to God, but the Jews themselves were an offering. Their lives were considered sacrificial offerings, raised up as examples so that all the peoples of the world would see the majesty of God and the goodness of his ways.

Jesus Christ was never referred to as a priest in his lifetime. He was called rabbi, or teacher, for he told of God's kingdom; but he never claimed to be initiating religious ritual. Jesus participated in ritual, but only that of any observant Jew. In the first Christian writings, Jesus is referred to as priest only in one place, the Letter to the Hebrews. Despite this, the early church fathers eventually concluded, Christ had become—through his life, death, and resurrection—a new mediator between human beings and God. He was an advocate, an intercessor; and these were priestly roles. So Christ was retroactively depicted as a priest, even a high priest.

Regardless, early Christianity was more involved with teaching—evangelizing, really—a new way to live and relate to God; so there was no immediate need for a ritual priesthood to be established. After all, Christians did not see themselves as distinct from Judaism for about a century after the death of Christ, and Judaism already had elaborate ceremonies and the priests to perform them.

On the other hand, the "priesthood of the believers"—the other element of Jewish tradition—was central to Christian belief, and taken quite literally. By baptism, each Christian participated in this royal priesthood. Their lives were to be a new light to the nations, demonstrating a way to live righteously on the earth and give honor to God. After all, the Messiah, God's son, had come to earth to set an example.

As the early Christian communities gathered together for prayer and mutual support, the classic forms of Jewish worship didn't seem appropriate, and were not easily tailored to fit this new, still-developing approach to God. So these first Christians developed their own simple ritual, centered around the Eucharist. It was a

reenactment and remembrance of the Last Supper, which itself prefigured the sacrifice of the Crucifixion. The Eucharist was an un-
bloody sacrifice that replaced the temple sacrifice with which the
earliest Christians were so familiar. A leader of each community or
household repeated Christ's words—"this is my body, this is my
blood"—and bread and wine were passed from hand to hand. This
was holy food, a renewal of the new covenant. It was a symbol of
their unity, a summoning of strength.

In the early church, as we saw in the previous chapter, this leader
was often called a bishop, signifying that he was akin to the president
of a ruling council. He saw to the spiritual lives of the community,
supervised the education of the catechumens, presided at the liturgy,
and either personally or through those he delegated looked after the
material wants of members in need. His primary qualifications centered around the good example he set and his ability to teach.

With the spread of Christianity, the bishops could no longer be
present in the far-flung communities, so presbyters—lay persons,
both men and women considered leaders in teaching and preaching,
but not necessarily liturgically proficient—took their place. They
presided over the Eucharistic ritual, which would eventually develop into the mass we know today. At one time, a portion of the
Eucharist, blessed by the bishop, was carried to each community for
its Sunday liturgy.

The presbyter was soon the ordinary celebrant of the Eucharist.
Most were men, and of these most were married. But there is also
fragmentary evidence that women—with whom Jesus traveled, and
whom he had proclaimed equal to men—served as the leaders of
Eucharistic worship.[1] Although presbyters were more and more frequently referred to as priests, there was extreme reluctance among
the early Christians to call them "priestly." The Christians well remembered how temple priests had often abused their position, and
they did not want to install another privileged group who would
claim special powers and unique access to God. Service to others—
not liturgical sacrifice—was considered the distinctive quality of
these early Christian priests.

As the theology and understanding of the priesthood continued to evolve into the Middle Ages, a marked change occurred. The biblical notion of service was gradually replaced by one perceived as more philosophical and erudite. The priest was considered not merely elected to the ministry, but somehow fundamentally changed, given certain "powers" that the ordinary lay person did not have. An indelible sign was imprinted on his soul through ordination, marking him as a priest forever.

As the doctrine of the Eucharist evolved toward transubstantiation—the belief that the substance of bread and wine actually changes into the substance of the body and blood of Jesus Christ—priestly duties centered more on the liturgical (or high priest) functions than on those as a leader of a community of believers. The precise execution of the Eucharistic sacrifice was considered all important. The line between clergy and lay people grew more and more distinct until priests were regarded as a group set both apart and somehow *above* the people. As the priesthood of the formally ordained grew in prominence, the priesthood of the believers receded as a dynamic—or even important—factor.

Although primitive forms of priestly ordination, such as the laying on of hands and recitation of prayers, were utilized even in the early church, elaborate ceremonies were developed to acknowledge this profound event. Vesting, presentation of the symbols of office, complicated invocations, blessings, and anointing called attention to this elevation. Still, in some ways, in its attempt to give praise to God, the church had returned to the era of the high priest, of the elaborate, complicated, difficult, and sometimes empty temple rituals that Jesus had railed against.

The emergence of a priestly class above the priesthood of all believers was one of the controversial Catholic teachings that led to the Protestant Reformation. The reformers maintained that ministry was the opportunity to preach and to serve—and that every Christian had direct access to God. The church saw only priests as properly sanctioned and exclusive mediators with a God-given power to offer fitting sacrifice and to forgive sins.

Still another church teaching that the reformers could not abide was mandatory clerical celibacy. Celibacy had always been looked upon as an admirable state in the pre-Christian and Jewish worlds— but never as a permanent life commitment. Throughout the first millennium of the church, most of the Christian priests and many bishops and popes were married. But the example of the unmarried Christ, the hermits who left the cities for lives of prayer and fasting, and the monks who gathered in same-sex communities, gave rise to the opinion that this was not only *acceptable*, but *desirable*, as a permanent state in Christian life. As celibates, truly religious persons could devote all their energies to God.

Other more worldly factors had also contributed to the church's advocacy of clerical celibacy. When a married Catholic priest or bishop died, his widow and children could, and did, lay claim to church lands. A professed celibate male left no legitimate heirs. There was also the vexingly intermingled relationships of church and state. Lay nobles had claimed the right to invest bishops and ab- bots with the symbols of their office, thereby assuring their alle- giance. Complicating matters, church hierarchy and secular royalty regularly intermarried, further blurring the lines. Pope Gregory VII (d. 1085) saw clerical celibacy as key to wresting the church from secular incumbrances, and by papal decree made it a requirement for ordination. The Second Lateran Council affirmed the requirement in 1139.

The Council of Trent, called as the church's answer to Protestant reformers, reaffirmed in the strongest terms the primacy and sepa- rateness of the clergy, instituted more uniform seminary training, and assured that celibacy would remain a requirement for those who aspired to the priesthood. Interestingly, though, the council took pains to be clear that celibacy laws were church laws, not divine laws, and therefore could be changed in the future if the will of the church so directed.

The Council of Trent left a lasting impact on the Catholic Church. It was perhaps the most far-reaching of all the church councils in terms of codifying dogma and practice. Remarkably, there was little change in Catholic teaching in the four hundred years that separated Trent from Vatican II. Catholics in the days before Vatican II were raised in a church whose theology and understanding of the priesthood was not materially different from that of the sixteenth century. The priest, with his mystical powers to bring Christ down onto the altar at mass, was set apart from the people, who were obligated to do his bidding obediently. He was their leader; he stood in Christ's place.

Vatican II looked back to Trent for precedent, but reached beyond, to the early church, to explore the nature of priesthood. Once again, as it had done for so many Catholic practices, the council reversed popularly held beliefs. The priest was to be a shepherd and co-worker, the council proclaimed, not a high priest set apart. His ministry—a term used purposefully to underscore service rather than the ecclesiastical prerogatives of Catholic priesthood—was threefold: preaching the word, performing the sacraments, and functioning as a community leader.

While affirming and redefining the crucial importance of the priest as mediator and guide, Vatican II dramatically resurrected the concept of a priesthood of believers, lost since the days of the early church practice. Priest and people were co-creators of God's kingdom on earth. Catholics—all Catholics—were chosen people, a light to the nations.

## PRIESTS: WHO THEY ONCE WERE— AND WHO THEY ARE

"During the past fifty years, societal, cultural and religious factors have challenged the once-entrenched cultic model of the priesthood," Father James J. Bacik has written. Bacik goes on:

> The cultic priest's main task was to provide the sacraments, most often mass and confession. He led a distinctive lifestyle by

remaining celibate, living in a rectory, and wearing clerical garb. Pastors worked as general practitioners, responsible for all aspects of parish life. Parishioners placed their pastors on a pedestal, as mediator between God and themselves. With the indelible character received at ordination, priests functioned as "other Christs," ruling and sanctifying the faithful.[2]

Many Catholics can remember the days when their parishes were literally teeming with priests of all ages, when a vocation to religious life was a serious consideration for many, and the priesthood commanded enormous prestige and respect.[3]

Things have changed. In 1982, there were 843 parishes that did not have a single priest in residence. Just ten years later, the number had more than doubled to 2,047.[4] Today, fully 10 percent of all Catholic parishes do not have a priest, and the number grows virtually week by week.

Between 1966 and 1969, an average of 932 men were ordained each year to the priesthood. Between 1975 and 1979, the number was 613; between 1990 and 1993, it had plummeted to 289.[5]

As the number of newly ordained priests diminish, the number of people who profess to be Catholics continues to grow, both in the United States and around the world. If each priest ordained today were assigned to his proportional number of new Catholics, he would find himself faced with a parish of 27,573 people!

In America, it is not difficult to see that the scarcity of priests we have just begun to experience will worsen—rapidly—as the priests who were ordained during the golden days of vocations, the 1950s, reach retirement age.

As Good Enough Catholics look to the 50,000 or so American priests who do remain, it is all too easy to point out glaring examples of priests who have betrayed both their sacred calling and our human trust. They are the pedophiles, the abusers, and the insensitive boors who have used their churchly position to unnecessarily bludgeon us. They are the poor homilists who have enervated us for years, the hapless administrators who have squandered both fiscal and human resources. They are the greedy, the lazy, the intellectually moribund, the spiritually proud, and the morally anemic.

And they are also the priests who have married us and buried our loved ones with grace, sensitivity, and dignity. They have patiently helped us through an annulment or deftly employed an internal forum to bring us back to the sacramental life of the church. When we were college students or grade school kids, they entered our lives with a message, a word, or a book that changed us forever. They are the priests who run and staff inner-city schools, hospices, and social service agencies. They have marched with workers for a just wage, or stood beside those afflicted with AIDS; and for years they have quietly handed out food and money to the poor from the back door of the rectory. They have served the diverse needs of suburban, urban, and rural parishes.

They are the priests who routinely have four masses on a Sunday, and infuse each with holiness and inspiration. They answer the phone in the middle of the night with good humor and readiness to serve. Too many times they quietly give up their day off. They don't strike back when we rage at them. And they don't back off when their bishop admonishes them for bending the rules, trying to make our spiritual paths a little less rocky.

They are also the men who watch our family drive off after mass for a Sunday outing—and sometimes, if we bother to look back, we can see that longing look in their eye as they go back to a lonely rectory.

On balance, we might conclude, these are a pretty remarkable group of men. Certainly, the majority are good enough priests for us Good Enough Catholics. But today, they are under public scrutiny as never before, while at the same time their diminished ranks are called upon to do many jobs they never expected, and for which they never trained—from counselor to financial planner, theologian to preacher. Little wonder that today's priests feel under enormous pressure. Their morale is a subject of near constant worry in many circles.

Yet recent studies of the Catholic clergy have come to a startling conclusion: Priests actually *like* being priests.

"Many of the pastors expressed gratitude that they could involve themselves in parish life and distance themselves somewhat from some of the institutional issues,"[6] a study funded by the Lilly Endowment revealed. "They are not men of theory who need conceptual clarity as a context for ministry," wrote Philip J. Murnion, the director of the National Pastoral Life Center and an expert on American priests. Reviewing a group of books about a cross-section of priests, he concluded, "Their lives are governed by some deeply embedded pastoral instincts and directed toward a half-articulated mission: imagination and adaption are essential elements."[7]

Priests like helping people. They like officiating at Catholic ritual. If they find themselves frustrated, it is not with their work (that is, with you and me); it is with the institution—a system, a hierarchy, a pope, a bishop, a bureaucracy that a good number would say impedes rather than assists them.

As for living a celibate life and holding on to the traditional clerical lifestyle and cultic model, American priests—especially older, experienced priests—are less enthusiastic. These priests, many of whom regard themselves as too old to even think of marriage, no longer see the benefit in the requirement that a man give himself wholly to the church, and never to another in marriage. They are willing to live somewhere other than a rectory; they are willing to allow lay people to share in their sacramental ministry.

Good Enough Catholics sometimes feel frustrated by those who insist that the only true church is the church of their youth; these priests often have a similar sensation as they come face-to-face with some of their newly ordained curates. "Older priests, who have worked their way through the profound changes of the council, often find it unsettling to be confronted with a new version of a style and approach they left behind," Father Bacik discovered. "Younger traditionalists often are not comfortable with clergy who have tried to adapt their ministry to the needs of the modern world. Unfortunately, these tensions can lead to serious polarization within a diocese and great stress and confusion within parishes."[8]

And so it is that a much larger percentage of recently ordained priests or men now in seminary training stand firmly behind the church's mandate of clerical celibacy—while a much smaller number of men who have experience in the priestly life hold the same position.

Father Karl Rahner (d. 1984), who helped to shape Vatican II's rethinking of priestly life, warned the Vatican unequivocally as the priest exodus continued unabated: "If in practice you cannot obtain a sufficient number of priests in a given cultural setting without relinquishing celibacy, then the church must suspend the law of celibacy."

> "Look, even if the priest is lousy, I can still focus totally on the readings. The words will always speak to you. So don't worry if the priest isn't everything that you want him to be. There's more to Catholicism than that."
>
> —VANESSA COOKE
>
> "Basically I'm very unhappy with the quality of priests today. When's the last time you heard a strong pro-life sermon?"
>
> —MARTY GERAGHTY

# THE DIVISIVE ISSUES

Much has been written about the place and propriety of an all-male priesthood and mandatory celibacy; this is not a place to further that debate in any great detail. But a brief review of the issues is in order.

The church's official teaching—reinforced repeatedly in our day by Pope John Paul II—is that the priesthood is limited to men because Christ, the first priest, was a man, and therefore set an irrevocable example. The priest at the altar stands in for Christ; and as Christ was a man, it cannot be any other way. Vatican II's *Lumen*

*Gentium* clearly taught that ordination involves a change not merely in degree, but in kind, and can only be conferred upon men.

Celibacy also is prefigured in Christ, church teaching and tradition hold. The priest, in essence, takes the church as his bride. His celibacy is a gift he offers up to God, as well as to the people of God—so that he might serve them wholly and unselfishly.

Many eminent theologians, scriptural scholars, and church historians, as well as the theological and biblical associations that have studied both issues, agree that there are indeed substantial, traditional arguments against ordaining women and rescinding the celibacy requirement. But, a good number—including participants in a study of these questions organized by the Vatican itself, and some of the most respected members of the hierarchy—have concluded that there is nothing in Scripture or in early church practice that actually precludes women liturgical leaders or married priests. In fact, both existed. An all-male, celibate priesthood came into being gradually, in response to historical, cultural, and economic forces.

Christ never commanded or in any way advocated an all-male priesthood, but this became common practice at a time in history when the societal role of women was considerably more circumscribed than it is today. Celibacy, as the Council of Trent proclaimed, is a matter of church law, not divine edict. As recently as late 1995, the Canon Law Society of America said the Catholic Church could ordain women as permanent deacons and that this "may even be desirable for the United States."[9]

Will women be ordained to the priesthood some day? Will celibacy be optional? Will the priesthood itself be offered for a period of a person's life, not all of it? If so, would this relieve the current shortage of priests—and perhaps even provide an even richer harvest of excellent clergy for the years ahead?

We do not know. Some may hope for change, but we cannot suspend our moral, spiritual, Good Enough Catholic lives as we await the outcome. And regardless, the transformation of our church—perhaps the most sweeping in so short a period of time in history—is already under way.

A new Catholic Church is being born, even as we struggle within the aging flesh of the old.

> "I know a Chicago priest who went to a meeting of fifty- to fifty-five-year-old priests—and not one of them had a good thing to say about celibacy."
>
> —PAT REARDON

# PRIESTS: WHO THEY WILL BE— AND ALREADY ARE

Even as the debate rages about who will be ordained, and about the very nature of the Catholic ordained priesthood, one thing is clear: Good Enough Catholics are already looking beyond this often vexing controversy. The revolution we are living through will, in ways we cannot yet see and may not ever understand or agree with, surely supplant the priesthood we once knew.

This calls for the Good Enough Catholic to assume a strange, seemingly contradictory, position—at once regarding and disregarding the priesthood. In other words, we need to speak of both our posture toward, and relation to, priests—and our readiness to see them shrink in importance.

For priests are our partners, our fellow pilgrims in our search for a Good Enough Catholic life. Like us, they are a varied lot, alternately quirky and stable, gifted and ordinary, inspired and tired, holy and sinful. They have their own misgivings about the state of the church, but—like us—are desirous of living moral lives, and somehow making the world a better place.

Let us not forget: they have dedicated their lives to the pursuit of God and of good. For the most part, they are devoted men. Yes, they have been found wanting in various ways, but the very basis of their lives is a spiritual premise, indeed a Catholic spiritual premise: selfless service to God and fellow human beings is the highest calling to which anyone can aspire. Who else do we have whose life is so focused? And who else do we have so close at hand, so accessible? There is nothing intrinsically wrong with the cultic component of the Catholic priesthood—the power and mystery of the sacraments are spiritual wellsprings we tap continually. The priesthood is a good, valid expression of our Catholic religious tradition—and it is necessary. In one form or another, it will always be necessary. And so, we must seek out priests who speak to our souls. "Simply put, the priest must be an authentically religious leader for his people; he must be, in the richest sense possible, spiritual director, mystical guide, shaman,"[10] writes Robert E. Barron, a professor of systematic theology.

If the Good Enough Catholic hopes to learn and be formed by the many wonderful priests that we have, it is necessary to invest time and to show interest in those who are already in your life or who will happen onto your path. We need to be open to their projects—whether it be Catholic education or liberation theology, a soup kitchen or a businessperson's prayer group. We need to listen to their sermons, and read their weekly parish bulletins or their books. And we need to talk back. After all, *we* are the reason they entered the seminary and were ordained. We must let them know how Catholicism works or fails in our lives.

Oftentimes, our priests are as confused as we are as to what is happening in our nation, our world, and our church. The journey of faith is also difficult for them. But they are our partners—and they are not going to run away (not all of them, or all at once, anyhow!) when the going gets tough.

With all that said, the Good Enough Catholic should equally *disregard* that we have formally ordained priests at all. In certain ways, we must set them aside.

The priesthood of the believers is not just some catchy, ultimately empty phrase. It is *us*. It is the premise on which Christianity is based. If the Good Enough Catholic takes seriously the honor and obligation of our common priesthood, it must be lived out. Jesus Christ did not appoint one nation, tribe, or group of people to proclaim his message about God's way to live a life; he looked out upon the crowds at the Sea of Galilee, at his neighbors on the narrow streets of Nazareth, at the worshipers at the Great Temple in Jerusalem—and he appointed them all. They were to be messengers of the Good News that God loves us all, unequivocally and forever, regardless of our level of religious observance or our place in life. All God asked is that they try—as best they could, each day, in each action—to love him and love their neighbor as they would also love themselves.

The revolution within the priesthood of believers that is happening in our lifetime—together with an ever-declining number of ordained priests—provides almost limitless opportunities for Good Enough Catholics to perform many of the functions we once thought were the exclusive domain of the clergy. Today, in virtually any parish in America, you have the opportunity to run its business; prepare its people for the sacraments; officiate at or administer those sacraments; counsel the young or old; feed, clothe, and house the needy; and preach the good news.

Or you can join the ever-growing number of lay missionaries—whose number has exploded by almost 600 percent in a recent five-year span—who work both overseas and at home. From recent college graduates to farmers and retired businesspeople, Catholics are the new missionaries, serving for a period of time and then returning to their secular lives.

Like a mammoth spiritual bazaar, a rich selection under one religious roof is proffered to today's Good Enough Catholic.

In my own case, I serve as a Eucharistic minister, visiting a local hospital one morning a week. I see from ten to twenty Catholics each Thursday morning—people who attend daily mass, and people who haven't been in church since they married that Baptist, Presbyterian, or Methodist thirty years ago. Almost instantly, I am involved intimately in their lives. I hear of the beauties and the blemishes of Catholicism. I hear from these patients—recuperating from a knee replacement, expecting a baby, or dying of cancer—that they are excommunicated, are not in a state of grace, love God, hate God, or don't know who God is.

There I stand, a Catholic lay person like themselves, a priest like themselves in the priesthood of believers. I bring a small book of prayers, the Eucharist, and myself. And as I stand there, I am ready to hear the stories of their lives and what has brought them to this hospital bed. We are in this together. We are Catholics. And for a few moments, in the presence of the Lord who rests in my tiny pyx, we two pilgrims—and those family members who may be there—hesitate on life's journey so that I might bring to them the bread of life.

When I was a boy, I thought of becoming a priest, and then again in midlife after I divorced. Somehow, it wasn't right for me; I found that out each time. So now, as a husband and father, I have this opportunity each week to perform what had once been a function of the formally ordained. Of course, it is not only the distribution of the Eucharist that is my weekly ministry. It is being able to be with another Catholic, to ask for strength and God's presence as we both struggle to make sense of our lives and make holy this moment together. It is a sign of our Catholic bond.

We hear of priestless Sundays across America, where there is no celebration of the mass. Of course, this is a disgrace; the mass is the centerpiece of our spiritual lives. In response to this potential spiritual loss, it would hardly do any good to simply disregard our current tradition and, with a parish coup, take over the altar and start offering mass. But we should never quietly settle for such a thing as a priestless Sunday. Catholics are a Eucharistic people; the mass and Holy Communion are rally, school, and meal.

What can be done? Some are gently trying to move the revolution along.

Father William Shannon, in an excellent article in *America* called "No More Circuit Riders, Please," lamented that the priest who whisks from church to church for a marathon of Sunday masses is killing both himself and the spirit of Christian community. Shannon called to mind Vatican II's dramatic shift—individual Catholics did not merely "attend" mass, but a community "celebrated the Eucharist." Pointing out that in an emergency, with no priest available, any one could baptize, Shannon asked: Why, under certain and well-defined circumstances, could not one of the community members, chosen from their midst, be sanctioned to officiate at the Eucharistic gathering of the community?

After all, this is *exactly* what was done in the early church. And look how it grew and prospered!

A priestless, mass-less Sunday was such an emergency, Shannon posited. The Eucharist is central to Catholic religious belief and worship. In a phrase invoked by Vatican II documents, the "needs of the times" require lay people to "zealously participate in the saving work of the church."[11] Was this not a moment to apply those words to a real need?

Some years ago, the archbishop of Milwaukee, Rembert Weakland, looked out to the priestless parishes he and his fellow bishops were seeing proliferate, and proposed publicly what a number of them were pondering privately: Why not elect one of the faithful to, in essence, be the parish—well—priest? Again, it was the practice of the early Christians.

In Seattle, parish closings have been halted; all parishes remain open, regardless of the availability of a priest. Over five hundred lay ministers are filling the gap. In Chicago, Father William Kenneally has offered an even more radical proposal. Looking out at the "minimally talented priests" he estimates comprise half the priesthood, he has said they simply should be encouraged to resign. Yes, it would exacerbate the priest shortage in the short run, but it would allow lay people to further fulfill their destiny as parish leaders.

Catholicism is too spiritually rich to allow its power to be diminished just because a limited number of people (and sometimes limited people) are sanctioned to perform its necessary rituals and ministries. This is the art, the delicate art, demanded of the Good Enough Catholic today: at once support your priests, but forge your

own way to a new and far more encompassing priesthood, that of all
of us believers.

> "One of the most important jobs of my early morning prayer
> group that meets once a week in the rectory is to emotionally sup-
> port our pastor."
>
> —MICHAEL TOBIN

> "I don't think of Ray Kemp as Father Ray Kemp, priest. I think
> of him as Ray Kemp, friend. We had this conversation at a cook-
> out—nothing about the Bible or spirituality, but after it I knew
> that this man was saying important things about my life. He was
> the bridge back for me. And he never preached. He talked to me
> like a friend."
>
> —DEE HARRIS

# THE GOOD ENOUGH CATHOLIC CHALLENGE:
## SUPPORT A PRIEST; BE A PRIEST

We can view with dismay or elation the shortage of priests. It is
either a tragedy or an opportunity. But we know for sure that
something is afoot, something not likely to be changed with a rash
of celibate vocations—by any measure, a quite unlikely event in
America. Too many Catholics have too much to offer to Catholic life to limit the scope of their ministry, their priesthood. And
the need is greater every day as the number of Catholics grows,
and the number of priests declines. The priesthood of all believers—that precious gift given to the first Christians—is also our
legacy.

And so, we must regard and respect the priests we have, while at
the same time looking beyond them so that we can be about our
Good Enough Catholic lives.

As for a Good Enough Catholic challenge to end this chapter, there is a choice.

Gregory Pierce proposed in one of his syndicated columns that we "Take a Priest to Lunch." Pierce said that our priests are not supported nearly enough, considering all that we ask of them. Are we more likely to thank our priest for choosing a life of service—or complain to him about the church's faults? Have we ever thought of inviting him to dinner or taking him along on a family picnic or trip to the zoo? He might love it.

So, do something nice for the best priest you know. A note, that lunch or dinner, a call, a small gift of a book that he might like—make an effort to let him know you appreciate what he's doing for you, our church, and our world.

The second option is to do something priestly yourself. If it helps, imagine yourself with a Roman collar; if it doesn't help, don't. Regardless, perform an action that is something one of the priesthood of believers would do. It might be a word to someone having a hard time at work, or it could be an act of kindness in return for some unkindness. Maybe it is something specifically Catholic—encouraging someone to come to a daily or Sunday mass with you. Or perhaps it is quietly just getting the right book into a person's hands.

One action, small as it might be, is your sign—and your validation—of ordination into this priesthood we all share.

## SELECTED READINGS

Daniel Donovan, *What Are They Saying About the Ministerial Priesthood?* New York: Paulist Press, 1992.

John Tracy Ellis, *The Catholic Priest in the United States: Historical Investigations.* Collegeville, Minn.: St. John's University Press, 1971.

Jean Galot, *Theology of the Priesthood.* San Francisco: Ignatius Press, 1984.

John P. McNamee, *Diary of a City Priest.* Kansas City, Mo.: Sheed and Ward, 1993.

Kenan B. Osbourne, *Priesthood: A History of the Ordained Ministry in the Roman Catholic Church*. New York: Paulist Press, 1989.

Edward Schillebeeckx and Johann-Baptist Metz, eds., *The Right of the Community to a Priest*. New York: Seabury, 1980.

Paul Wilkes, *In Mysterious Ways: The Death and Life of a Parish Priest*. New York: Avon Books, 1992.

# EPILOGUE
## The Good Enough Catholic

As I was nearing the end of this book, and wondering what I might say in conclusion, I came across a passage that so accurately summarizes the value of Catholicism that it actually made me smile—perhaps because I had spent thousands of words, and Mitch Finley had managed to sum it up in just twenty-nine:

> You will find in the Catholic Church the most reliable opportunity to discover the truth about yourself, about other people, about life, and about the world we live in.[1]

Yes, there are certainly other ways than following Catholic precepts to feed our gnawing spiritual hunger, to help us live as moral people, and to begin the needed transformation of ourselves, our homes, neighborhoods, workplaces, communities, and nation. And, even within our own faith, there are many ways of living as a Catholic other than the one presented in this book. The Good Enough Catholic approach offers but one path.

But I think it is a way that makes sense, both as a practical lifestyle and as a holy pursuit.

For I believe the Good Enough Catholic approach is first and foremost a response to an internal longing, not external pressure. The Good Enough Catholic does not pursue Catholicism (or even Good Enough Catholicism) to please the pope, a pastor, parent, spouse, children, friends—or even one of those wonderful nuns who policed our moral lives years ago. This is not a matter of guilt. We want to live better, holier lives, because in our hearts and in our souls, we know we will gain something from it. Our spiritual hunger can only be satisfied with true spiritual nourishment. In certain ways, we have no choice.

Yes, Catholicism is demanding, and people may refuse to return to it—or turn to it—because of an inchoate fear that it will cause them to change the way they live.

It will.

But as we all attempt to live lives that respond to the deepest stirrings of our being, Catholicism is a good place to be, a place where love and grace are available to saint and sinner alike, a place with a spiritual infrastructure so strong and so varied that we have enormous and continuing assistance as we build our own temporal dwellings upon this earth. We can quibble with this rule or that, this person or that; but for the most part Catholicism embodies good and wise rules, practices, and people that will help to deepen our spiritual and moral selves. The more we practice its ways, the easier they become and the more we benefit.

I have attempted in these pages to show that living as a Good Enough Catholic means acquiring an attitude, a life skill, not merely practicing a science. Morality is not a physical law like gravity. The church has no specific blueprint for society or for our lives; but her constant admonition to practice love and seek justice point a clear way. Changing situations, both in the world and in ourselves, call for different responses. A fast rule at one point becomes a rule to be broken at another. That is why we must rely, in turns, upon our church and upon ourselves.

But it is here that Catholicism sustains the Good Enough Catholic. For although each one of us must confront the unique set of circumstances that is our life, we are not alone. Behind each of us frail individuals is a mighty church whose rich history and current teachings provide us with the guidance we need to lead moral lives, a church that provides "ways of thinking, modes of analysis."[2] We have a church whose sacramentality gives us the spiritual sustenance we need to go on. We have a religious belief that continually tests us, asks for the best we can be, makes outrageous demands—and yet is ready with unfathomable, embarrassing forgiveness when we fall short.

And in still another way we are not alone.

If the Good Enough Catholic way makes sense to us, it equally makes sense to others. We have the assurance that there are ever-growing numbers of Good Enough Catholics who are discovering that a proper reading and practice of their ancient faith offers the means for personal sanctification, and an answer to the profound cultural crisis of modern American society. Catholicism is not as linear, dogmatic, and inflexible as they once believed; it is human, it is divine. Like us.

Good Enough Catholics can be in the vanguard of those who, by the example of their lives, show what a proper, realistic, modern expression of Catholic belief—in short, what authentic spirituality—can yield. They can distinguish themselves as "a certain kind of people"—people not ashamed to show charity in the workplace, not ashamed to perform those unasked-for acts of goodness, privately and publicly. People with ". . . distinctive habits of the heart, of the mind, and of the will—disciplined habits of doing and of being by which we come to define ourselves and others come to know who we are," as *Newsweek*'s Kenneth L. Woodward has written.[3] Catholics not ashamed to say they are Catholic, and that Catholic belief motivates their lives.

Good Enough Catholics can also be the transmitters of Catholicism, those who will hand the faith down to future generations. In the past, this was the province of the ordained and consecrated women and men, institutional personnel. That day has past, as a generation of unchurched Catholics born in the 1960s and 1970s know too well. The era of the lay Catholic is here, for there are so many more of us—one billion worldwide, and 65 million in the United States, by far the largest religious group in America. We are well placed in all economic, professional, corporate, and cultural spheres. We are in boardrooms and backrooms; in the arts, science, education, and politics. We are everywhere.

But Catholicism is far more than sheer numbers of people, an unparalleled network of schools, universities, hospitals, and social-welfare agencies, or an impressive ecclesiastical network that reaches to every square inch of this nation. The Catholic sense of mystery—or mysticism—holds our true transforming power.

> There is a unique treasure imprinted in the imagination of every Catholic. It is the suspicion that embedded in the ordinary lies the extraordinary, the miraculous, the salvific. . . . Catholics see the shopping mall, the school house, the kitchen table, the factory, the courtroom and the hospital as altars of sorts—places where the ordinary, mundane labors of life may be offered up, blessed and transformed into things of beauty.[4]

Catholicism is a faith that at once draws lines, and forgives. It is a faith that makes demands, and makes allowances. It is a sprawling, vast canopy that encompasses people who have a stunning variety of religious expressions. All that is asked for entry into this most inclusive club is that we seek the God who first sought us.

"The great challenge to us religious people, it seems to me," wrote British physician Dr. Sheila Cassidy, "is not how to spread the gospel, but how to live it. It is only when Christ's teaching of love is lived naturally, unselfconsciously, that it takes hold, catches fire in a society."[5]

Naturally, unselfconsciously—exactly what being a Good Enough Catholic is about.

*Mary Anne Barry*, Chicago, is the mother of five and grandmother of seven. She is a retired clinical social worker who is active in work with spina bifida children and the Catholic bishops' Campaign for Human Development.

*Marielsa Bernard*, Silver Spring, Md., is a lawyer who does substantial pro bono work for the poor and indigent.

*John Butler*, Clinton, Md., is a management consultant.

*Vanessa Cooke*, Wheaton, Md., is the assistant principal and guidance counselor at Elizabeth Seton, an all-girls Catholic high school in Maryland.

*Paula Dawson*, Hardwick, Mass., is a preschool teacher and mother of two grade school–age children.

*Shilpi D'Costa*, Silver Spring, Md., is a native of Bangladesh who works in the medical field; she recently married Stanley Dean.

*Stanley Dean*, Silver Spring, Md., is a native of Pakistan who is studying to become a pharmacist.

*Minnie Diana*, Silver Spring, Md., was born in the Dominican Republic.

*John Fialka*, Washington, D.C., is an investigative reporter for the *Wall Street Journal*; he is the father of two grown children.

*Marty Geraghty*, Evanston, Ill., is a commercial real estate broker and the father of six children.

*Maureen Geraghty*, Washington, D.C., one of the six Geraghty children, is a reporter for *The Chronicle for Higher Education*.

*Hal Gordon*, Washington, D.C., is the executive director of a community action group.

*Dana Green* is a professor at St. Mary's College of Maryland and a retreat leader.

*Emilie Griffin*, New Orleans, is an advertising executive and the author of *The Reflective Executive: A Spirituality of Business and Enterprise* (Crossroad, 1993).

*James "Dee" Harris*, Hyattsville, Md., is a Nissan salesman.

*Marty Hegarty*, Chicago, a former priest, is an organizational consultant.

*Jim Helein*, Arlington, Va., is a video editor and newly married.

*Father Raymond Kemp*, Washington, D.C., is a parish priest who conducts homily workshops on "Preaching the Just Word."

*Cappy Kustusch*, Chicago, is the mother of five children, whom she home-schools. She is a born-again Christian and also attends evangelical churches.

*Suzanne Lefevre*, Evanston, Ill., is the treasurer of a Fortune 500 subsidary. She recently gave birth to her third child. She is married to Tom Lenz.

*Tom Lenz*, Evanston, Ill., is a planner at a Chicago urban research institute.

*Le Trong Phu*, Silver Spring, Md., escaped from Vietnam as one of the "boat people." He works with recent immigrants at Associated Catholic Charities of the Archdiocese of Washington.

*Dorothy Papachristos*, Chicago, is a street gang worker, the mother of two grown children, and foster parent of gang members.

*Patrick Reardon*, Chicago, is an urban affairs writer for the *Chicago Tribune*; he is the father of two young children.

*Leon Roberts*, Brooklyn, N.Y., is a church music director and composer.

*Magalie Salas*, Adelphi, Md., was born in Puerto Rico and graduated from Georgetown Law School. She is a lawyer with the Federal Communications Commission and the mother of two school-age children.

*Lena Shipley*, of Waterloo, N.Y., is the coordinator of the CCD program at St. Mary Parish. She is the mother of two young children.

*Gail Smith*, Chicago, is a third-grade teacher at St. Gertrude's Catholic school and the mother of one school-age child.

*Allen Stryczek*, Chicago, is a business systems consultant for a large bank. He and his wife have served as foster parents for teenagers.

*David Suley*, Silver Spring, Md., is an executive in a nonprofit agency. He is married and the father of two children.

*Joan Sullivan*, Chicago, calls herself "a woman in transition." Divorced, she has been a foster parent.

*Carolyn Sweers*, Evanston, Ill., single, is a retired schoolteacher.

*Dorothea and Michael Tobin*, Chicago, are the parents of seven children. Michael is a psychoanalyst.

*Betty and Numa Torres*, Silver Spring, Md., emigrated from El Salvador. They have two children and are active in Marriage Encounter.

*Father Jack Wall*, Chicago, is the pastor of Old St. Patrick's.

*Beata Welsh*, Chicago, is a transportation consultant and mother of two school-age children.

*Dick Westly*, Chicago, is a writer and philosophy professor at Loyola University; he has been a member of the same prayer group for twenty-five years.

*Natasha Witschy*, Evanston, Ill., is a public school teacher in Chicago and the single parent of two teenage children.

*Mary Murphy Zastrow*, Chicago, is the mother of three children and a kindergarten aide. Her husband, Peter, a convert to Catholicism, is a postman.

There is a wealth of Catholic information available via your computer. Home pages and discussion groups are constantly changing and new ones starting up. Using one of the major search engines like Alta Vista, Yahoo, or Lycos will yield a bountiful harvest. Here are just some of the sources you may want to consult.

## Discussion Groups

**http://www.bcinet.net/goodenuf/**

This is your own discussion group, Good Enough Catholics. You can exchange information about living as a Catholic today, and find exciting parishes, projects, and people.★

**listserv@vm.temple.edu**

A group of Vatican II Catholics who exchange information and experiences. To become a member of this group, send E-mail to above address with: "Sub Vatican2 (your first name) (your last name)"

**listserv@listserv.syr.edu**

Originally envisioned as forum for Catholic women religious, now also has lay members—male and female—from other traditions. Feminist issues are explored in a nonadversarial way. Send E-mail to above address with: "Sub Sister-L (your first name) (your last name)"

Compuserve

Type "Go Catholic" for about two dozen topic areas.

America OnLine

Go to keyword "Religion," and select the "Catholic community" newsgroup.

★Provided, thanks to Rebecca Folmsbee of Southport, NC.

# Resources

**http://www.catholic.org/colweb/dioceses.html**
Directory of parishes, mass schedules, the local Catholic newspaper, and many other resources for the Catholic community.

General Catholic information:
**http://www.catholic.net**
**http://www.cs.cmu.edu/Web/People/spok/catholic.html**
**http://www.wsnet.com/~alapadre**

**http://www.zpub.com/un/pope**
The unofficial Pope John Paul II home page.

**http://www.vatican.va**
Vatican home page.

**http://www.interpath.com/~mdoyle/regnews/regnews.html**
A Southern review of Catholic newspapers and resources.

**http://www.osb.org/osb/**
The Order of Saint Benedict.

**http://www.epix.net:80/~byzantin/byzan.html**
Byzantine Catholic Page.

**http://www.archdiocese-chgo.org/commenu.html**
Catholic Common Ground Project to bring together varying points of view.

**http://www.partenia.fr/**
French Bishop Jacques Gaillot's "Cybersee."

**http://www.knight.org/advent/cathen/cathen.html**
Catholic Encyclopedia.

**http://www.ccseb.com/ddh/index.html**
Dorothy Day House, Berkeley, CA.

**http://bingen.cs.csbsju.edu/~roliver/bro1.html**
Suggested links from Brother Richard Oliver.

**http://microweb.com/burnside/sfbay.htm**
San Francisco Bay Catholic in the original spirit of Vatican II.

**http://astro.ocis.temple.edu/~arcc**
Association for the Rights of Catholics in the Church.

# ❧NOTES❦

### INTRODUCTION

1. James J. Bacik, "The Practice of Priesthood: Working Through Today's Tensions," *Church*, Fall 1993, 12.

### CHAPTER I. JESUS CHRIST:
### WISTFULNESS, WISHFUL THINKING, AND REALITY

1. From a treatise by St. Cyprian on the Lord's Prayer, quoted in *The Liturgy of the Hours*, vol. 2 (New York: Catholic Book Publishing, 1976), 267–68.
2. Cullen Murphy, "Who Do Men Say That I Am?," *Atlantic Monthly*, December 1986, 38.
3. *New York Times*, 25 December 1994, 1.
4. Dick Westly, *In the Meantime: A Thomas More Newsletter*, Issue 13 (Chicago, Ill.; n.d.), 7.
5. Richard P. McBrien, ed., *Catholicism* (New Edition) (New York: Harper San Francisco, 1994), 400.
6. Colossians 3:12–14.

### CHAPTER 2. MASS AND THE EUCHARIST:
### THE SOURCE

1. Robert A. Wolfe, "The Parish Church: Shaping Our Catholic Identity," *Catholic World*, May/June 1994, 143.
2. Second Vatican Council, "Constitution on the Sacred Liturgy," at note 10.
3. Quoted in Tom McGrath, "Why Get Up and Go to Mass?," *U.S. Catholic*, December 1994, 7.

## CHAPTER 3. THE SACRAMENTS:
### DIVINE INTERVENTIONS

1. William O'Malley, "Understanding Sacraments," *America*, 7 March 1992, 188.
2. Quoted in Arthur M. Schlesinger, Jr., *Robert Kennedy and His Times* (New York: Ballantine, 1978), 983.


## CHAPTER 4. PRAYER AND SPIRITUALITY:
### THE TRUE PATH

1. 1 Peter 4:2–3a.
2. Richard Foster, "Just Do It: How to Jump Start Your Prayer Life," *U.S. Catholic*, February 1993, 25.
3. Dennis Hamm, "Rummaging for God: Praying Backward Through Your Day," *America*, 14 May 1994, 22–23.
4. Matthew 6:7–14.
5. Thomas Merton, *New Seeds of Contemplation* (New York: New Directions, 1972), 104.
6. Basil Hume, "Joy of Our Desiring," *The Tablet*, 29 April 1994, 406.
7. Merton, *New Seeds of Contemplation*, 18.
8. Exodus 35:20.
9. James Martin, ed., "How Can I Find God?," *America*, 30 September 1995, 15.
10. Janet Joy, *A Place Apart: Houses of Prayer and Retreat Centers in America* (Trabuco Canyon, Calif.: Source Books, 1995).
11. Mary Luke Tobin, "How Do You Rate Your Prayer Life?," *U.S. Catholic*, May 1990, 9–10.


## CHAPTER 5. MORALITY, CONSCIENCE, AND SIN:
### THE ARCHITECTURE OF CHARACTER

1. Thomas G. Long, "God Be Merciful to Me, a Miscalculator," *Theology Today*, July 1993, 166.
2. Quoted in *The Liturgy of the Hours*, vol. 3 (New York: Catholic Book Publishing, 1975), 59.
3. McBrien, *Catholicism*, 925.
4. Merton, *New Seeds of Contemplation*, 32.
5. Joseph H. McKenna, "The Optimism of Sin," *America*, 12 February 1994, 18–19.
6. James K. Healy, "God's Forgiveness as a Hand on the Shoulder," *National Catholic Reporter*, 18 February 1994, 2.
7. Fred Sontag, "New Beginnings," *Encounter*, Winter 1994, 61–68.

## CHAPTER 6. WORK:
### THE ART OF CO-CREATION

1. William J. Byron, "Spirituality on the Road to Re-employment," *America*, 20 May 1995, 15.
2. *Gaudium et Spes*, paras. 33–34; quoted in *The Liturgy of the Hours*, vol. 2 (New York: Catholic Book Publishing Co., 1976), 1801–2.
3. William L. Droel and Gregory F. Augustine Pierce, *Confident and Competent: A Challenge for the Lay Church* (Chicago: ACTA Publications, 1991), 43.
4. Michael Lerner, in a 17 May 1995 letter from the Foundation for Ethics and Meaning.
5. John S. Driscoll, "God as City Editor," *Nieman Reports*, Summer 1993.

## CHAPTER 7. MARRIAGE (AND DIVORCE):
### THE MORAL GREENHOUSE

1. Quoted in John L. Thomas, *Beginning Your Marriage* (revised by David M. Thomas) (Chicago: ACTA Publications, 1994), dedication page.
2. McBrien, *Catholicism*, 857.
3. Donald W. Wuerl, "A Catholic/Jewish Dialogue: A Catholic Vision of Marriage, Divorce, and the Family," *Vital Speeches of the Day*, 1 July 1992, 551.
4. John S. Grabowski, "Divorce, Remarriage, and Reception of the Sacraments," *America*, 8 October 1994, 24.
5. Ibid.
6. Grabowski takes his quotation of Ratzinger from Ladislas Orsy, *Marriage in Canon Law: Texts and Comments, Reflections and Questions* (Wilmington, Del.: Michael Glazier, 1986).
7. Grabowski, "Divorce, Remarriage, and Reception of the Sacraments," 20.
8. "What Gift Does the Church Bring to Your Wedding?" (interview with Joseph Champlin), *U.S. Catholic*, June 1992, 22.

## CHAPTER 8. SEX, ABORTION, AND BIRTH CONTROL:
### OF LIFE AND OF LOVE

1. Charles E. Curran, "Catholic Social and Sexual Teaching: A Methodological Comparison," *Theology Today*, January 1988, 438.
2. Richard McBrien, ed., *The HarperCollins Encyclopedia of Catholicism*, 422.
3. *New Catholic Encyclopedia*, vol. 17 ("Supplement: Change in the Church") (Washington, D.C.: Publisher's Guild, 1988), 505.

4. Andrew M. Greeley, "Sex and the Single Catholic: The Decline of an Ethic," *America*, 7 November 1992, 342–59.

5. For further discussion on this point, see Marie Theresa Coombs and Francis Kelly Nemeck, *Discerning Vocations to Marriage, Celibacy, and Singlehood* (Collegeville, Minn.: Michael Glazier, 1994).

6. Gerald D. Coleman, "Sexual Activity Among Teenagers," *Church*, Summer 1991, 41.

7. Catherine Walsh, "Perspectives," *America*, 11 February 1995, 5.

8. Julie Clague, review of A. E. Harvey, *Promise or Pretense? A Christian's Guide to Secular Morals*; *The Tablet*, 20 May 1995, 639.

9. John Korte, *Simple Gifts: The Lives of Pat and Patty Crowley* (Kansas City, Mo.: Andrews and McMeel, 1979), 98–99.

10. Quoted in John Marshall, "A Watershed for the Church," *The Tablet*, 10 June 1995, 740.

11. *Longergan Studies Newsletter*, vol. 11 (1990), 7–8.

12. Bernard Haring, *Free and Faithful in Christ: Moral Theology for Clergy and Laity* (vol. 1: *General Moral Theology*) (New York: Seabury, 1978), 280–81.

13. Quoted in John F. Dedek, *Contemporary Medical Ethics* (New York: Sheed and Ward, 1975), 130.

## CHAPTER 9. PARISH: A HOME FOR THE SPIRIT

1. Walter M. Abbott, ed., *The Documents of Vatican II* (New York: Herder and Herder, Association Press, 1966), 60.

2. "Small Faith Groups Help the Good News Hit Home" (interview with Arthur Baranowski), *U.S. Catholic*, January 1992, 6–13.

3. Ibid.

4. See, for example, Thomas A. Kleissler, Margo A. Lebert, and Mary C. McGuinness, *Small Christian Communities: A Vision of Hope* (New York: Paulist Press, 1991); and Arthur Baranowski, *Creating Small Faith Communities: A Plan for Restructuring the Parish and Renewing Catholic Life* (Cincinnati, Ohio: St. Anthony Messenger Press, 1989), and *Praying Alone and Together: An 11-Session Prayer Module for Small Faith Communities* (Cincinnati, Ohio: St. Anthony Messenger Press, 1988).

## CHAPTER 10. FAMILY: THE GENTLE CRUCIBLE

1. Second Vatican Council, "Decree on the Apostolate of the Laity," in Abbott, ed., *The Documents of Vatican II*, 11.

2. William Urbine and William Seifert, *On Life and Love: A Guide to Catholic*

*Teaching on Marriage and Family* (Mystic, Conn.: Twenty-Third Publications, 1993), 2.

3. National Conference of Catholic Bishops, "Follow the Way of Love" (pastoral letter), 17 November 1993, 11.

4. Mitch Finley, *Your Family in Focus: Appreciating What You Have, Making It Even Better* (Notre Dame, Ind.: Ave Maria, 1993), 12.

5. National Conference of Catholic Bishops, "Follow the Way of Love," 8.

6. Arthur Jones, "Teaching the Faith," *National Catholic Reporter*, 28 May 1993, 2.

7. Patrice J. Tuohy, "Religious Symbols Belong in Your Home," *U.S. Catholic*, April 1993, 19.

8. Quoted in Dolores R. Lecky, "Children in Jeopardy: Who Cares?," *Church*, Spring 1995, 5.

9. "The Narrow Road" (editorial), *America*, 16 April 1994, 3.

CHAPTER II. COMMUNITY:
A WAY TO LIVE TOGETHER

1. Robert N. Bellah, et al., *Habits of the Heart* (Berkeley: University of California Press, 1985), viii.

2. Quoted in "Americans Giving Less Money, Time to Charity; Catholics Lead Retreat," *National Catholic Reporter*, 28 October 1994, 6.

3. From *Rerum Novarum* quoted in Mel Piehl, "A Wealth of Nations," *America*, 3 May 1991, 284.

4. Ibid.

5. Eugene Kennedy, in a review of Alan Ehrenhalt, *The Lost City: Discovering the Forgotten Virtues of Community in the Chicago of the 1950s* (New York: Basic Books, 1995); *New York Times Book Review*, 24 December 1995.

6. In late 1995 the National Conference of Catholic Bishops, defying the sentiment of many American Catholics, soundly criticized the cuts in social welfare programs proposed in Congress.

7. Bellah, et al., *Habits of the Heart*, 295.

8. Amitai Etzioni, *The Spirit of Community: Rights, Responsibilities, and the Communitarian Agenda* (New York: Crown, 1994), 247.

9. *Gaudium et Spes*, at para. 32.

10. Bellah, et al., *Habits of the Heart*, vii.

11. Quoted in Amitai Etzioni, "Restoring Our Moral Voice," *The Public Interest*, Summer 1994, 107.

12. Quoted in *The Liturgy of the Hours*, vol. 4 (New York: Catholic Book Publishing Co., 1975), 1342.

CHAPTER 12. CHURCH TEACHING:
THE ART AND PRACTICE OF BELIEF

1. Quoted in Brennan R. Hill, *Exploring Catholic Theology* (Mystic, Conn.: Twenty-Third Publications, 1995), 1.
2. From the first instruction of St. Vincent of Lerins, Cap. 23, PL 50; quoted in *The Liturgy of the Hours*, vol. 4 (New York: Catholic Book Publishing, 1975), 667–68.
3. McBrien, *Catholicism*, xii.
4. Robert L. Wilken, "The Christian Intellectual Tradition," *First Things*, June/July 1991, 15.
5. *Gaudium et Spes*, at paras. 9–10.
6. "Decree on Ecumenism," November 1946; quoted in Richard A. Mc-Cormick, "*Humane Vitae* 25 Years Later," *America*, 17 July 1993, 12.
7. The December 1995 statement from the Congregation on the Doctrine of the Faith, claiming infallibility for the teaching that women could not be ordained priests, was *not* proclaimed *ex cathedra* by the pope.
8. Clifford Longley, "Asking Too Much," *The Tablet*, 6 January 1996, 7.
9. From Claudel's *Tradition and the Life of the Church*, quoted in an obituary for Yves Congar in *The Tablet*, 1 July 1995, 854.
10. John T. Noonan, Jr., "Development in Moral Doctrine," *Theological Studies*, vol. 54, December 1993, 662–67.
11. John Henry Newman, "Essay on the Development of Christian Doctrine"; quoted in Noonan, "Development in Moral Doctrine."
12. Hill, *Exploring Catholic Theology*, 3.
13. Henri de Lubac, "Memoir sur l'occasion de mes ecrits," quoted in Christopher Walsh, "De Lubac's Critique of the Postconciliar Church," *Communio*, Fall 1992, 408.
14. Quoted in "Vatican Limits Dissent," *The Tablet*, 11–19 July 1990, 665.
15. Brian Jordan, letter to congregants of St. Camillus Parish, Silver Spring, Md., 2 December 1994.

CHAPTER 13. CHURCH AUTHORITY:
THOUGHTFUL OBEDIENCE

1. McBrien, ed., *The HarperCollins Encyclopedia of Catholicism*, 955.
2. Richard P. McBrien, in a review of David Edwards, *What Is Catholicism? An Anglican Responds to the Official Teaching of the Roman Catholic Church*; *The Tablet*, 7 January 1995, 19.
3. Quoted in Hill, *Exploring Catholic Theology*, 273.
4. Ibid.
5. 1 Timothy 3:2–5.

6. Quoted in McBrien, *Catholicism*, 756.

7. *Christus Dominus*, at paras. 12–13, 16.

8. Bernard Cooke, "Papal Pomp Contrasts with Simplicity of Jesus," *National Catholic Reporter*, 3 March 1994, 10.

9. Quoted in Philip S. Kaufman, *Why You Can Disagree and Remain a Faithful Catholic* (New York: Crossroad, 1995), ix.

10. Ibid.

11. National Conference of Catholic Bishops, "Human Life in Our Day" (pastoral letter); Washington, D.C., 15 November 1968.

12. Alain Woodrow, "Pope-Watching Goes Pop" (review), *The Tablet*, 25 September 1995, 1205.

CHAPTER 14. PRIESTHOOD OF PRIESTS,
PRIESTHOOD OF BELIEVERS

1. Karen Jo Toriesen, *When Women Were Priests: Women's Leadership in the Early Church and the Scandal of Their Subordination in the Rise of Christianity* (San Francisco: Harper, 1993).

2. James J. Bacik, "The Practice of the Priesthood," *Church*, Fall 1993, 5.

3. In this discussion of the priesthood, I would be remiss if I did not mention the women religious, the nuns who were an equally important part of our secular and religious education. Catholic schoolchildren probably had much more contact with nuns than with priests; and these women religious were indeed the backbone of our parishes.

4. E. T. Gomulka, "The Priest Shortage," *America*, 16 April 1994.

5. Ibid.

6. Jerry Filteau, Catholic News Service wire story on the Lilly Endowment–funded study of Catholic clergy; quoted in *North Carolina Catholic* (newspaper of the Catholic Diocese of Raleigh), 30 July 1995.

7. Philip J. Murnion, "Ministry as a Project: Reflections on Ordained Priesthood," *Church*, Fall 1992, 51.

8. Bacik, "The Practice of the Priesthood," 7.

9. Jerry Filteau, "Within the Authority," *North Carolina Catholic*, 5 November 1995.

10. Robert E. Barron, "Priest as Bearer of the Mystery," *Church*, Summer 1994, 10.

11. Shannon, 11.

EPILOGUE

1. Mitch Finley, *Catholic Is Wonderful: How to Make the Most of It* (Williston Park, N.Y.: Resurrection Press, 1994), 14.

2. Margaret O'Brien Steinfels, "The Laity," *Commonweal*, 10 September 1993.
3. Kenneth L. Woodward, "Ushering in the Age of the Laity," *Commonweal*, 9 September 1994, 9.
4. National Center for the Laity, *Initiatives*, June 1995, back page.
5. Sheila Cassidy, "Easter in Ordinary," *The Tablet*, 15–22 April 1995, 480.

# ✥ACKNOWLEDGMENTS✥

A book like this required ears, eyes, hearts, inspiration, and wisdom far beyond what could be mustered by this single author.

Many of my friends and acquaintances contributed names, ideas, and contacts, and I am deeply grateful to each of them. Almost without exception, they each also contributed a knowing chuckle when I first mentioned the title of the book. Thanks for your help—and for that chuckle. Believe me, it kept spurring me on.

Good Enough Catholics told me of their lives. Their candor, faith, and moral beauty infuse these pages.

Father James Bacik of Toledo, Mary Kate Codd Davidson of Wilmington, North Carolina, and Greg Pierce of ACTA Publications in Chicago were good enough to read through the entire manuscript, correct my many mistakes, and add their insights. Monsignor Philip Murnion of the National Pastoral Life Conference was most helpful in steering me toward "Good Enough" parishes and pastors.

At Ballantine Books, Kayley LeFaiver designed a most beautiful dust jacket, Nora Reichard meticulously saw the manuscript through production, and Sally Marvin prepared the book for its launch into the world. Matt Doyle and Ingrid Shafer helped with the electronic resources. Mark Edington assisted in forming the book in its early stages, then expertly copyedited it before publication. Clare Ferraro, my editor at Ballantine, believed in me and the idea behind this book from its conception—she is a Good Shepherd indeed.

❀INDEX❀

PAUL WILKES is the author of eleven nonfiction books, a novel, and was the host, writer, director, or producer of seven PBS documentaries.

He has written for numerous national magazines, such as *The New Yorker, The Atlantic,* and *The New York Times Magazine* and is a former reporter for the *Baltimore Sun* and the *Boulder* (Colorado) *Daily Camera.*

He has written extensively about the role of religious belief in individual lives as well as the place and impact of religion in public life.

He has been a visiting writer and guest lecturer at Clark University, University of Pittsburgh, Columbia University, Holy Cross, Boston University, and Brooklyn College. He is currently a visiting distinguished professor at the University of North Carolina at Wilmington.

Mr. Wilkes has been honored for his body of work with a Distinguished Alumnus Award from Columbia University's Graduate School of Journalism, where he received his advanced degree, and with a By-Line Award from Marquette University, where he graduated.

A practicing Catholic, he lives in Wilmington, North Carolina, with his wife Tracy, a social worker, and two young sons, Paul Noah and Daniel Thomas. The Wilkes family are parishioners at St. Mary Church.